THE CLASSIC GARDEN

THE CLASSIC GARDEN

GRAHAM ROSE

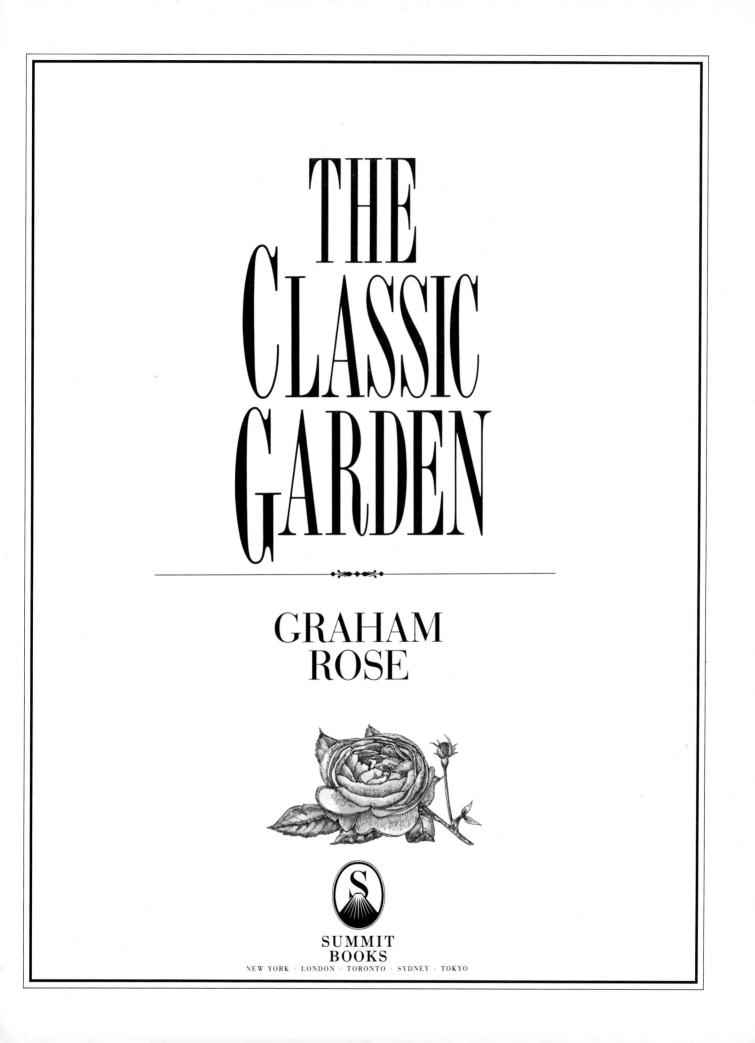

SUMMIT BOOKS

NEW YORK · LONDON · TORONTO · SYDNEY · TOKYO

A Dorling Kindersley Book

SUMMIT BOOKS

Simon & Schuster Building
Rockefeller Center
1230 Avenue of the Americas
New York, New York 10020

SUMMIT BOOKS and colophon are trademarks
of Simon & Schuster Inc.

Designed by Peter Luff
Manufactured in Italy

10 9 8 7 6 5 4 3 2 1

ISBN 0-671-68840-5

CONTENTS

INTRODUCTION 7

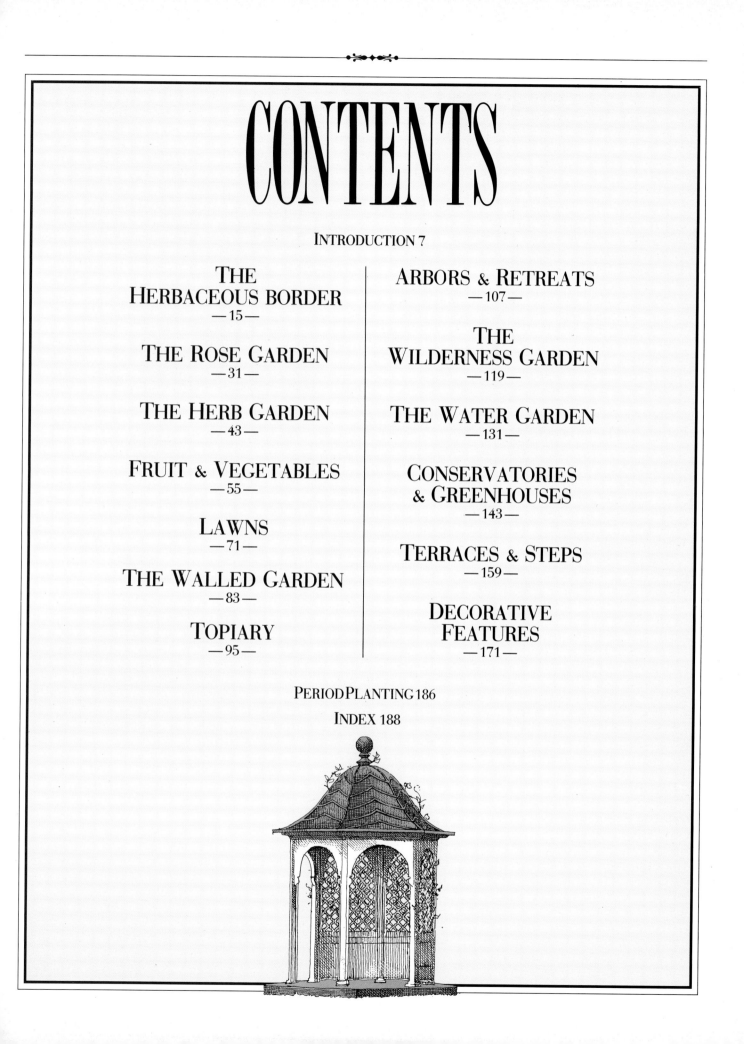

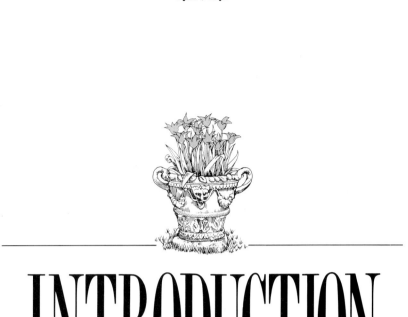

INTRODUCTION

Gardening has to some extent always been a retrospective activity. For a gardener, there are few more poignant reflections than the thought that to mold and plant a piece of ground is to participate in a ritual that has taken place for centuries.

A richly satisfying feature of such a reverie is that it has virtually no geographical boundaries. Throughout history, the joys and frustrations of the gardener have been common to people working land everywhere. They were as valid for the gardeners of Victorian country houses as they were for early Virginian colonists, and they would have been shared by the gardeners of French châteaux as much as by the makers of medieval *pleasances* years before them.

Sometimes the retrospection that characterizes gardening has served to fuel a reaction, encouraging innovation in new startling new directions. At other times, the result of this process has been affectionate nostalgia, a desire to recreate the finest elements of gardens of bygone times.

It is this latter kind of gardening, which borrows ideas and practices from the past, reinterprets and then places in the present that forms the subject of this book.

· THE SEARCH FOR STYLE ·

In gardening – as indeed in any creative activity – style is dynamic. Over the centuries, the pendulum of fashion has swung many times between freedom and formality, lingering at one extreme before initiating its accelerating descent towards another.

The triggers for this constant change in what is considered desirable or beautiful are many. Sometimes, change is brought about by the evolution of ideas, as one approach is shaped into another by experiment and modification. At other times, it is initiated by some outside influence – often the traditions belonging to another culture, or indeed those of another period. In looking at the gardens of earlier periods, it is easy to be bemused

CLASSIC DECORATION
The combination of weathered stone, terracotta pots and informal plants makes an enchanting scene at the meeting point between a house and its garden.

by the multiplicity of themes and fashions. But, in reality, what we see is a very compressed representation of the march of events. In the past, before the advent of rapid communications, change was often slow to the point of imperceptibility. The widespread adoption of any style of gardening could take tens if not hundreds of years, and even when the well-informed and fashionable had abandoned it for its successor, there were always gardens in which the old ways of doing things – whether planting flower gardens, growing vegetables in geometric beds, or clipping hedges into exotic shapes – were rigorously adhered to. Precisely because the history of gardening has been shaped by so many different influences, today's traditional gardener has many different styles to choose from. In the past, gardening style has ranged from the almost mathematically severe to the wholly naturalistic. And herein lies the pleasure of traditional gardening. If your taste is for formality, you might wish to recreate a seventeenth-century knot garden, in which symmetry and pattern are paramount. On the other hand if you wish to create a garden in which more natural forms take precedence, the Victorian wild garden, or the eighteenth-century grotto, may well provide the models that you seek. In gardening, the achievements and traditions of the past act very much as the pattern-books for the present with countless ideas awaiting exploration and development.

A LIVING MENAGERIE
In a traditional garden, the whimsical and eccentric have just as much a place as the serious and formal.

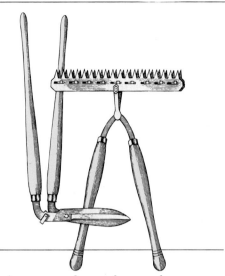

In planting our gardens today, we have at our disposal an extraordinary range of plants from all over the world. Given this rich palette, it is easy to become so engrossed in the plants themselves that another equally important part of traditional garden design – the inclusion of classic decorative features – becomes neglected. A traditional garden is not simply a horticultural experience, but also an artistic one.

Before the great waves of plant collecting in the eighteenth and nineteenth centuries, far fewer plants were available to gardeners. Until this time, great importance was attached to ornament, not in the form of plants, but in the form of man-made objects disposed at appropriate points to catch the attention. These structures were an essential counterpoint in garden design.

· TRADITIONAL FEATURES TODAY ·

There is no substitute for the sweeping spaces of the great gardens made in former times that we visit and enjoy. Their vistas, grand walks and the room they have for indulgence in particular aspects of gardening are worlds apart from the standard suburban plot. Few today can afford the capital investment needed to build the more ambitious features that are part of many traditional gardens. Even the building of a substantial brick wall costs more than many gardeners would dream of spending. However, the underlying aesthetic principles of traditional gardening remain unchanged. Garden buildings can indeed prove

costly if made of authentic materials, and it is by no means easy to find craftsmen with sufficient skill to construct them properly. However, classic garden ornament need neither be lavish nor expensive. As more and more gardeners are discovering, doing everything on a grand scale is not quintessential to the successful period garden. Even the smallest decorative object, carefully chosen and thoughtfully placed, can have a great impact, and one of the aims of this book is to show how such objects can be used, and what forms they can take.

· TIME AND TECHNIQUE ·

There are ways of translating grand techniques for the smaller space. The most obvious perhaps, is to look at aspects of the large traditional garden separately – the herb garden, the rose garden, water, fanciful or formal topiary, and borders, for example – with a view to using them in isolation in a smaller garden. To this end, the chapters of this book deal with each of these aspects in turn. It will act as your guide, reviewing the ways in which they have been treated in the past and describing how they can be adapted for use today. However strong our affection for the past, it would be misleading to imagine that traditional gardening is simply a matter of following the practices of our

THE WORKING PAST
The hand-light is just one example of a gardening bygone that can be used to adorn today's period garden.

gardening forebears without any departure from their methods. It is not possible to recreate the past, and to do so would be to throw away many of the advantages that today's gardener undoubtedly enjoys.

One problem facing anyone who seeks to perpetuate gardening traditions is that much of the gardening we might wish to recreate depended on techniques that made few concessions to the clock. The upkeep of gardens in the past consumed a great deal of labor, and large teams of gardeners were employed in tending and maintaining ornamental grounds.

Not only was labor more plentiful, but it has to be admitted that gardeners were also more patient, being prepared to wait a considerable time for results. Whether preparing the soil to a peak of perfection, raising plants from seeds and cuttings, shaping fruit trees to give the best crops or fashioning topiary, results rather than speed were the prime consideration.

The right tools, as well as a sufficiency of time were essential in this pursuit of perfection. Gardeners of the past had perhaps a greater appreciation of the importance of selecting the tools for a job, and as the following pages show, a well-tended garden would have an armory of forks, spades, pruners, gatherers, scythes and sickles as well as large stocks of pots, bell-jars, hand-lights and forcers. The great range of these implements was a testimony to the attention to detail prevalent in those times.

THE AGE OF CRAFTSMANSHIP
An antique garden seat shows an artistry characteristic of a time when mass-production had yet to be invented.

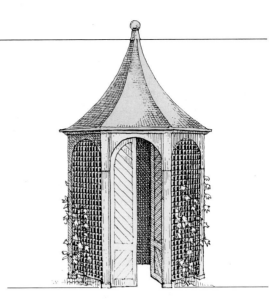

Few of us today have either the means or the time to create gardens that must be maintained by such laborious techniques. Decisions therefore have to be made about which techniques to follow, and which to pass over in favor of the less time-consuming modern alternatives outlined in the following chapters.

On a practical level, traditional gardening is a matter of compromise, the art being to compromise in those areas that will save time or expense without having a disadvantageous effect on the result. This applies especially to long-term projects such as topiary. If you have time, you could develop maiden trees into topiary over a period of several years, as would have been done in former times. But if you are impatient to achieve the effect that topiary would have on the ultimate design of your garden, you may well decide to pay for well-shaped container-grown shrubs instead, and be content to shape them with shears and secateurs as they develop.

· PATTERNS FROM THE PAST ·

After a period of innovation and modernism in gardening, which has in many ways reflected the same process in the field of architecture, we seem at present to be entering a more reflective age. More and more of us today feel the desire to perpetuate past traditions rather than spearhead new ones.

Seeing fine examples of topiary, sitting in inviting period conservatories, or discovering darkly surprising grottos may be all it takes to instill the drive to reproduce the same effect around your home. It is the aim of this book to provide you with all you will need to create a successful classic garden today.

THE HERBACEOUS BORDER

*The flight from formality — A Victorian duet —
The great autumn dig — Sweetening the soil — Classic
proportions — Variations on the theme — Some border
favorites — Screen planting — The mixed border*

THE ALMOST CASUAL INFORMALITY THAT CHARACTERIZES A TRADITIONAL herbaceous border might well convince innocent spectators that they are looking at nature indulging in an Elysian rampage. Such borders were described by the English Victorian writer Percy Lubbock. The effect, to use his words, was one in which "not a flower could look constrained," which had "a bushy luxuriance of phlox and rosemary," and where there was "a mazy confusion of everything that gleams and glows and exhales a spicery of humming fragrance." The lasting impression the border created was that of "rambling and crowding in liberal exuberance" in which "everything bloomed tumultuously."

AN AIR OF ABUNDANCE
The essence of a traditional herbaceous border is not so much a profusion of colors as a profusion of forms, as this border in the White Garden at Sissinghurst demonstrates.

**PLANTS FROM
THE NEW WORLD**

*As trade and exploration
expanded in the eighteenth
and nineteenth centuries,
many plants were carried
between continents. On
arrival, they were then bred
commercially and made
available to gardeners for
the first time. The Americas
were a particularly rich
source of border perennials
for European gardens,
providing – among other
species – phlox, dahlias,
hostas, alstroemerias and
evening primrose. This last
plant was particularly
popular because its blooms
open just before dusk, when
most other flowers have
closed up.*

ALSTROEMERIA

EVENING PRIMROSE

What man, a visitor might have reflected, could possibly have contrived such a triumphant profusion of leaf and flower, such a harmonious spectrum of vibrant color?

The answer to such a question may well have lurked close at hand. If, from his discreet cache in the shrubbery, the head gardener glimpsed their obvious wonder, he would have chuckled and felt satisfied. Yet again his show feature had accomplished its mission of inducing a memorable delirium. The gasps of admiration would have been his recompense for the hours of backaching work that continued throughout the year, reaching a crescendo every autumn.

For in the great traditional herbaceous borders of the past, nature concealed not only art, but also sheer manpower expended on a massive scale. The border may have looked a "mazy confusion" but in reality it was a carefully prepared horticultural set-piece that required rigorous planning and perfect execution.

The challenge today lies in reproducing something of that tumultuous effect with a fraction of the space and labor available in former times.

· OBSCURE BEGINNINGS ·

It is difficult to know just when the herbaceous border first appeared, or who was responsible for it. Certainly the plant ingredients of the herbaceous border – hardy perennials such as oriental poppies, red-hot pokers, agapanthus, alstroemeria and plantain lilies, all of which could be grown together *en masse* – poured into Europe from the eighteenth century onwards as plant collectors scoured the globe.

There are charming contemporary watercolors of a great herbaceous border that existed at Arley Hall in Cheshire as early as 1845. While the plants seem to have been more formally grouped than in the classic border, the overall effect in summer was very similar to that of the great herbaceous borders that later figured so prominently in many English country gardens.

· THE FLIGHT FROM FORMALITY ·

Rather more easy to establish than the date of the herbaceous border's first appearance is the notion that originally lay behind it. For most of the nineteenth century the idea prevailed that a good garden consisted of a series of rigidly geometric carpet beds set in grass and packed with bright annual plants arranged to form patterns. This persisted for the first half of the twentieth century in municipal parks, and vestiges of it are still to be seen.

These annual plants had to be raised by the thousand from seed in heated glasshouses, a propagation program of baffling complexity that began early in the year and ran right through into the summer. Keeping the beds bright and beflowered from spring through until autumn often involved changing the plants several times per season. Color and symmetry were paramount, with little concern being felt about the unnaturalness of the display. It was inevitable that after a period of such stifling and often unimaginative formality, a reaction would eventually set in.

· A VICTORIAN DUET ·

The two figures most closely associated with the break from carpet beds and rigid planting were Gertrude Jekyll and William Robinson. Jekyll's background as a painter and Robinson's experience as a plantsman gave each of them a nostalgia for the freer attitude towards planting to be found in some simpler cottage gardens. Here, flowering plants had continued to be grown long after anything so vulgar had been banished from the immediate surrounds of the great houses.

In the eighteenth century the "landscape" movement *(see p.122)* had swept flowering plants aside to be replaced by an idealized landscape of grassy parkland with gentle slopes, copses of native trees and distant glimpses of impressive water features. Flowers were grown to decorate the house, but they were kept out of sight in remote, walled kitchen gardens.

Cuttings, offsets and seeds from these gardens must certainly have been smuggled out to grow alongside the rhubarb and the gooseberries in thousands of humble cottage gardens. It was in these gardens that natural, liberal exuberance was to be found.

Much has been made of the claim that William Robinson was responsible for pioneering the idea of the herbaceous border after he moved to England in the 1860s. But what he proposed seems to be much more what today we would consider a mixed border *(see p.29)*, which includes a year-round skeleton of evergreen shrubs. Robinson's real contribution to border-making was probably his influential advocacy of a freer, "wilder" and more natural use of plants than many of his contemporary Victorian gardeners favoured.

After 1890, Gertrude Jekyll certainly developed the art of border-making to its high point. In writing about it so cogently she was responsible for making it a mandatory feature of her style in garden schemes from that time onwards. She used her talents, which were originally channeled into painting and designing embroidery, to teach how Robinson's tenets could be adopted to the greatest effect.

· AN EYE FOR COLOR ·

Among Gertrude Jekyll's many contributions to the art of gardening, one of the most invaluable was her approach to the use of color. Nowhere is this more clearly shown than in some of the herbaceous borders she designed.

Color selection obviously involves a good deal of subjectivity. In carpet bedding, color contrasts of the strongest possible kind were always in vogue. But in her work with herbaceous borders, Jekyll looked for a very different effect. She created swathes of plants that produced a painterly impression, with subtle color transitions as the eye roamed the length of the border.

Partly through her work it became accepted that most color changes from one area of a border to another had to be introduced gradually. The margins of a red area, for example, would display plants whose blooms were a very pale pink, while the more obtrusive reds would be confined to the central areas of that block. Very pale pinks, it was felt, could be blended satisfactorily with very pale yellows, and this was the way of linking bold reds and very intense yellows in adjacent blocks. In the same way, pale pink could happily be married with pale lilac and

thus used to link red blocks to blocks containing dark blues and bright purples.

· THE GREAT AUTUMN DIG ·

In creating a traditional herbaceous border to suit today's garden, there are, as we shall see, some "short cuts" that can be taken. This is fortunate, because in these days of more casual gardening, it is astonishing to discover just how much work the creation and maintenance of a traditional herbaceous border entailed.

The tasks marched in step with the weather of the English seasons, with new beds being made and old ones refurbished during the period of the great autumn dig. A complicated series of operations had to be accomplished in the usually short weather "window" between the moderately dry summer and the wet autumn. This was the only time, between the seasons of active growth, when so much groundwork was possible. If left until later, the soil became heavy and waterlogged.

We tend to forget, in these days of sophisticated mechanization, that such work required the skills of a formidable garden staff. In a larger household it often comprised more than 10 people if the two or three apprentices (the "improvers," who would have recently left

LABORING ON THE LAND

This team of gardeners, photographed in about 1900, shows how much labor was needed to maintain the grounds of an English country house. The head gardener sits near the center, while around him are ranged the under-gardeners and general laborers, while at the front is an apprentice or improver. Although the gardeners may well have enjoyed their work, the conditions in which they lived could be less than congenial. Garden staff were usually poorly paid, and they and their families often lived in cramped quarters attached to the walled kitchen garden.

RECREATING A JEKYLL BLUE BORDER

L IKE ALL TRUE ARTISTS, MANY DESIGNERS OF CLASSIC GARDENS BELIEVED that rules could be broken to good advantage. One result of this was the monochromatic border, pioneered by Gertrude Jekyll. In this, flowers of a single color are allowed to dominate, so that the variations in color normally present in a traditional herbaceous border become transformed into changes of tone.

In her writings, Jekyll set down detailed records of some of her planting plans, making it possible to recreate her work today. The blue border shown here was originally designed to be a double feature some 75 feet (23 m) long – dimensions that are far too generous for most modern gardens. However, such was the attention to detail of Jekyll's planning that a much smaller length of the blue border is still extremely effective.

As with all traditional borders, the depth from front to back, rather than the length, is crucial if the right effect is to be obtained. The blue border is 12 feet (3.5 m) deep. This allows plants to be grouped so that they rise gently from the front, progressing through species of medium height, to truly imposing plants such as delphiniums at the back.

BLUE BORDER PLANTING PLAN

AREA SHOWN PLANTED UP

1 **White perennial pea** *Lathyrus latifolius* 'Albus'
2 **Delphinium** *Delphinium × belladonna*
3 **Variegated corn** *Zea mays*
4 **White tree lupine** *Lupinus arboreus*
5 **Rue** *Ruta graveolens*
6 **Yucca** *Yucca filamentosa*
7 **Sea holly** *Eryngium giganteum*
8 **Lithospermum** *Lithodora diffusa*
9 **Sea holly** *Eryngium × oliverianum*
10 **Lily** *Lilium monadelphum*
11 **Plumbago** *Plumbago auriculata*
12 **Yucca** *Yucca recurvifolia*
13 **White hollyhock** *Alcea rosea*
14 **Yellow meadow rue** *Thalictrum flavum*
15 **Corn** *Zea mays*
16 **White lupine** *Lupinus polyphyllus*
17 **Alkanet** *Anchusa angustissima*
18 **Madonna lily** *Lilium candidum*
19 **Clematis** *Clematis heracleifolia* var. *davidiana*
20 **Phacelia** *Phacelia campanularia*
21 **Delphinium** *Delphinium × belladonna*
22 **Lily** *Lilium longiflorum*
23 **Plumbago** *Ceratostigma plumbaginoides*
24 **Variegated coltsfoot** *Tussilago farfara* 'Variegata'
25 **White snapdragon** *Antirrhinum majus*
26 **Gentian sage** *Salvia patens*
27 **Yellow snapdragon** *Antirrhinum majus*
28 **Clematis** *Clematis recta*
29 **Silver grass** *Miscanthus sinensis*
30 **Plantain lily** *Hosta sieboldiana*
31 **Delphinium** *Delphinium grandiflorum*
32 **Goat's beard** *Aruncus dioicus*
33 **Plantain lily** *Hosta plantaginea* 'Grandiflora'
34 **White foxglove** *Digitalis purpurea* 'Alba'
35 **Yellow lupine** *Lupinus polyphyllus*
36 **White lupine** *Lupinus polyphyllus*
37 **Mullein** *Verbascum phlomoides*
38 **Variegated manna grass** *Glyceria aquatica* 'Variegata'

WHITE LUPINE
Lupinus polyphyllus
A short-lived perennial propagated by division.

YELLOW MEADOW RUE
Thalictrum flavum
Foam-like flowers on stately, robust stems

CORN
Zea mays
An annual planted for its foliage.

YUCCA
Yucca filamentosa
A stemless yucca grown for its foliage and flowers

DELPHINIUM
Delphinium × belladonna
A majestic plant that requires careful staking

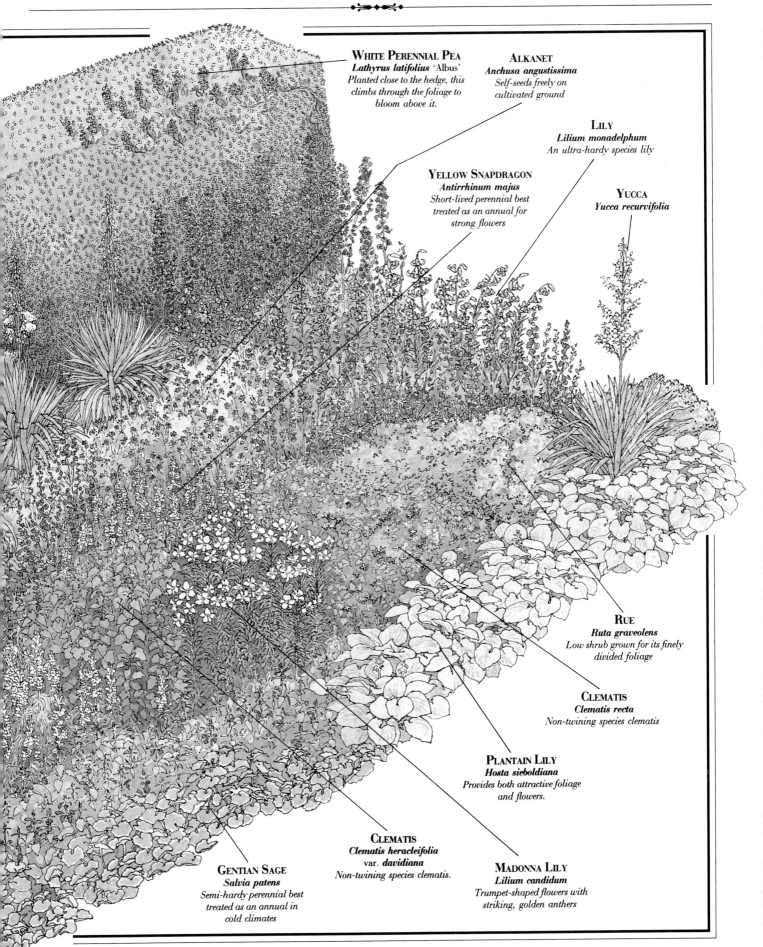

WHITE PERENNIAL PEA
Lathyrus latifolius 'Albus'
Planted close to the hedge, this climbs through the foliage to bloom above it.

ALKANET
Anchusa angustissima
Self-seeds freely on cultivated ground

LILY
Lilium monadelphum
An ultra-hardy species lily

YELLOW SNAPDRAGON
Antirrhinum majus
Short-lived perennial best treated as an annual for strong flowers

YUCCA
Yucca recurvifolia

RUE
Ruta graveolens
Low shrub grown for its finely divided foliage

CLEMATIS
Clematis recta
Non-twining species clematis

PLANTAIN LILY
Hosta sieboldiana
Provides both attractive foliage and flowers.

GENTIAN SAGE
Salvia patens
Semi-hardy perennial best treated as an annual in cold climates

CLEMATIS
Clematis heracleifolia
var. *davidiana*
Non-twining species clematis.

MADONNA LILY
Lilium candidum
Trumpet-shaped flowers with striking, golden anthers

TURFING
SPADE WITH
SIDE-CUTTING
FLANGES

TRIANGULAR
TURFING
SPADE

SEMICIRCULAR
TURFING SPADE

school) were included among their number.
Then, as now, the workload was heaviest when
new beds were to be created on land under grass.
It was only after the turf had been laboriously
removed and set aside for use elsewhere in the
garden that the digging itself could begin.

· THE BACKBREAKING ART OF TRENCHING ·

Most of the best borders were made on soil that
had been cultivated down to more than 3 feet
(1 m). Excavating to this depth was accomplished in several stages by adopting a procedure
known as *trenching*. The purpose of trenching,
and indeed any form of digging, is to aerate the
soil and improve drainage while removing every
scrap of the roots of perennial weeds. In trenching, the soil was also deepened and the subsoil's
fertility improved, making it fit to support the
growth of the deeper-rooted perennials.

True trenching on a site that had a deep
covering of topsoil involved digging down to the
equivalent of two spade-depths or *spits*. The
topsoil would be excavated and then the base of
the trench probed and broken up with a fork,
making it easier for plant roots to penetrate deep
into the ground. At this point, some organic
matter would be added to improve the subsoil's
fertility and enable it to hold moisture. When this
had been done, a small quantity of this improved

subsoil would be dug out and mixed with the
topsoil before it was replaced. The result was that
every time the bed was trenched, the depth of
useful soil beneath it would gradually increase.

On land with a thin topsoil lying over thick
clay, gardeners would set aside the topsoil and
laboriously dig out the clay. The topsoil would
then be put into the bottom of the trench and the
abandoned clay replaced by an equivalent
volume of high-quality loam that was brought
in from elsewhere.

Even the best loam was never likely to drain
satisfactorily if it sat on a solid bed of clay, and to
remedy this, trenches in clay were often dug a
further 6 inches (15 cm) deep and the extra space
filled with coarse gravel or broken bricks. Rainwater could percolate easily through this layer,
and a hollow tile drain set along one edge would
conduct the water away.

Where a truly impenetrable barrier such as
solid rock made deep trenching impossible,
gardeners fell back on an inferior technique
known as *bastard trenching*, in which the topsoil
was dug only to a single spit.

· SWEETENING THE SOIL ·

Few people today would have either the time or
the inclination to dig down through the top yard
of their garden to create a border. However, to
the gardener of the last century, it was an

essential part of the process of border-making. Much of the soil depth demanded by the head gardeners of old was to accommodate long tap-roots and provide a sufficiently rich supply of nutrients. They went to extraordinary lengths to ensure that the soil had high fertility and the correct texture. Treatments were as varied as the characters of the gardeners who applied them. Each gardener had his own mysterious formula in which he placed his faith. However, while they all guarded the fine details of their procedures with the jealousy of medieval alchemists, they all used similar sources of both nutrients and soil-conditioning agents in their mixtures.

In an age when horses were still used for transport and hens, pigs and cows were kept quite close to the centers of towns, animal manure was always the most significant additive to the beds. It was used in massive quantities. One or two large barrow-loads were forked into every square yard of the freshly dug soil. In their efforts to make truly heavy soils more tractable

gardeners often added lime, coarse sand, wood ash, bone meal and basic slag to the soil. Other additions included *shoddy* (the leftovers from woollen yarn manufacture) and even meat meal, something which on health grounds is certainly not recommended for gardens today.

· SHALLOW BEDS ·

The attention to soil quality was what made the best traditional herbaceous borders – the variety of plant forms they offered reflected the amount of effort that had gone into pampering their roots. This richness can still be obtained in smaller gardens by planting in a smaller area. However, for a garden that does not have the space for larger perennials, there is the expedient of using more compact herbaceous plants.

There are these days a great many splendid alpine versions of common border plants. Minia-ture campanulas, poppies, violas, roses, golden-rod, asters, hardy geraniums, phlox, dianthus, scabious, potentillas and many others have long

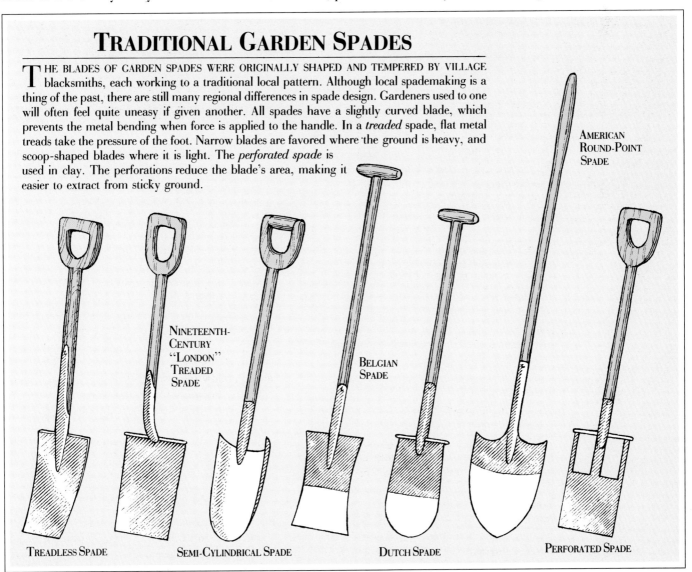

TRADITIONAL GARDEN SPADES

THE BLADES OF GARDEN SPADES WERE ORIGINALLY SHAPED AND TEMPERED BY VILLAGE blacksmiths, each working to a traditional local pattern. Although local spademaking is a thing of the past, there are still many regional differences in spade design. Gardeners used to one will often feel quite uneasy if given another. All spades have a slightly curved blade, which prevents the metal bending when force is applied to the handle. In a *treaded* spade, flat metal treads take the pressure of the foot. Narrow blades are favored where the ground is heavy, and scoop-shaped blades where it is light. The *perforated spade* is used in clay. The perforations reduce the blade's area, making it easier to extract from sticky ground.

AMERICAN ROUND-POINT SPADE

NINETEENTH-CENTURY "LONDON" TREADED SPADE

BELGIAN SPADE

TREADLESS SPADE

SEMI-CYLINDRICAL SPADE

DUTCH SPADE

PERFORATED SPADE

FORMALITY AND FREEDOM

This double border (above) is laid out on formal lines, flanking a path that leads deep into the garden. Much of the border's charm derives from the combination of informal plants seen within a formal layout. In the less structured border (right) herbaceous plants are massed in front of an old wall, giving a delightful impression of unruly abundance.

been available and recently breeders have even produced tiny chrysanthemums. These plants have shallower roots, and are small enough to allow them to be planted close together without them appearing overcrowded. It is possible to make a small area of a much shallower bed – even on a balcony or in a roof garden – produce a rich tapestry of color throughout a long season.

The particular advantage of alpine plants when used in this way is that, provided the drainage is good, they will thrive on soils of low fertility, making much of the work involved in enriching traditional beds superfluous.

· CLASSIC PROPORTIONS ·

The best model for making a traditional border is, of course, an old existing one, and the best time to see it is in the height of summer. By following the original details of shape, positioning and planting, while at the same time reducing the overall dimensions, you should be able to capture some of the cascading grandeur present in a border on the largest of scales.

Traditional borders are surprisingly deep. Early manuals dictated that borders should never be less than 4 feet (1.2 m) and preferably at least

8 feet (2.4 m) from front to back. In fact, borders of 10 to 14 feet (3–4 m) deep were more usual in the gardens of grand houses because it was felt that only with such dimensions could a sufficient variety of plants, flowering from late spring to late autumn, be displayed. The grand effect was also much to do with the height of the planting of the back end of the bed, gradually reducing towards the front – a transition that needs considerable depth.

The conclusion for the modern gardener is clear: in reducing the dimensions of a border, depth, rather than length, is the crucial dimension, and it should not be over-compressed. The narrower the border becomes, the less is the space for the interplay of flower forms and colors.

· VARIATIONS ON THE THEME ·

While the majority of herbaceous borders took the form of long rectangles there were many variants. Sometimes they had serpentine backing hedges or walls, which curved in and out. In others, the front edges were scalloped.

Nineteenth-century gardening books are full of illustrations showing the various ways, by using pegs and string lines, that the geometry of beds on paper plans could be translated into

PLANTING AND WEEDING

Trowels and hand-forks, which are essential for close work in a herbaceous border, are tools with an ancient pedigree, and have appeared in many different styles. Trowels and forks are used for planting and weeding where access is easy. When border plants start growing in the spring, the long-handled fork and pronged hoe make it easier to work the ground without damaging the foliage.

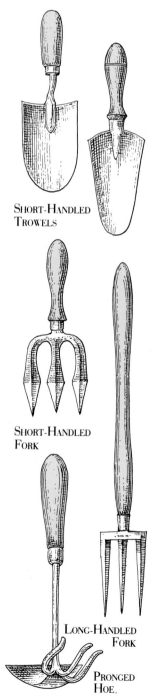

SHORT-HANDLED TROWELS

SHORT-HANDLED FORK

LONG-HANDLED FORK

PRONGED HOE.

actual scaled-up shapes on the ground. Circles, ovals and spirals were favored for free-standing "island" beds. These had one advantage, in that they could be enjoyed from all sides, but they were more exposed to wind and the taller plants therefore needed more staking.

The best herbaceous borders were always positioned to ensure that the plants in them received the maximum sunlight. One technique was to incline the level of the soil upwards towards the back of the bed. This also allowed the smaller plants to be seen more clearly. The only exception would be beds specifically designed to show off shade-loving plants such as Solomon's seal, lungwort, mimulus and brunnera. The other major factor determining their location was the desire that they should feature prominently in the vista from the main sitting rooms and terrace. The border was something to show off to guests during a pre-dinner stroll.

· PROTECTION FROM THE ELEMENTS ·

To provide the plants with the best possible conditions for growth, traditional borders were frequently backed by walls of mellow stone or brick 10–15 feet (3–4.5 m) high. These screened the plants from damaging cold winds. Tall thick hedges of dark evergreen yew were preferred by many as a foil for brightly colored border blooms. Alternatively, trelliswork, heavily planted with climbers, could be used as a backing for borders in places where it had a role to play in the overall garden design. While they did not act as such solid barriers to the wind, hedges and trellises slowed it down very effectively and created less damaging turbulence in the relative shelter of their lee side.

Because old borders were frequently backed by hedge plants, roses, or espaliered fruit growing on walls or trellises, a narrow path was usually left along the back. This prevented the roots of the background plants and the border plants from competing too vigorously. It also enabled the gardeners to get to the back of the bed to weed or tie up some of the taller plants like hollyhocks. If you have the space, it is a very practical feature, well worth including.

While few gardens today are bounded by walls reaching 10 feet (3 m) or more, a wall that just reaches the tops of the tallest plants will provide adequate protection from the wind. Wooden fencing is best clothed with climbers on a support, such as trelliswork of a traditional design *(see p.27)*, that can be detached when fence maintenance is necessary. As an alternative, you might choose to use dark green wood-preservative to tone the fence itself. Backing hedges are easily planted, but be wary of

evergreens such as cypresses that grow too rapidly and swamp the plants in front of them.

· PLANTING PLANS ·

Expressing the accumulated experience of nearly a century of making herbaceous borders Coutts, Edwards and Osborn, curators at Kew Gardens in 1930, wrote that "arranging herbaceous plants in borders according to their height" was still the most effective way of planning a border.

It was a maxim of Gertrude Jekyll's that no soil should be visible in a border in summer. To ensure that this was so, annual or biennial plants were used to fill any gaps between the perennials. These were either sown directly into the border, or transplanted from boxes in the greenhouse, frames or open ground elsewhere.

In the best borders, few plants went into the ground individually (thereby avoiding a trap into which today's more parsimonious gardeners often fall). Most of the larger plants like irises, lupines, peonies, delphiniums, phlox, asters, bergamot, day lilies and red-hot pokers were planted in groups of four to five or eight to nine. The smaller the plant when mature, the larger the number in the group. Smaller plants were set at 8 inches (20 cm) apart, medium-sized plants at 15 inches (40 cm) and really tall plants at 2-foot (60 cm) intervals.

The groups of plants were arranged to produce interweaving, irregularly shaped drifts of massed harmonious color rather than formally arranged isolated patches. But care was taken in spacing the groups to see that extra-vigorous plants, such as lupines and peonies, were not allowed to choke their neighbors.

· SOME BORDER FAVORITES ·

Among the towering favorites for the back of the border hollyhocks, delphiniums, red-hot pokers, gaillardias, goldenrods, Michaelmas daisies, evening primrose and acanthus were the most frequently planted. As plants of intermediate height, few gardeners ignored the appeal of gladiolus, alstroemeria, euphorbias, foxgloves, irises, peonies, lupines or oriental poppies. In this middle rank of the border there was a bewildering choice of plants – it also included astrantia, Solomon's seal, phlox, plantain lilies, lilies, bergenias, brunneras, carnations, astilbes, penstemons and chrysanthemums. At the front edges came the smallest plants, species such as thrift, trilliums, lady's mantle, hardy geraniums, columbines, polyanthus, pinks, auriculas, primulas, violas, saxifrages, alyssum and nasturtiums seeded directly into place.

As Gertrude Jekyll often pointed out to her disciples, the plan was never allowed to be too stiff because freedom and irregularity provided much of the charm of the herbaceous border. This meant that while generally obeying the rule of arranging the plants according to their height, it was successfully disobeyed by placing taller plants at intervals towards the front edge of the border. Plants like greenhouse-reared castor oil plants were often used in this way, and today abutilons are often used for the same purpose.

· SCREEN PLANTING ·

As it develops through the season, a good border presents a dynamic rather than a static picture as particular plants grow, flower and die back. The great gardeners were able to plan and exploit the sequence of border happenings to best effect. They could plan that during each week of the season from spring through to the first autumn frosts, there would always be something attractive and in flower in each sector of the bed. And, cleverer still, they were masters of screen planting, ensuring that plants that flowered early always had some slower starters placed in front of them. These would grow up to screen the early-flowering plants as they died back and became untidy.

Considered individually, the design problems created by the plants' different sizes, shapes, flowering times and colors may appear easy to solve. Since they occur simultaneously, integrated solutions are necessary, and that demands a real mastery of the border-maker's art.

· SUPPORTING ROLES ·

Having transformed a planting plan into a finished border, the team of gardeners in a large household would then turn their attention to ensuring that it produced the best possible display. One of the most important jobs they had to carry out was staking the growing plants.

As the season progressed, border plants, nourished by a fertile soil, produced luxuriant, fleshy stemmed growth, which was no match for the wind and rain of the English climate. Staking was essential to prevent tall plants from collapsing and ruining the display.

Any plant whose stems reached 2½ feet (75 cm) or more was supported. The prescription was that "each strong shoot of very tall plants should have its separate stake to preserve the natural contour of the plant." Bamboo was the first choice for this work. Most plants that did not exceed the specified height were cradled in a ring of string stretched between three or four stakes set around the base of the plant and leaning slightly away from it. Plants that produced only one or two tall central spires of flowers were attached to a single upright stake.

We have a great deal to learn from the techniques that were used in supporting plants. Victorian gardeners used raffia (also known as *filis* or *bass*) and soft "tarred" string for tying the plant stems to stakes. They took care not to tie them too tightly to avoid damaging the plants and to leave them looking as natural as possible. To the same end, stakes were painted dark green or brown· to make them less obvious among the foliage.

Twiggy branches of hazel were prized as stakes for multistemmed plants. Their flexibility was a bonus because they gave slightly in the wind, so preventing the delicate flowers becoming damaged. Cut deal was often used to make particularly strong stakes for supporting plants like the larger-flowered dahlias, which have heavy heads. The stakes' pointed ends were sometimes charred in a fire before being dipped in creosote to preserve them.

When, towards the end of the nineteenth century, metal technology became highly evolved, and rigid wire and steel rod was available in many grades, ingenious manufac-

PRUNING AND DEAD-HEADING
Every year, the abundant growth of the herbaceous border has to be carefully tended in order to maintain the display for as long as possible. This gardener shows the traditional equipment for the job – a basket for collecting prunings, spent flowers and weeds, and a wooden barrow for removing them to the compost heap. When carrying bulky materials, the barrow was fitted with high sides to cut down the number of journeys that had to be made.

PLANTING A COMPACT HERBACEOUS BORDER

ALTHOUGH THE HERBACEOUS BORDER WAS originally developed as a feature for larger gardens, there are ways in which it can be modified to suit a more restricted space. The border here shows what can be done within the more limited confines of a typical modern garden. It is 5 feet (1.5 m) deep, and 9 feet (2.75 m) wide. Instead of having a backing hedge, it is bounded by a tall trellis over which climbing plants can scramble and flower.

The plants used include many that found favor in Victorian times and also a few, such as ornamental gourds, that are less expected, and create added interest when seen at close quarters. The planting plan also features spring-flowering bulbs, such as crocuses, narcissi and tulips, which provide color while the perennials are still in early growth without competing with them.

No part of a garden entirely looks after itself, and the border requires some maintenance if a consistently good display is to be produced year after year. Most of the plants will flourish with little attention apart from weeding and cutting down in the autumn.

COMPACT BORDER PLANTING PLAN

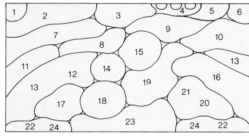

1. **Japanese honeysuckle** *Lonicera japonica* 'Halliana'
2. **Hollyhock** *Alcea rosea*
3. **Michaelmas daisy** *Aster novae-angliae* 'Harrington's Pink'
4. **Ornamental gourd** *Cucurbita pepo* var. *ovifera*
5. **Delphinium** *Delphinium* 'Butterball'
6. **Rose** *Rosa* 'Mermaid'
7. **Lupine** *Lupinus* 'George Russell'
8. **Bearded iris** *Iris* 'Tangerine Sky'
9. **Delphinium** *Delphinium × ruysü* 'Pink Sensation'
10. **Goat's beard** *Aruncus dioicus*
11. **Astilbe** *Astilbe × arendsii*
12. **Narcissus** *Narcissus* 'Cheerfulness'
13. **Alstroemeria** *Alstroemeria ligtu* hybrids
14. **Martagon lily** *Lilium martagon* 'Marhan'
15. **Regal lily** *Lilium regale*
16. **Masterwort** *Astrantia major*
17. **Chrysanthemum** *Chrysanthemum rubellum*
18. **Peony** *Paeonia lactiflora* 'Globe of Light'
19. **Phlox** *Phlox paniculata*
20. **Plantain Lily** *Hosta* 'Thomas Hogg'
21. **Tulip** *Tulipa* 'White Triumphator'
22. **Polyanthus primrose** *Primula* Polyanthus group
23. **Water avens** *Geum rivale*
24. **Crocus** *Crocus vernus*

BACKING TRELLIS Painting the trellis white will emphasize its decorative value until the plants climb over it

ORNAMENTAL GOURDS *Cucurbita pepo* var. *ovifera* Self-supporting climbers producing unusual fruit.

REGAL LILY *Lilium regale*

JAPANESE HONEYSUCKLE *Lonicera japonica* A very vigorous honeysuckle that quickly produces a floral screen behind the border

HOLLYHOCK *Alcea rosea*

LUPINE *Lupinus* 'George Russell' Plants need replacing after about three years

BEARDED IRIS *Iris* 'Tangerine Sky'

ALSTROEMERIA *Alstroemeria ligtu* hybrids. In cold areas, these should be lifted each autumn and replanted in spring

POLYANTHUS PRIMROSE *Primula*

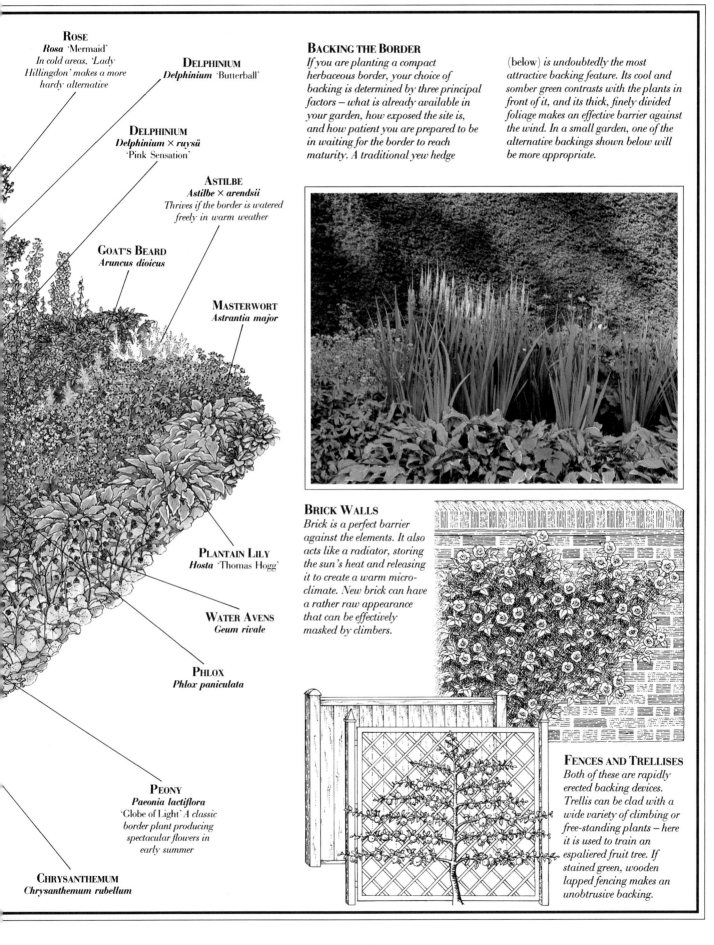

ROSE
Rosa 'Mermaid'
In cold areas, 'Lady Hillingdon' makes a more hardy alternative

DELPHINIUM
Delphinium 'Butterball'

DELPHINIUM
Delphinium × *ruysü*
'Pink Sensation'

ASTILBE
Astilbe × *arendsii*
Thrives if the border is watered freely in warm weather

GOAT'S BEARD
Aruncus dioicus

MASTERWORT
Astrantia major

PLANTAIN LILY
Hosta 'Thomas Hogg'

WATER AVENS
Geum rivale

PHLOX
Phlox paniculata

PEONY
Paeonia lactiflora
'Globe of Light' *A classic border plant producing spectacular flowers in early summer*

CHRYSANTHEMUM
Chrysanthemum rubellum

BACKING THE BORDER

If you are planting a compact herbaceous border, your choice of backing is determined by three principal factors – what is already available in your garden, how exposed the site is, and how patient you are prepared to be in waiting for the border to reach maturity. A traditional yew hedge (below) is undoubtedly the most attractive backing feature. Its cool and somber green contrasts with the plants in front of it, and its thick, finely divided foliage makes an effective barrier against the wind. In a small garden, one of the alternative backings shown below will be more appropriate.

BRICK WALLS

Brick is a perfect barrier against the elements. It also acts like a radiator, storing the sun's heat and releasing it to create a warm micro-climate. New brick can have a rather raw appearance that can be effectively masked by climbers.

FENCES AND TRELLISES

Both of these are rapidly erected backing devices. Trellis can be clad with a wide variety of climbing or free-standing plants – here it is used to train an espaliered fruit tree. If stained green, wooden lapped fencing makes an unobtrusive backing.

turers developed designs for plant supports. Many of these are still made and can be used today in the same way as in former times.

· THE AUTUMN REFIT ·

In late autumn, when all the problems involved in creating new borders had been overcome, gardeners on large estates would turn their attention to maintaining those that were already well established. Borders that had been in place for three or four years, and begun to perform less splendidly in the summer because the soil had become too consolidated, weed-infested and to some degree exhausted, needed considerable work. Most of the plants whose flower color, size and vigor had deteriorated would be dug out and their crowns heeled into temporary beds in the vegetable garden. The only plants left in place would be those that perform best if

undisturbed, such as irises, lilies, delphiniums and peonies. When most of the border was cleared, it would be fully or bastard trenched depending on its condition before replanting.

Such techniques have changed little over the years. A spade, border fork, dividing knife and a little patience are still the essential tools required to keep border perennials at their best.

Refurbishing the borders in this way allowed new arrangements of the plants to be tried and enabled notable new varieties or families to be included. Throughout the nineteenth and early twentieth centuries, more and more herbaceous plants were discovered by plant explorers. They were brought out of wild places in many parts of the world to be improved by selection and hybridization and thus provide new plants for the border. Both gardeners and their patrons were always anxious to try them. In England, compe-

TOOLS FOR TRANSPLANTING

THE VICTORIAN PASSION FOR IRONMONGERY IS PARTICU-larly well demonstrated in the variety of tools that they used for lifting and moving plants. Small plants would be moved by placing the transplanter over the plant, and then pushing it home into the soil. Once the transplanter was in position, it would be locked, either by applying pressure to its

handles, or by operating its locking mechanism, which could be a sliding ring, rack or lever. When the root-ball was gripped firmly, it would be pulled up intact. To move a larger plant, a circular trench was first made around the plant, and then a cylinder transplanter dropped into it. Its two halves were then brought together and locked, and the plant lifted.

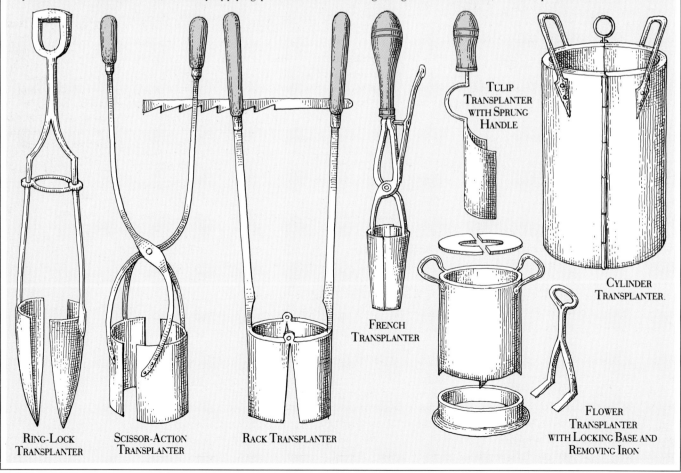

TULIP TRANSPLANTER WITH SPRUNG HANDLE

CYLINDER TRANSPLANTER.

FRENCH TRANSPLANTER

FLOWER TRANSPLANTER WITH LOCKING BASE AND REMOVING IRON

RING-LOCK TRANSPLANTER

SCISSOR-ACTION TRANSPLANTER

RACK TRANSPLANTER

tition to grow them was notoriously keen. It frequently led to disputes when gardeners or their masters were discovered discreetly pillaging neighboring gardens for cuttings of rare plants recently introduced.

Usually the subjects of this gardening brigandage were improved or differently colored versions of many of the plants which had been available to gardeners before the epoch of great herbaceous border-making began. Today, the clamor for new varieties has somewhat abated as the preference for the natural look has gained the upper hand. Furthermore, those novelties that are produced can readily be bought, and so the temptation to engage in such pillage has largely (if not wholly) gone.

Apart from any new plants to be included, most of the plants used in the renovation were obtained by dividing healthy sections of crown and root from the plants previously removed from the border. These offshoots are found towards the margin of the crown. They were carefully separated from it by steeping in water to remove all the soil, disentangling the roots, and cutting the crown with a short knife.

Cuttings of summer shoots and stems, rooted in pots or boxes, were the other major source of plant material used to renew borders. Gardeners also frequently devoted a section of their greenhouses to raising herbaceous perennials from seed collected from the borders in the autumn.

· THE MIXED BORDER ·

Before the Second World War, houses could still be found in Britain that had sufficiently large staff of gardeners to maintain herbaceous borders in the old way. But it has become increasingly difficult to afford their management, even on a reduced scale. Consequently, another expedient has evolved: the mixed border, which in many ways harks back to the ideas of William Robinson a century ago.

Robinson was a keen advocate of mixing flowers with trees and shrubs. A mixed border makes use of this idea by having shrubberies with a cultivated edge and tongues of dug soil projecting into the gaps between the shrubs. It is in these gaps that the herbaceous perennials are planted, creating swathes of color in the spring and summer.

Herbaceous plants in situations like this require less labor all round. They need little staking because of the screening provided by the shrubs, and these days unseen drip irrigation equipment and electronically controlled taps can take all the work out of watering. Furthermore, because the perennials are mingled with shrubs, the border never develops the traditional her-

baceous border's very dead look in the winter.

Even with a mixed border, there does remain the problem of weeding, which used to call for so much time with fork and hoe. Applying herbicides to any kind of border is clearly very difficult, but measures can be taken to suppress the weeds and prevent them gaining a hold.

Weeding the areas between shrubs in a mixed border can be greatly reduced if, before planting, the soil is clad with a black plastic sheet hidden below a masking layer of coarse ground tree bark. Another very acceptable low-maintenance solution is to make all the garden into a mixed border, mingling trees, shrubs and herbaceous plants very freely. The ground is then topped with very coarse grit or attractive gravel laid over weed-suppressing black plastic. Areas of the garden to be used as paths or sitting areas are simply left unplanted.

By using this short cut, the herbaceous border can be made if not work-free, at least manageable. The effort is well rewarded because, apart from their contribution of color to a garden, herbaceous borders alone bring with them the excitement of watching the annual development of plants from insignificant crowns in bare earth in the winter, through the full glory of their flowers in spring and summer, to their frequently beautiful autumn demise.

EASY-CARE PLANTING
The border at the foot of this old greenhouse is composed of shrubs and perennials, and gives a delightful impression of color and profusion in return for relatively little maintenance. The shrubs suppress much of the weed growth that occurs in a traditional herbaceous border, where the ground is left bare in winter.

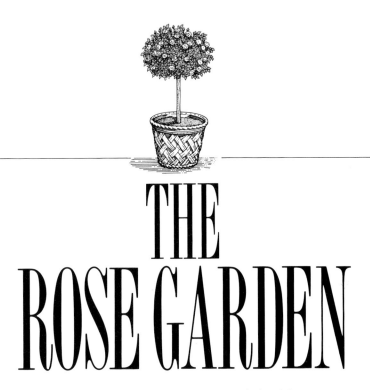

THE ROSE GARDEN

Dogs and Damasks — Cross and double-cross —
The nineteenth-century rose garden — Rose management
— Victorian rose care — Arches, tunnels and garlands
— Old roses for new gardens

Iᴛ ɪꜱ ɴᴏᴛ ᴅɪꜰꜰɪᴄᴜʟᴛ ᴛᴏ ɪᴍᴀɢɪɴᴇ ᴛʜᴇ ᴇxᴄɪᴛᴇᴍᴇɴᴛ ᴏꜰ ᴘᴀꜱꜱᴇɴɢᴇʀꜱ ᴏɴ ᴛʜᴇ first trading vessels from Europe, calling into Canton in the middle of the sixteenth century. Apart from encountering a highly developed culture more ancient than their own, the keen gardeners among them must have gasped with astonishment when they entered the Fa Tee nurseries on the outskirts of the town. For there they would have encountered hundreds of roses growing in pots, roses with an allure quite different from that of the roses then common in Europe. They were smoother stemmed, less prickly and, more importantly, capable of flowering several times during the season, with peaks in early summer and early autumn. Finally, and most astonishing to European eyes, some of them were *yellow*.

The fact that these Chinese roses were grown in pots made it relatively easy for travelers who recognized the great significance of their characteristics to bring some of them home to Europe. In doing so, they made it possible to conceive of the rose garden as the separate entity that we know today. Before the introduction of the Chinese strains to western Europe, a garden planted only with roses would have been a dreary place except for a

SUMMER ROSES
Such is the charm and variety of cultivated roses that, uniquely among garden plants, they are often planted exclusively to produce spectacular color and heady perfume.

FROM A MEDIEVAL GARDEN

This woodcut from Gerard's Herbal, which was first published at the end of the sixteenth century, shows a cultivated variety of the white-petalled Rosa alba. The flamboyant flowers and double petals of this specimen demonstrate that even at this early date, garden roses had been the subject of extensive improvement on wild forms.

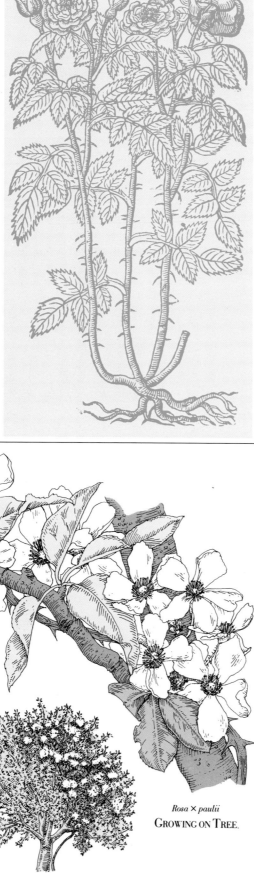

NATURAL SUPPORT

Although many wild roses are free-standing, others have a more straggling and lax habit, and rely on neighboring plants for support. In a garden, these species roses and their hybrids make an effective display when allowed to climb through trees.

Rosa × paulii
GROWING ON TREE.

few brilliant weeks in early summer, when the roses burst into bloom.

· THE FAME OF THE ROSE ·

Despite their short flowering season, the blooms of European roses were so admired that few gardens were without them. As well as the charm and light fragrance of their flowers, there were the culinary and medicinal properties of their hips, and the fact that sweet perfumes could be extracted from their petals. From the earliest days of European gardening, these useful features assured them of a place in most gardens.

Certainly, by the time the Romans came to dominate Europe, they had developed the growing of roses into a high art. Roses were so appreciated for their ritual, decorative and useful roles (their petals being used to make perfume and create fragrant and soothing pillows) that they were grown in large nurseries south of Rome. To help overcome the great problem of their seasonality, the Romans even had roses grown in Egypt and shipped to Rome while still in bud.

Today's professional growers of California, southern France or Italy, who organize local parades and battles-with-roses to publicize their industry, might well be jealous of the scale of Roman rose festivities. Emperors like Nero regularly ordered the streets and temples to be strewn with millions of blooms during festivals.

· DOGS AND DAMASKS ·

The roses that the Roman throngs crushed beneath their feet were almost certainly selected from the few species of wild rose known to have existed in Europe at that time. Naturally occurring variants of these roses, or hybrids between them, would have provided the raw material from which choice blooms could be created. Notable among these parent roses were *Rosa canina*, the common hedgerow dog rose, which usually has simple pink blossoms and *Rosa gallica*, which usually has semi-double red blooms and is thought to be a native of southern Europe. Both these species flower briefly but gloriously in early summer, producing distinctive hips in autumn.

By the Middle Ages, Damask roses were added to the list. They are highly fragrant with clear pink blooms. The summer Damasks are thought to have originated as natural hybrids between *Rosa gallica* and *Rosa phoenicia*, a species found in the Middle East. The autumn Damasks, which are only distantly related, were probably brought back to France from Persia by the Crusaders. These possess some ability to reflower in the autumn, and were the only roses in Europe with that capacity, prior to the introduction of truly reflowering or "remontant" roses from China.

· CROSS AND DOUBLE-CROSS ·

This handful of European species and their hybrids are likely to have been found in mediaeval *garths*, the tiny gardens created high up among the turrets of fortresses, remote from the stink and clamor in the courts below. They were also known to be present in cloisters and *paradises*, which were often created as isolated areas beyond the apse of monastery churches, and used for quiet contemplation.

Later, in Tudor gardens, another rose began to appear alongside them. The newcomer was *Rosa moschata*, which is believed to have been brought into Europe via Spain by the Moors. They valued it for its musky odor and for the fact that its flowers were borne in clusters, not as single widely separated blooms as was the case in all the other species then available.

In the early seventeenth century, Dutch rose breeders were probably responsible for producing the heavy-bloomed Centifolia or cabbage roses, whose pinks do not fade in strong sunlight. Their offshoots, the moss roses, which have a moss-like growth on their sepals and flower stalks, came from the same source. It is likely that these two groups of roses resulted from crosses between *Rosa gallica*, *Rosa phoenicia* and *Rosa moschata*. The Centifolia roses in particular must have been warmly welcomed by late seventeenth- and eighteenth-century gardeners because they brought greater variety to their gardens.

Although most of these earlier rose hybrids were short-seasoned singles, they were also extremely pretty, and many of them have survived to be grown today. Rosa Mundi, a sport, or chance variant, of *Rosa gallica* is a good

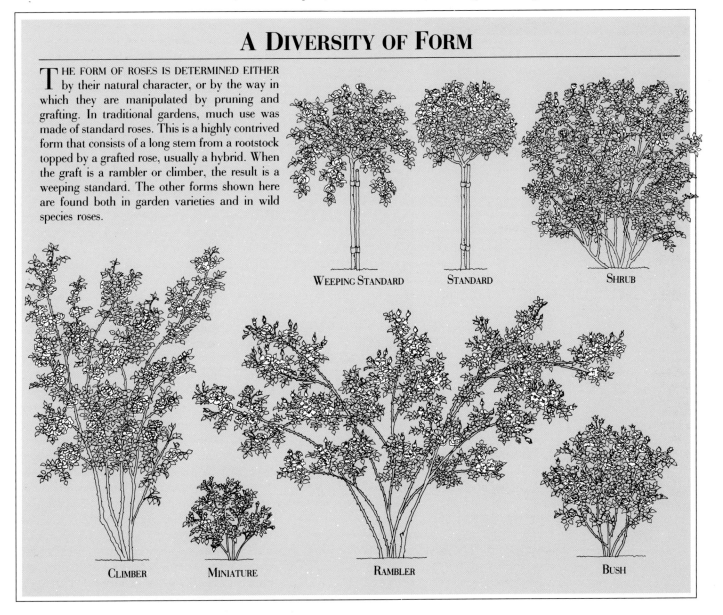

A DIVERSITY OF FORM

THE FORM OF ROSES IS DETERMINED EITHER by their natural character, or by the way in which they are manipulated by pruning and grafting. In traditional gardens, much use was made of standard roses. This is a highly contrived form that consists of a long stem from a rootstock topped by a grafted rose, usually a hybrid. When the graft is a rambler or climber, the result is a weeping standard. The other forms shown here are found both in garden varieties and in wild species roses.

WEEPING STANDARD   STANDARD   SHRUB

CLIMBER   MINIATURE   RAMBLER   BUSH

A ROSE SEAT
Growing a rose around a seat allows its delicious perfume to be fully appreciated. The rose seen enveloping this bench at Mottisfont Abbey in Hampshire is 'Constance Spry'. Despite the old-fashioned appearance of its flowers, this is in fact an outstanding modern shrub rose (see p.41) produced by crossing old varieties.

example. With its vivid pink petals distinctly striped with white, it is as chic as anything a modern designer could dream up. Its charms, however, are too fleeting to tempt anyone to grow it *en masse* in a bed and allow it to dominate the planting in a garden. This is presumably why, until the early 1800s, roses were used as we use specimen plants today. The documentary and pictorial evidence we have suggests that they were located individually, where they could be sufficiently prominent when looking their best, but where their presence would not be too intrusive when their charms began to fade.

· A FRENCH REVOLUTION ·

When the introduction of remontant Chinese roses made the exclusive planting of roses a possibility, one of the first to realize their potential was Napoleon's first wife, the Empress Joséphine. She was an extraordinary figure in the history of rose growing, and her origins were as exotic and her story as remarkable as that of the flowers she favored.

Marie Joséphine Rose Tascher de la Pagerie, to give her her original name, was a mixed-race child born on the Caribbean island of Martinique. Accepted into the island society as the offspring of the wealthy plantation-owning class, she attracted the attention of the aristocratic Alexandre de Beauharnais, who married her and took her to Paris. Her husband was guillotined in 1794, but this did not prove at all a setback to Joséphine, who became such a brilliant figure in

the salons that she was introduced to Napoleon, who married her in 1796.

After being crowned Empress in 1804, Joséphine tired of a surfeit of court life and frequently fled Paris to the house at Malmaison which Napoleon had had built for her. Here she created a splendid garden, which included a *jardin à l'anglaise*, streams with cascades, a temple of love, and what we can consider one of the world's first genuine rose gardens. This was an innovation in garden design, with paths meandering between bed after bed of roses, grown as bushes or standards, in pure stands on bare soil. Sometimes the paths ran beneath rambler-clad pergolas and arches, among roses on pillars and obelisks, or between trellis screens and metal frames on which the roses were espaliered.

As opposed to making romantic, natural-looking pictures in the rose garden at Malmaison, Joséphine created something highly contrived and charming which, for its management, demanded the techniques of high gardening. Its stagey style earned it the name *gardenesque*.

As well as the many hybrids of the species roses, which had been selected in Europe prior to the 1770s, Joséphine was able to include a host of new repeat-flowering China roses, of which three forms — crimson, pale pink and intense pink — were initially available.

· THE BIRTH OF MODERN ROSE BREEDING ·

Had she lived a little longer, Joséphine would have been able to plant two further types of repeat-flowering roses with exotic origins. In 1819, the Paris nurseryman Louis Noisette introduced a pink-flowered climber that developed from a cross between *Rosa moschata* and the pink Chinese species *Rosa chinensis*. The cross was made in America by an acquaintance of his brother Philippe.

From the island of Bourbon (now named Réunion) in the Indian Ocean came the first roses to bear that name. They were launched on the market by the Paris nurseryman M. Jacques in 1822. Owners of estates on Réunion surrounded their gardens with hedges of roses — usually a row of *Rosa chinensis* and a row of *Rosa damascena* because their matted prickly stems discouraged marauding animals and people. An estate owner noticed one plant very different from the others, and in 1817 the director of the island's botanic garden realized that this unique plant must be a hybrid between *Rosa chinensis* and *Rosa damascena*. He sent cuttings back to Jacques in France in 1819.

By 1824, a significant yellow rose had arrived

AN ANCIENT LINEAGE

FEW GARDEN PLANTS ARE SO REDOLENT OF GARDENING history as old roses. Although they frequently flower only for short periods, and may be difficult to prune because they are very thorny, old roses have a relaxed form and a charm that some of the more recent hybrids undoubtedly lack. The restrained hues and delightful perfumes of old roses such as the Gallicas, Centifolias and Damasks make the periods when they are not in flower a time of pleasant anticipation. The tremendous range of rose varieties has been produced in two ways. In the first, new characteristics appear spontaneously in plants known as *sports*. In the second, new varieties are cultivated by the deliberate or accidental crossing of two parents.

SPECIES ROSE
All cultivated roses spring originally from wild species roses, of which there are hundreds worldwide. Some species roses, such as the European dog rose Rosa canina, shown here, are occasionally grown in their wild form in gardens.

ALBA ROSE
Albas are hybrid roses of ancient origin. They flower once in early summer, and are highly resistant to disease. Alba Maxima, or the Great Double White, shown here, is a medieval variety.

GALLICA ROSE
The Gallicas are among the most ancient of cultivated roses, flowering once in early summer. This is Rosa Mundi, or Rosa gallica 'Versicolor', the oldest striped rose, which probably dates from the fifteenth century.

CENTIFOLIA ROSE
Centifolia roses, also known as cabbage and Provence roses, are ancient hybrids that have long been grown for ornament, and also to produce rose perfume. This is Rosa × centifolia.

BOURBON ROSE
Bourbons were a favorite of Victorian gardeners, who prized their rich perfume and also their ability to flower repeatedly. This variety, 'Madame Pierre Oger', was discovered in the 1870s, and became one of the most widely grown of the Bourbons.

CHINA ROSE
China roses have a long history of cultivation in the East, but their introduction to Europe dates back only to the late eighteenth century. Like most China roses, 'Mutabilis' has little scent, but makes up for this by having a long flowering period.

MOSS ROSE
These roses are characterized by a moss-like growth that covers their stems and buds. The mutation that causes moss roses has arisen a number of times on Damask and Centifolia roses. This is 'Nuits de Young', a compact Damask moss raised in 1845.

RAMBLER ROSE
Ramblers are vigorous roses that have large panicles of small flowers. Their parentage is complicated, being hybrids of species from Europe and the Far East. Rosa multiflora, shown here, is a wild rambler from China.

BLOOM SHADES

Victorian gardeners used special shades to protect blooms intended for cutting or showing from the sun and rain. The shade's metal collar was attached to a spike, and this was driven into the ground next to the plant.

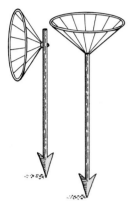

NAMES TO REMEMBER

In a well-run rose garden, the many different rose varieties would be labeled so that they could be readily identified. Early labels were ornate objects made of ceramic or zinc, either tied to the plants or pushed into the ground. The lettering would be painted or engraved. For everyday gardening, plainer zinc labels would be marked with a lead pencil – simple but surprisingly permanent.

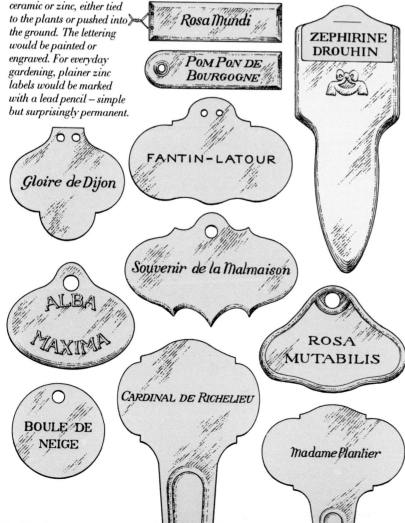

from China. This was *Rosa gigantea*, which had long, light yellow petals and the delicate fragrance of China tea. Crosses between *Rosa gigantea* and *Rosa chinensis*, which were both vigorous ramblers, provided stocky bushes with high-centered buds. These became known as Tea roses.

With all this new genetic material available and a more highly developed understanding of sexual reproduction in plants, rose breeders began the vast hybridization programs that have led to the astonishing range of roses we have available today. The use of Tea roses in crossing ultimately led to the production of the high-budded Hybrid Teas. From their first appearance they have played a dominant role in rose gardens which, until today, have mostly followed the style created by Joséphine at Malmaison.

· MINIATURES AND MONSTERS ·

Two further species roses have had a strong influence on the appearance of our garden roses. Some time before 1868, *Rosa multiflora*, whose small flowers are borne in clusters, arrived in Europe from Japan. When crossed with the Hybrid Tea roses, it yielded a whole range of dwarf Polyantha roses. From these, the larger-flowered Floribundas later developed. By 1891, the strident reds and yellows of *Rosa foetida* (the ill-named Austrian briar, which actually comes from Iran and Kurdistan) had been transferred to other hybrids, increasing the rose-breeder's palette still further.

The tiny-flowered Scottish burnet rose *Rosa pimpinellifolia* gave breeders the ability to miniaturize blooms, and the tough Japanese shrub rose *Rosa rugosa* also donated some of its rugged characteristics to hybrid roses.

By the end of the nineteenth century, rose nurseries were able to offer gardeners bush or standard plants that varied in height between 18 inches (45 cm) and 10 feet (3 m), with climbers capable of reaching 25 feet (7.5 m) or more against sheltered walls. Their blooms could vary from tiny white florets borne in clusters, to crush-petalled Bourbons as big as tennis balls.

· THE NINETEENTH-CENTURY ROSE GARDEN ·

The huge choice of roses available by the middle of the last century allowed rose gardens to be made to many different designs. Plants of different heights might be arranged in tiers on flat land, or similarly sized plants could be laid out on steps on sloping land to form "rose cascades." The varieties were sometimes chosen so that they flowered at different times, ensuring that the beds remained interesting and allowing their predominant colors to change throughout the season.

Even for people as staid as our nineteenth-century forebears, it is astonishing to see quite how formal their rose gardens could be. One favored plan involved planting five oval lines of roses of increasing height inside one another to form a floral crown. The planting was completed by stationing eight equally spaced standard roses around the crown like soldiers guarding a monarch's funerary bier. The bed was approached by paths from the four cardinal points which led to a perimeter path around the bed from which the view would barely change as the visitor progressed.

Paintings like Monet's *Femmes au Jardin*, which dates from 1867, demonstrate the appeal which rose gardens had for artists in the nineteenth century. It also shows that it was the practice to plant the roses in bare ground, which was kept free of weeds and all other plants. Reacting against the carpet-bedding craze in the second half of the century, many gardeners seem to have turned to roses as substitutes for the annuals that were formerly used to plant up

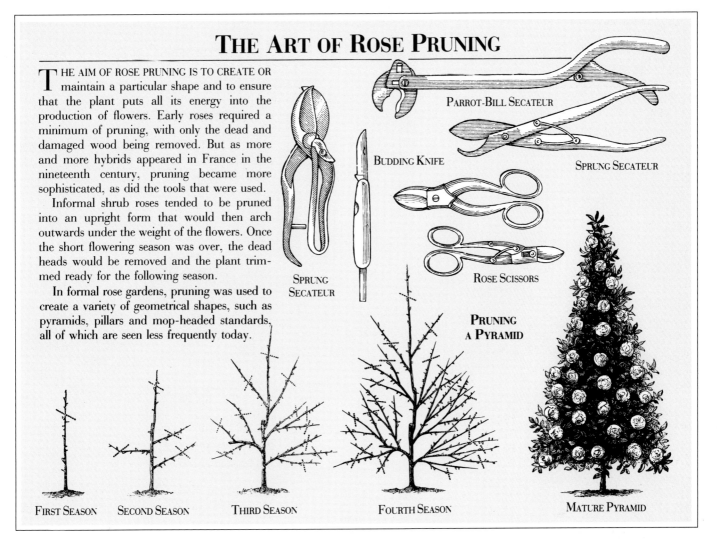

THE ART OF ROSE PRUNING

THE AIM OF ROSE PRUNING IS TO CREATE OR maintain a particular shape and to ensure that the plant puts all its energy into the production of flowers. Early roses required a minimum of pruning, with only the dead and damaged wood being removed. But as more and more hybrids appeared in France in the nineteenth century, pruning became more sophisticated, as did the tools that were used.

Informal shrub roses tended to be pruned into an upright form that would then arch outwards under the weight of the flowers. Once the short flowering season was over, the dead heads would be removed and the plant trimmed ready for the following season.

In formal rose gardens, pruning was used to create a variety of geometrical shapes, such as pyramids, pillars and mop-headed standards, all of which are seen less frequently today.

PARROT-BILL SECATEUR

BUDDING KNIFE

SPRUNG SECATEUR

SPRUNG SECATEUR

ROSE SCISSORS

PRUNING A PYRAMID

FIRST SEASON SECOND SEASON THIRD SEASON FOURTH SEASON MATURE PYRAMID

---

flower beds. This approach to rose cultivation continues to this day.

· ROSE MANAGEMENT ·

With the development of sophisticated rose gardens, and the breeding of hybrid varieties, the workload of the traditional gardener was greatly increased. The species roses of earlier centuries required little attention. Because they were essentially wild plants, they were easily propagated by cuttings, and could be allowed to grow on their own roots. Pruning, too, was a simple operation.

With the introduction of new hybrids, which were needed in their hundreds if they were to make an acceptable "show," all that changed. Gardeners were expected to become first-class rosarians, possessing all the necessary skills to keep the roses both in bloom and in health.

One of the first things they had to learn was to recognize useful and superfluous wood: what to prune away to stimulate good growth and flowering in the following season, and when it should be done. Most of the newer hybrids made better roots and performed more uniformly when

grafted on to the more vigorous roots of species roses. Gardeners had to learn to identify suckers growing from the rootstocks and to remove them effectively, so that they did not deprive the hybrid stems of nutrients for growth.

To ensure a sufficient supply of roses to replace losses or fill further beds, gardeners had to become masters of the art of budding, which was the most widely adopted form of propagation. This involved removing a bud from some recently flowered young wood of the hybrid, and inserting it beneath the bark, low down on a stem emerging from the rootstock. It was an operation that was carried out in nursery beds in the kitchen garden, and it required surgical skills of a high order that could only be learned by example and much trial and error.

· VICTORIAN ROSE CARE ·

For much of the nineteenth century, symmetry in plants was highly respected, and gardeners were always vigilant to ensure that neither developing buds, blooms nor foliage were damaged by insect or disease attack. By the 1890s, a range of

PRACTICAL PEST CONTROL

Victorian gardeners could remove aphids from their roses with the aphid brush, *an ingenious little device small enough to be carried in the pocket. The soft brushes dislodged aphids without doing any damage to the plant.*

SPRUNG APHID BRUSH

CREATING A VICTORIAN ROSE WALK

THE ART OF GROWING ROSES IN FORMAL WALKS IS SOMETHING that is undergoing a resurgence in popularity as gardeners rediscover this traditional alternative to the more familiar rose bed. The walk shown here has six different varieties of rose, nearly all of nineteenth-century origin. Some flower once in summer, while others are remontant, giving a longer display. The arrangement includes four classic rose shapes. In the typical nineteenth-century manner, the walk is devoted solely to roses, with no other blooms competing for the attention.

RAMBLER 'ALBÉRIC BARBIER'
Not as old as the other varieties in this grouping, 'Albéric Barbier' was raised in 1900. It has large, pale yellow flowers and deep green foliage and makes an excellent variety for training up a wall.

STANDARD 'BOULE DE NEIGE'
A row of "shrub standards" of this white Bourbon rose, introduced in 1867, provides the walk with height and form. The trunks should be about 4 feet (1.2 m) high.

SHRUB 'CÉCILE BRUNNER'
This Polyantha rose was raised in 1881. It forms a small shrub that produces large flower panicles throughout the summer.

SHRUB 'FANTIN-LATOUR'
Named after the painter, Henri Fantin-Latour, at the end of the nineteenth century, the origin of this Centifolia rose is unknown. Its buds are initially deep pink, the flower opening to reveal white petals with a pink flush.

SHRUB 'MADAME HARDY'
A Damask raised in the 1830s, this rose has brilliant white flowers with green centers. The flowers are slightly cupped, and the petals densely clustered.

PILLAR 'ALBÉRIC BARBIER'
To produce a pillar, the rose's stems are trained on a cylinder of stakes, or stakes that support wire netting. Severe pruning maintains the geometric shape.

PLANTING THE WALK

The walk should be marked out before planting so that each bed is 20 feet (6 m) long and about 4 feet (1.2 m) deep. The individual plants should be positioned so that each shrub rose is approximately 5 feet (1.5 m) from its neighbor. The standards are planted within the gaps left between the shrubs.

The roses should reach their mature dimensions in about three to four years.

ROSE WALK PLANTING PLAN

1 'ALBÉRIC BARBIER'

2 'CÉCILE BRUNNER'

3 'BOULE DE NEIGE'

4 'FANTIN LATOUR'

5 'MADAME HARDY'

6 'KÖNIGIN VON DÄNEMARK'

7 'ALBÉRIC BARBIER'

SHRUB 'KÖNIGIN VON DÄNEMARK'

This striking Alba rose, first grown in 1826, is generally held to be one of the best of all old varieties. Its flowers have deep pink centers with paler petals towards the edges.

fungicides was available to keep roses blemish-free. They included sulphur dust to counteract powdery mildew and Bordeaux and Burgundy mixtures, based on copper sulphate and used to protect against downy mildew. Insecticides were also available, including nicotine decoctions, extracts of derris and pyrethrum, and arsenic-containing compounds like Paris Green and London Purple. There were efficient syringes and knapsack sprayers to apply these substances.

Most of these measures were precautionary and had to be taken before the pest or disease arrived. Spraying was therefore carried out with military precision according to a tight operational schedule.

Selective weedkillers at this time were unknown, so in most gardens the topsoil was lightly disturbed to ensure that no weed was ever allowed to grow beyond its first visible seedling stage. Copious watering, too, was considered *de rigueur* in dry weather because, although roses will tolerate some drought, they are much more beautiful if never stressed for water. The ability of organic matter to improve water retention in the soil led to all rose growers placing great faith in heavy mulching with animal manure – particularly stable manure – early in the spring. They also applied fertilizers such as dried blood and bone-meal at this time.

To boost the supply of nutrients for mid- and late-season blooming, the diligent gardener was advised to make summer top-dressings with fertilizers high in potassium. Wood ash was favored in the early days of rose-growing, but this was replaced by mineral potash when

SWAMPED BY FLOWERS

The sight of a vigorous rambling rose in full flower, as seen here at Sissinghurst, is one of the glories of a traditional garden in early summer. Large ramblers can reach considerable proportions within a surprisingly short time.

supplies from Alsace and elsewhere became more readily available late in the nineteenth century.

· ARCHES, TUNNELS AND GARLANDS ·

Many nineteenth-century rose planting plans were too formal and required too much mainten-ance to be in tune with modern tastes. However, despite the general propensity to excessive order and decoration, elements in the nineteenth-century rose garden are well worth including in a garden today.

Apart from laying out their roses in geometri-cally shaped beds, the Victorians experimented a great deal with different forms of supports. Arches, made out of bent metalwork, were very popular as a decorative feature over paths. Separate sections could be linked together to form extensive tunnels. The simplest types of these metal supports were, for Victorian garden decorations, fairly plain: flat strips of iron formed the main structure of the frame, while horizontal metal rods provided support for the plants. For this reason they are well suited to many modern gardens. The use of an arch as a gateway, even in a garden where space is at a premium, creates an enticing feeling and breaks up a view.

As well as tying or training roses to rigid structures, nineteenth-century rose gardeners made climbers and ramblers spread along swags of stout rope or chain to provide a garland effect. Sometimes their flexible younger stems would be intertwined within the supporting frame and all the side-branches removed until they had reached a certain height. When those stems had become woody and strong, the supports would be removed to leave bizarre but decorative man-made "trees." Although not everyone would want to experiment with this effect, simple swags and garlands make an attractive and traditional eye-catcher. An equally interesting feature is created by growing roses in a flowing mass.

· OLD ROSES FOR NEW GARDENS ·

Many twentieth-century rose varieties are the products of the single-minded pursuit of such characteristics as repeat-flowering and large bloom size. In order to achieve these qualities, the delicate nature and fragrance of old roses, not to mention their pleasing foliage and shape, has been sacrificed. Intensive breeding has brought its own problems. Modern roses often require extensive pruning, mulching and spraying to

CLASSIC ROSE SUPPORTS

THE USE OF SUPPORTS FOR GROWING ROSES REACHED its heyday in the last century, when a wide variety of forged iron arches, tunnels and umbrellas could be found in gardens. All of these had the advantage of giving familiar plants an unfamiliar shape, and they made eye-catching architectural features that enhanced formal planting schemes. Growing roses on supports is fairly easy, because compared with many garden plants, roses will tolerate a great amount of interference in the way they grow.

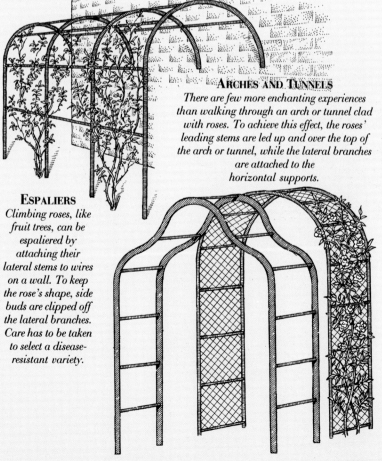

ARCHES AND TUNNELS
There are few more enchanting experiences than walking through an arch or tunnel clad with roses. To achieve this effect, the roses' leading stems are led up and over the top of the arch or tunnel, while the lateral branches are attached to the horizontal supports.

ESPALIERS
Climbing roses, like fruit trees, can be espaliered by attaching their lateral stems to wires on a wall. To keep the rose's shape, side buds are clipped off the lateral branches. Care has to be taken to select a disease-resistant variety.

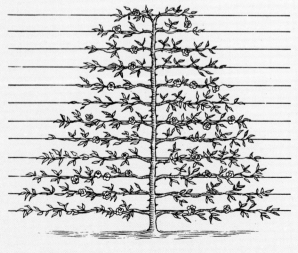

keep them in peak condition. However, as we near the end of another century of rose breeding, more and more gardeners are beginning to appreciate the subtler qualities of old roses, and this is reflected in a steadily increasing supply of many traditional favorites, some of which date back to medieval times.

As well as supplying these truly old varieties, rose growers today often stock modern varieties that have the outward appearance of old roses, but which lack some of their disadvantages. These modern shrub roses are hybrids between old roses and species roses. They are large and vigorous, but unlike old roses, are repeat-flowering. They require hardly any maintenance, resist disease well and produce charming loose and fragrant blooms as a result of the most rudimentary pruning. When grown alongside old roses, they make a delightful contrast to the lifeless, waxy blooms of Hybrid Teas that monopolize so many rose beds.

· ROSE-GROWING IN COMPACT GARDENS ·

As gardens become smaller, breeders have recently concentrated on producing space-saving dwarf or even truly miniature roses. These, together with the more compact bush and standard hybrids, can also be used to good effect in mixed borders.

One way to enjoy roses where space is limited is to allow them to grow up shrubs and trees. Although any two plants growing together will compete to some extent for light, many roses will thrive in this situation. The rose needs to be chosen with care, because, as in topiary, it is often a mistake to buy a variety that will grow quickly. Prodigious growth often means constant attention. A rambler such as *Rosa filipes* 'Kiftsgate' can produce shoots that grow 12 feet (3.5 m) in a season, which can be a problem if your neighbors do not share your enthusiasm for its rampant nature.

If you are attracted to the idea of a pure rose bed of the traditional type, it is possible to achieve an eye-catching yet compact summer display without suffering a long barren period in winter and early spring. Planting spring bulbs followed by forget-me-nots will mask the rose stems until the first buds open. Some ground-cover plants will also hide the earth without robbing too much nutrient from the roses.

ROSES IN CONTAINERS
Roses have compact root systems, making the smaller varieties suitable for growing in containers. The square-sided wooden tub is a traditional container that has long been used for rose-growing. Originally made to be seen on terraces and in orangeries (see p.144), it is ideal for today's balconies. As with all container-grown shrubs, roses must never be allowed to dry out completely.

UMBRELLAS
In Victorian times, gardeners used several techniques to make "trees" out of climbing roses. This nineteenth-century umbrella frame has a broad dome over which the branches from the main stem are allowed to fall.

FESTOONS AND SWAGS
Ramblers or climbers can be trained along swags of rope that are supported by stout posts. Light wooden arches give a similar effect, and both are useful for backing a formal rose bed, or for marking garden boundaries in a decorative way.

CASCADE
By combining several stems inside this framework, the mature plants spill out of the top producing a cascade of blooms. When planted with vigorous roses, supports like this can make imposing garden features within two or three seasons.

THE HERB GARDEN

Growing herbs in containers — Culinary and medical herbs — The Renaissance herb garden — Herb gardening in colonial America — Growing herbs informally

IT WAS GROWING HERBS FOR CULINARY, MEDICINAL AND COSMETIC purposes that seems to have kept the beacon of high gardening alight in the Dark Ages, between the fifth and eleventh centuries. By then, herb gardening was already an ancient art. The first herbals, or written guides to herbs, were produced by the Chinese over three thousand years earlier. Knowledge of herbs gradually spread westward, reaching the Middle East a millennium later, where it was recorded on stone tablets by the Sumerians, before arriving at the shores of Europe.

Over the ages, much debate has centered on exactly which plants have a proven medicinal value. In the earliest herbals, belief in magic enshrouded the supposed properties of many of the plants listed, and it was not until classical times that any attempt was made to assess the real merit of the herbs available. Hippocrates, the father of Western medicine, listed a total of four hundred useful species. By the time the Greek physician Dioscorides wrote his great work *De Materia Medica* in the first century BC, the useful list had increased to six hundred.

In many ways, herb gardening today owes a great deal to *De Materia Medica*. This monumental herbal was painstakingly hand-copied and it spread throughout Christendom, remaining in daily use for fifteen hundred

HISTORY IN HERBS
Once treasured for their practical properties, herbs are now increasingly appreciated for their beauty and the sense of history they bring to a garden.

THE RAISED BED
This medieval woodcut shows a gardener working with a raised bed, in which earth is banked up behind retaining boards. Raised beds are ideal for growing herbs because they ensure good drainage.

years. It informed and guided herbalists from classical to medieval times, and helped them to create the herb gardens and physick gardens attached to temples, monasteries and great houses. It is these gardens, with their carefully arranged plots of medicinal and culinary plants, that are the inspiration behind so much herb gardening today.

· HERBAL RETREATS ·

The earliest Middle Eastern herb gardens were attached to temples and sacred groves and were tended by priests. In Egyptian reliefs and Persian paintings the gardens were shown as being formal and rectilinear, and they were usually protected from wild animals by walls or fences. The plants were confined to long, narrow beds with paths and irrigation channels between. There was frequently a rectangular central tank or pool that acted as a source of much-needed water, and the humid atmosphere produced by the water would have carried the scent of the plants, especially in the evening when the air began to cool.

Herb gardens of this type can make attractive features today in gardens where formality is the keynote. In recreating them, authenticity in design is easier to achieve than authenticity in the choice of plants, because there are no detailed records of exactly which plants were grown. However, it is safe to assume that lavender and myrtle were among them, and it is known for certain that scented roses, particularly the Damasks *(see p.32)*, would have been grown among the herbs on supports.

Today, the threat of wild animals has been replaced by that of burglars, and for this reason alone, walls still have their value. However, as an

alternative, the same feeling of enclosure can be produced by an evergreen hedge of a species such as the pencil-shaped American incense cedar. This New World tree resembles the cypresses of the Middle East, but unlike them it is fully hardy. It produces a resinous fragrance, especially when the leaves are touched.

· GROWING HERBS IN CONTAINERS ·

Herbs are particularly well suited to being grown in containers, because most of them – the woody species especially – appreciate moderately dry, well-drained soil. Some herbs, especially the mints, have very invasive roots, and growing these in containers prevents them spreading in an uncontrolled way.

Besides growing their herbs in open beds, the Romans were exponents of the art of growing them in pots. One of the reasons for this was that much of their gardening was urban, being carried on within the confines of high-rise tenements where the only places to grow plants were balconies and windowsills.

Herbs are especially rewarding plants for today's town gardeners. Taking only a little space, they scent the air beautifully and produce a supply of material for the kitchen, as well as being highly decorative.

To break away from the purely functional approach of having single plants in small pots, ready for use in the kitchen, it is worth using larger pots and massing a number of smaller plants together. Just as in a garden border, this will give a much more striking effect. With larger plants such as tarragon, rosemary and lavender, a single specimen can be allowed to grow into a large bush, which can be clipped to shape.

One of the joys of growing herbs in containers is that their position is never fixed. As soon as you tire of one arrangement, you can try another, perhaps bringing the ones in flower into a prominent position, and "retiring" those that have passed their prime.

· THE MEDIEVAL HERB GARDEN ·

Our best information about medieval herb gardens comes from an early planting plan for an idealized monastery garden, which was found among the manuscripts at the monastery of St. Gall in Switzerland. The kitchen garden was stationed next to the poultry runs, and consisted of 18 narrow rectangular beds where dill, coriander and chervil were grown among the cabbages and carrots. There were sixteen plots in the *herbularius*, which was set just outside the infirmary, where sage, rue, rosemary, lilies and roses were among the many herbs to be grown. As well as being used as medicine, medieval

CONTAINERS FOR HERBS

B Y USING CONTAINERS, AN HERB GARDEN CAN BE CREATED almost anywhere, from a town balcony to a garden doorway within easy reach of the kitchen. As with all container gardening, careful siting is needed to ensure the best results. A position in full sun encourages the production of aromatic oils, but exposure to strong winds will damage leaves and impair growth. The ideal site is both light and sheltered.

Herbs differ in their soil requirements. Those from Mediterranean hillsides, such as sage and rosemary, are adapted to life on poor, well-drained ground. This can be created in a pot by mixing loam with an equal volume of horticultural grit. Many Mediterranean herbs grow naturally on limestone, and adding lime to the mixture will keep them in good health. Plants from damper habitats, such as mint or chives, require a richer soil that retains moisture.

Most annual herbs do not require a great depth of soil, although there are exceptions to this rule, such as borage, a fast-growing plant that has a deep tap-root. Biennials, such as parsley, will thrive if given sufficient depth of soil from their first year. If they are confined in an inadequate volume of soil, they may well be stressed into flowering early, at the expense of producing leaves. Woody perennials, such as sage and rosemary, should be planted singly and moved to larger pots as they grow, autumn being the best time to make the change.

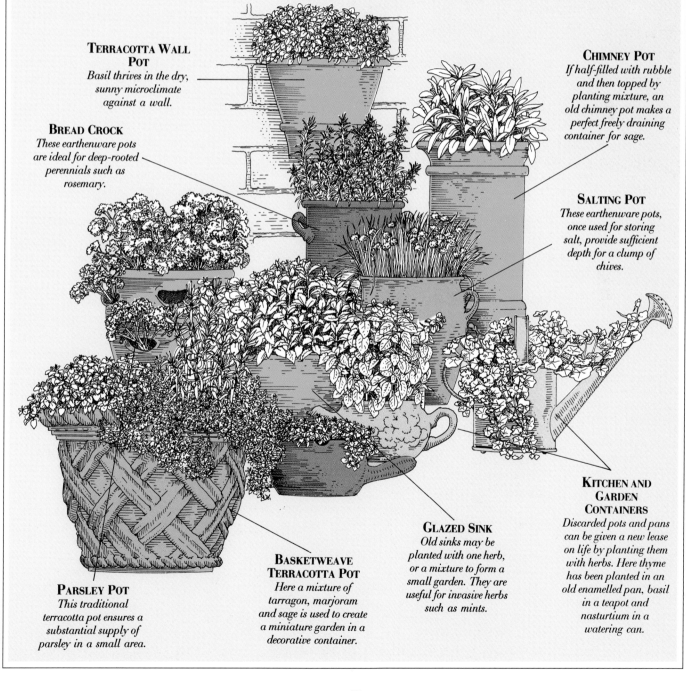

TERRACOTTA WALL POT
Basil thrives in the dry, sunny microclimate against a wall.

BREAD CROCK
These earthenware pots are ideal for deep-rooted perennials such as rosemary.

CHIMNEY POT
If half-filled with rubble and then topped by planting mixture, an old chimney pot makes a perfect freely draining container for sage.

SALTING POT
These earthenware pots, once used for storing salt, provide sufficient depth for a clump of chives.

KITCHEN AND GARDEN CONTAINERS
Discarded pots and pans can be given a new lease on life by planting them with herbs. Here thyme has been planted in an old enamelled pan, basil in a teapot and nasturtium in a watering can.

GLAZED SINK
Old sinks may be planted with one herb, or a mixture to form a small garden. They are useful for invasive herbs such as mints.

BASKETWEAVE TERRACOTTA POT
Here a mixture of tarragon, marjoram and sage is used to create a miniature garden in a decorative container.

PARSLEY POT
This traditional terracotta pot ensures a substantial supply of parsley in a small area.

herbs had an important culinary value. Their use in the kitchen was not simply a matter of imparting a delicate flavor to the dish of the day. Rather, it was a question of rendering a meal actually fit to eat. Without refrigerators or cool rooms in summer, medieval cooks had to deal with meat and dairy products that were nearly putrid, and strong herbs were needed to disguise their unwholesome flavor. The situation was little better in winter. At that time, only essential breeding stock could be kept during the winter months, and there was no question of using these animals to provide fresh meat. So all meat had to be preserved, either by drying and smoking, salting or pickling. Again, herbs would be used to mask the flavor.

· DESIGNS AND THEMES ·

In the more decorative medieval gardens, herbs were grown in a checkerboard pattern. Squares were either planted with a single type of herb, or left unplanted and given a covering of sand or gravel. This kind of herb garden is simple to recreate and works well on a small scale with herbs such as thyme, although a certain amount of trimming is needed to maintain the strict squared pattern as the plants grow and spread into their naturally rounded clumps.

WITHIN EASY REACH
A herbal window box (above) *creates an attractive prospect from inside a house and also makes collecting herbs for the kitchen a simple matter. The herbs growing in this box are golden thyme, basil, rue, tarragon, marjoram and mint.*

DIVIDED BY PATHS
In this compact herb garden (right) *red brick paths separate beds of mixed herbs. The herbs contained in the beds include purple sage, scented geranium, salad burnet, hyssop, chives, thyme, tarragon, mint and sorrel.*

BORDERED WITH BOX
The gardens at Ham House (opposite) *feature clipped box hedges that are used to form boundaries to large beds of lavender and cotton lavender. Both these herbs were widely grown in England in the seventeenth century, when the gardens were laid out.*

A MEDICINAL HERB GARDEN

HERBS PROVIDE MANY OPPORTUNITIES FOR THEMATIC GARDENING. This circular herb garden has both a medicinal and a chromatic theme. The herbs it contains are all reputed to have medicinal properties, and they are predominantly yellow in flower, with grey tones prevailing in their foliage.

The planting arrangement in this garden is permanent because all of the plants – except two – are perennials. The two exceptions are the evening primrose and mullein, both of which are biennials. These will self-seed in well-drained soil, and so to ensure a continuity of plants, some first-year plants should be left to flower the following year. Clipping the woody perennials after they have flowered will preserve the garden's ordered appearance.

MEDICINAL HERB GARDEN PLANTING PLAN

1 **Southernwood**
   Artemisia abrotanum
2 **Lavender cotton**
   Santolina chamaecyparissus
3 **Lavender**
   Lavandula angustifolia
4 **Chamomile**
   Chamaemelum nobile
5 **Roman wormwood**
   Artemisia pontica
6 **Feverfew**
   Chrysanthemum parthenium
7 **Comfrey**
   Symphytum officinale
8 **Yarrow**
   Achillea millefolium
9 **Evening primrose**
   Oenothera biennis
10 **Mullein**
   Verbascum thapsus
11 **Lady's mantle**
   Alchemilla mollis

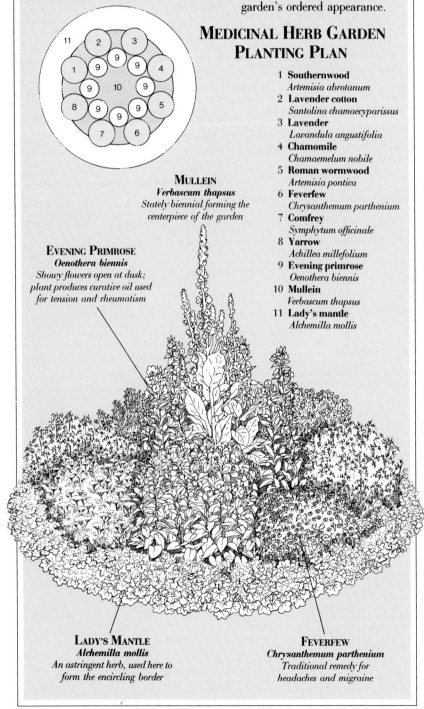

MULLEIN
Verbascum thapsus
Stately biennial forming the centerpiece of the garden

EVENING PRIMROSE
Oenothera biennis
Showy flowers open at dusk; plant produces curative oil used for tension and rheumatism

LADY'S MANTLE
Alchemilla mollis
An astringent herb, used here to form the encircling border

FEVERFEW
Chrysanthemum parthenium
Traditional remedy for headaches and migraine

Like vegetables, herbs in medieval monastery gardens were often grown in raised beds, surrounded by boards, to improve drainage. These raised beds make an excellent framework for a period herb garden, because they allow the herbs to be densely packed without making maintenance impossible. In a small modern garden, a miniature *herbularius* can be squeezed into a single raised bed. If you have more space, it is a fairly simple matter to arrange perhaps four beds so that they meet at a central feature, such as a simple seat.

For those interested in a thematic approach, an herb garden of this type can be divided into sections according to the herbs' uses, with culinary herbs, medicinal herbs, herbs for scent and herbs for dyes each occupying their own separate beds.

· CULINARY AND MEDICINAL HERBS ·

A bed of culinary herbs can be based around a semi-permanent planting of perennials that includes chives, bay, fennel, lavender, marjoram, mints, French tarragon, sage, sorrel and thyme. These offer a good variety of colors and forms, and their shrubby or herbaceous nature gives a bed an interesting structure. Most of these plants will survive severe winters although, in very cold areas, bay is best grown in a container and brought indoors until spring.

Plants such as basil, borage, chervil, dill, garlic, nasturtium, parsley and summer savory are either annuals, or are best treated as annuals. Their seeds should be sown or their bulbs planted indoors in early spring, and the young plants grown on in pots to be set out when any risk of frost has passed. They too offer an interesting variety of shapes and sizes that can enrich the bed in summer.

The period gardener has almost an embarrassment of choice when it comes to growing medieval medicinal herbs. Apart from the better-known remedies such as pot marigold or calendula, feverfew and comfrey, hundreds more were ground, mixed, decocted and infused. Powdered yarrow, thyme and woodruff were sniffed like snuff to cure headaches and clear the head. Infusions of basil were used to reduce fevers, while coughs were soothed with a syrup made from hyssop and honey. A gargle of sage, plantain and rosemary with honeysuckle flowers was recommended for treating sore throats, and sunflower seed mixed with honey was said to loosen tight chests.

The "virtues" of plants were held to be almost limitless, especially where they pertained to digestion. Gentian and peppermint, or centaury in wine, were considered excellent for aiding digestion and rhubarb or violet syrups were frequently prescribed laxatives.

A compress of crushed nasturtium seed and grated potato (a plant recently arrived from the Americas) was used to soothe tired eyes, and the seeds of fennel, love-in-a-mist or fenugreek would, it was believed, help nursing mothers.

Some of these remedies, which were passed from generation to generation, undoubtedly worked, and many modern synthetic constituents in medicines contain the refined forms of the active drugs present in these plants. While the effects of other plants among them may be debatable, their interest and the attractive appearance of the majority fully earn them their place in today's gardens.

· PERFUMES AND DYES ·

In medieval times, many herbs were used indoors for their perfume. Rush floor covering, although warm, rapidly became pestilential and malodorous. But it could be kept relatively free of fleas and sweet-smelling by strewing herbs such as wormwood, rue, hyssop, lavender, santolina and meadowsweet over it at regular intervals.

Flies were discouraged by hanging bunches of fresh tansy in the vicinity of meat carcases. Rosemary, lavender and southernwood were used in cupboards and chests to keep the linen smelling sweet. The water in which linen was washed was also sweetened with infusions of sweet marjoram, rosemary, apple mint, rose petals, violets or clove carnations. Soapwort was frequently used to produce a cleansing lather, particularly favored when washing delicate fabrics. Scrubbing wooden floors with bunches of rosemary and lavender crushed out their oils, which spread like a polish and left the room smelling fragrant.

Most of these plants are highly decorative, especially soapwort, a vigorously spreading plant that produces loose clusters of delightful pink flowers over a long season. Not all the dye plants are as attractive as this, but they are certainly interesting subjects for the more adventurous herb gardener. They include agrimony, which gives fawns and brownish greys, bloodroot, which gives an orange, sorrel a yellowish green, pot marigold a yellow, madder a red and woad one of the few blues.

· THE RENAISSANCE HERB GARDEN ·

While relatively unsophisticated herb garden designs with their rectangular beds might have served medieval monks perfectly well, they did not satisfy the owners of manor houses in the fifteenth and sixteenth centuries. During this period, herbs were still very much in demand,

but, to fit in with the spirit of the times, they were grown in more elaborate and decorative ways than before.

Many English landowners, heavily influenced by the gardens of continental Europe, had herbs grown in beds defined by looping patterns of lavender and germander hedges, which resembled intricate knots. A plan for one knot is given on page 96.

Growing herbs within the confines of low hedges, which may themselves be herbs, combines great formality with high decorative appeal. It can be very effective to commit an entire hedged bed to a single flowering herb – lavender, for example – giving a spectacular and pungent display at the height of the summer. As in *potagers (see p.57)* clipped bay trees in containers can be used to punctuate and give height to the scheme.

· HERB GARDENING IN COLONIAL · · AMERICA ·

When the early colonists reached North America, they brought with them many of the then prevalent ideas about herb garden design. Their herb gardens played a vital role in ensuring their comfort and good health, and gradually their innovations led to the distinctive designs that are still to be found today in American herb gardens.

Initially, timber was the most readily available material, and logs were used to make colonial homes and also to edge the beds of herb gardens. If, as was often the case in settlements on the eastern seaboard, the ground was marshy, boards would be used to create raised beds for better drainage. This was a style echoed in the nineteenth century when, as in Europe, American gardeners had easy access to the tough timber railroad ties. These make an ideal framework for an herb garden, although it is essential that they should not be heavily creosoted as this poisons plants.

In the late seventeenth century, when settlements had become more solidly established and brickmaking was common, bricks were used to make herb gardens in the Dutch style. Good reconstructions of these can be seen today in towns like Williamsburg – appropriately named after the Dutch monarch who had recently succeeded to the English throne.

Old bricks, laid without mortar on a base of sand, make a delightful and easily maintained herb garden. They can be used both to create the paths that divide the borders in a symmetrical arrangement, and also to make the walls of the borders themselves, if these are to be raised above ground level. A wooden fence surrounding the entire garden will provide an attractive

PAVING IN BRICK
Brick paths, like brick walls (see p. 84), are laid in traditional arrangements known as bonds. The bond not only creates a pleasing pattern, it also ensures that the bricks interlock tightly. To be durable, a brick path should be laid over a layer of rubble. This is then covered with mortar to a depth of about an inch (2.5 cm) and the bricks pressed in. When the mortar has set, a dry mixture of sand and cement is brushed into the joints.

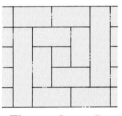

SPANISH BOND

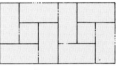

HALF-BASKETWEAVE BOND

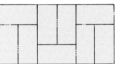

WHIRLING SQUARE BOND

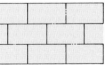

STACK BOND

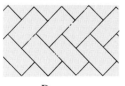

RUNNING BOND

DIAGONAL HERRINGBONE BOND

MAKING A COLONIAL HERB GARDEN

THE EUROPEAN COLONIZATION OF NORTH AMERICA brought together two traditions of culinary and medical herb use. The arriving settlers planted European herbs in their newly formed gardens, and as well as raising plants that were familiar to them, they also gradually discovered the properties of native herbs. Colonial herb gardening in North America developed its own distinctive style, echoed in the garden shown here. A picket fence surrounds the entire garden, which is divided up by brick paths meeting at a central bee skep. The paths are edged with boards, which prevent invasive plants from spreading over the brick.

COLONIAL HERB GARDEN PLANTING PLAN

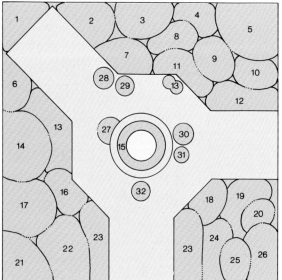

FENNEL
Foeniculum vulgare
A tall, elegant perennial; leaves, seeds and stems impart an aromatic flavor to food

ALECOST
Balsamita major tanacetoides
Perennial of medium height; introduced to North America by the first settlers for its tonic properties

LAVENDER
Lavandula angustifolia

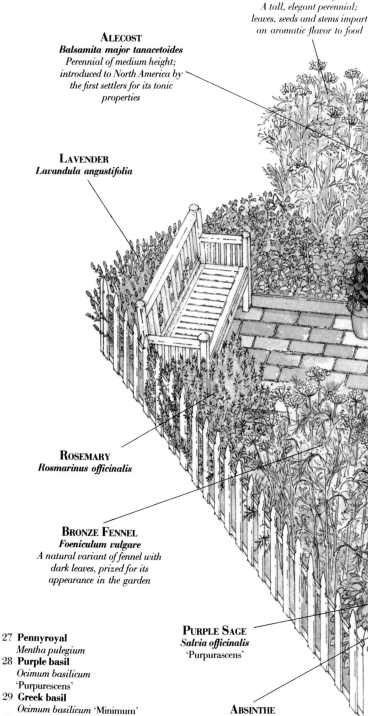

ROSEMARY
Rosmarinus officinalis

BRONZE FENNEL
Foeniculum vulgare
A natural variant of fennel with dark leaves, prized for its appearance in the garden

PURPLE SAGE
Salvia officinalis
'Purpurascens'

ABSINTHE
Artemisia absinthium
Silver-colored with deeply dissected bitter leaves; a European plant used to repel insects, now found in the wild in North America

1 **Lavender**
  Lavandula angustifolia
2 **Soapwort**
  Saponaria officinalis
3 **Fennel**
  Foeniculum vulgare
4 **French tarragon**
  Artemisia dracunculus
5 **Joe Pye weed**
  Eupatorium purpureum
6 **Rosemary**
  Rosmarinus officinalis
7 **Bowles' mint**
  Mentha rotundifolia 'Bowles'
8 **Alecost**
  Balsamita major tanacetoides
9 **Pot or French Marjoram**
  Origanum onites
10 **American sweet cicely**
  Osmorhiza claytonii
11 **Spearmint**
  Mentha spicata
12 **Variegated apple mint**
  Mentha suaveolens 'Variegata'
13 **Chives**
  Allium schoenoprasum

14 **Bronze fennel**
  Foeniculum vulgare purpureum
15 **Hyssop**
  Hyssopus officinalis
16 **Lemon thyme**
  Thymus × *citriodorus* 'Variegata'
17 **Purple sage**
  Salvia officinalis 'Purpurascens'
18 **Golden thyme**
  Thymus 'Doone Valley'
19 **Pot marigold**
  Calendula officinalis
20 **Sage**
  Salvia officinalis
21 **Absinthe**
  Artemisia absinthium
22 **Bergamot or bee-balm**
  Monarda didyma
23 **Parsley**
  Petroselinum crispum
24 **Golden marjoram**
  Origanum vulgare 'Aureum'
25 **Variegated sage**
  Salvia officinalis 'Icterina'
26 **Lovage**
  Levisticum officinale

27 **Pennyroyal**
  Mentha pulegium
28 **Purple basil**
  Ocimum basilicum 'Purpurescens'
29 **Greek basil**
  Ocimum basilicum 'Minimum'
30 **Bay**
  Laurus nobilis
31 **Basil**
  Ocimum basilicum
32 **Lemon verbena**
  Aloysia triphylla

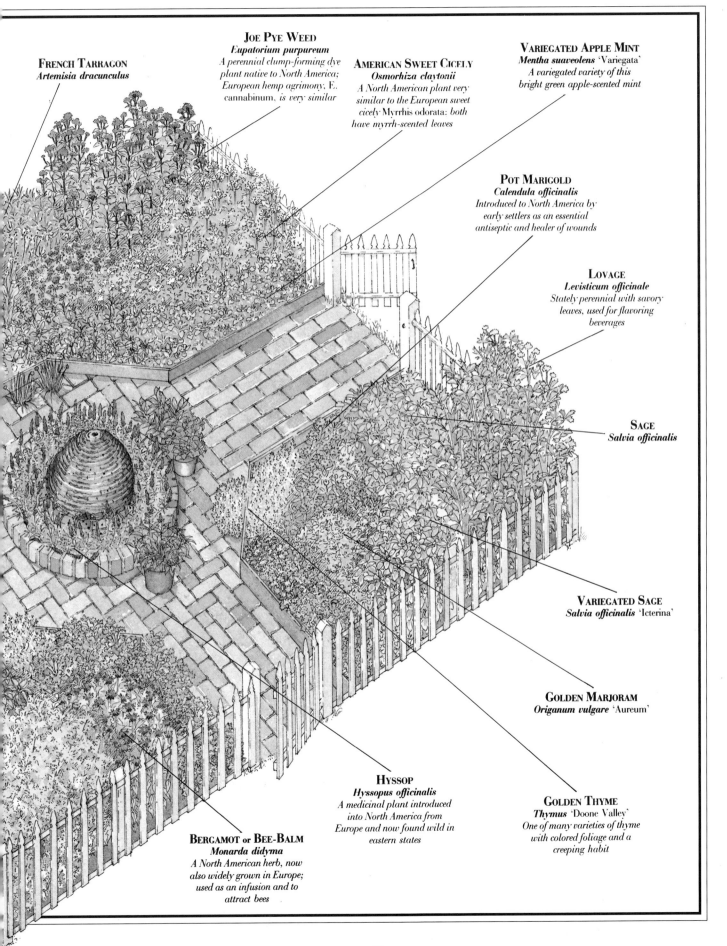

FRENCH TARRAGON
Artemisia dracunculus

JOE PYE WEED
Eupatorium purpureum
A perennial clump-forming dye
plant native to North America;
European hemp agrimony, E.
cannabinum, *is very similar*

AMERICAN SWEET CICELY
Osmorhiza claytonii
A North American plant very
similar to the European sweet
cicely Myrrhis odorata: *both*
have myrrh-scented leaves

VARIEGATED APPLE MINT
Mentha suaveolens 'Variegata'
A variegated variety of this
bright green apple-scented mint

POT MARIGOLD
Calendula officinalis
Introduced to North America by
early settlers as an essential
antiseptic and healer of wounds

LOVAGE
Levisticum officinale
Stately perennial with savory
leaves, used for flavoring
beverages

SAGE
Salvia officinalis

VARIEGATED SAGE
Salvia officinalis 'Icterina'

GOLDEN MARJORAM
Origanum vulgare 'Aureum'

GOLDEN THYME
Thymus 'Doone Valley'
One of many varieties of thyme
with colored foliage and a
creeping habit

HYSSOP
Hyssopus officinalis
A medicinal plant introduced
into North America from
Europe and now found wild in
eastern states

BERGAMOT or BEE-BALM
Monarda didyma
A North American herb, now
also widely grown in Europe;
used as an infusion and to
attract bees

HERB GARDEN DESIGNS

Many of the plants grown in herb gardens are perennials, and as such they have a natural tendency to spread year by year. Some herbs, such as the thymes, spread slowly like advancing blankets. Others, including soapwort and, most notorious of all, the mints, spread rapidly by underground stems. To restrain excessive growth, herb gardens are often divided into easily maintained beds. The herb ladder (right), made out of wood or brick, confines the plants within manageable rectangles. In a variant of the cartwheel garden (below) the plants are grown inside sectors of the wheel, while the center is decorated with a sundial.

frame. Weathered wood looks unobtrusive and will not distract attention from the plants, while traditional white picket fencing gives the garden a well-tended appearance.

· CLOCKS, CARTWHEELS AND ·
· LADDERS ·

In Britain, most decorative herb gardens were swept away by the eighteenth-century landscape movement *(see p.122)* in which herb plants had no role. However, since herbs remained essential whether fashionable or not, they continued to be grown. They were hidden from visitors inside the walls of kitchen gardens, often being planted in simple beds similar to those used by the monks of earlier times. When herbaceous plants regained their popularity in the nineteenth century, simple

herbs could not compete for attention with the host of dazzling new plants that began to pour into Europe from abroad.

It was only toward the end of the nineteenth century and in the first quarter of the twentieth that innovative designers such as Gertrude Jekyll began to reintroduce herbs. However, instead of planting in traditional ways, they created new designs that have since become a tradition in their own right.

One of the most popular of these designs is the "herb clock" or "herb cartwheel." This consists of a circular bed paved with brick or fine stone slabs. It is usually surrounded by a wall, hedge or trelliswork, and often contains some eye-catching central feature such as a sundial, a statue on a plinth or even a lily pond.

In a circular herb garden, the planted area consists of unpaved segments of the circle with a single, or at the most two or three, different types of herb confined within each individual segment.

Two other early twentieth-century designs that merit a place in gardens today are the paved rectangle and the herb ladder. The paved rectangle has beds around its edges and patterns of beds within its central area. In the herb ladder, lines of bricks make up the framework of the ladder, into which the herbs are set. For really rapid results you can of course grow herbs within the framework of an old wooden ladder.

· PREPARING AN HERB BORDER ·

The renewed interest in older, less flamboyant garden plants makes herbs more welcome in gardens than they once were. One way to grow them informally but effectively is in a mixed herb border.

The essential difference between an herb border and a full-blown herbaceous border is that many more annual plants can be included. Also, the level of fertility required for success is much lower. This is because many of the more fragrant or flavorsome herbs – the species of particular interest to cooks or aromatherapists – grow naturally in rocky or gravelly sun-scorched places. Here, the soil is generally poor, rainfall low and the drainage good.

If you are making an herb border, it helps to have it in a sunny spot and to ensure that the ground is well dug before the planting starts. While a little organic material can be mixed into the top of the subsoil to ensure moisture retention, there is no need for anything more than this. Digging the border over thoroughly every four or five years will provide both the opportunity for dividing and renewing the perennial herbs, and getting rid of every scrap of deep-rooted perennial weed. Most herbs seem to relish tough competition, but it is better that they should compete with each other, jostling for space and creating an impression of abundance.

Although many of the culinary herbs used today are fairly tolerant of a wide range of garden soil types, in nature they seem to enjoy slightly alkaline conditions. If your garden is on acidic or neutral soil, adding lime before planting, or when the border is being dug up for maintenance, will keep the herbs in good condition.

· GROWING HERBS INFORMALLY ·

The tradition of growing herbs informally has its origins in cottage gardening. In a cottage garden, herbs would normally be grown around the kitchen door, where they were close to hand, and no attempt was made to organize them into rigid decorative beds.

The result of this free and easy approach is a profusion of plants of all shapes and sizes. Some cottage garden herbs, such as the more stately umbellifers – angelica, caraway, lovage, and fennel – are imposing plants indeed, and merit a place in today's informal garden for their architectural qualities alone. Others provide interest of a different kind. The foliage of lungwort, for example, which is spangled with patches of silver, would have been seen in many cottage gardens, often as an edging plant along the margins of the garden path.

As with vegetables, there is no hard and fast gardening rule that dictates the placing of herbs in a garden. Plants such as columbine, chicory, foxglove, bergamot and evening primrose are colorful enough for any flower garden. Hemp agrimony, or its American relative Joe Pye weed, makes a dramatic clump every summer, rapidly growing from ground level to a height of up to 4 feet (1.2 m). At the other end of the scale, thyme will form a delightful carpet if allowed to grow among the stone slabs of a path. As most herbs tend to be robust plants, planting in unlikely locations can produce impressive results.

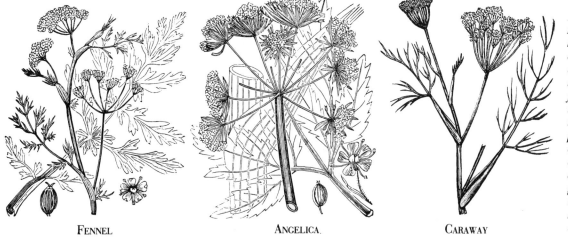

FENNEL

ANGELICA.

CARAWAY

ARCHITECTURAL HERBS
Robust and stately herbs have an imposing presence at the back of an herb border (above). The two tall plants visible here are fennel and angelica, both umbellifers, or members of the carrot family. The plants in this family, which also include caraway, dill and lovage, are characterized by their rapid growth and often majestic, umbrella-shaped flower-heads – ideal qualities for an informal herb border.

FRUIT &
VEGETABLES

The potager — Decorative vegetable growing
— The kitchen garden — Plants from the past —
Bell-jars and hand-lights — Using a hot bed —
The art of growing fruit — The history of the pear
— In search of excellence — Pruning and pest control —
Shaping fruit trees — Techniques for training

A TRUE APPRECIATION OF THE PASSING SEASONS IS ONE OF THE greatest pleasures that a garden can provide, and nowhere is this more true than in the growing of food. At one time the eager anticipation of such seasonal delights as fresh asparagus, strawberries, pears, raspberries, plums and apples spurred gardeners on as they labored over their crops. Today, with the advent of cheap air freight, our sense of seasonality has become blurred. In most supermarkets, strawberries can be bought during every month of the year, and when anything as exquisite as a strawberry becomes common – when we no longer have to wait for the arrival of the first fruit – some joy vanishes, and our lives are poorer.

Seen against this background, it is easy to understand why the cultivation of fruit and vegetables in gardens was held in higher esteem than

PLEASING PRODUCTIVITY
A scattering of decorative objects among crops ensures that a vegetable garden pleases the eye as much as the palate.

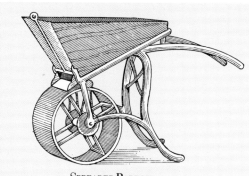

SPREADER BARROW

HAND AND WHEELBARROWS

THE EARLIEST GARDEN BARROW – THE HANDBARROW – WAS IN EXISTENCE before medieval times. It had no wheels, and was carried by two gardeners rather like a stretcher. By contrast, a wheelbarrow enables an unaided gardener to lift heavy weights with ease, because the barrow has a lever action, with the wheel acting as a fulcrum. The first barrows with wheels were fashioned almost entirely out of wood, the only metal being an iron hoop around the wheel. When the material to be moved was light but bulky, high sides enabled a greater volume to be carried.

BOX BARROW

WOODEN-WHEELED BARROW
WITH REMOVABLE TOP

IRON WHEELBARROW

WHEELBARROW

WROUGHT-IRON WHEELBARROW

HANDBARROW

HARDWOOD BARROW WITH WROUGHT-IRON WHEEL

it is today. In many cases, growing food was a matter of simple necessity. But where space and labor were both plentiful, the techniques of providing food were developed and refined into a highly decorative and imaginative art.

· THE *POTAGER* ·

In large gardens of the fifteenth and sixteenth centuries, fruit and vegetable growing was subjected to the same degree of formality as the rest of the garden. As tastes grew more sophisticated, so did the designs of the beds. In some of the greatest French gardens, fruit and vegetables were laid out in extraordinarily elaborate arrangements, with each bed being bounded by a low hedge of clipped box.

One of the greatest of these gardens or *potagers*, as they were known, was that at the château of Villandry. Created in the sixteenth century, the *potager* fell into disuse, but from the turn of this century, a restoration program has gradually recreated its former glory.

A walk around Villandry's *potager* is an extraordinary experience. Dozens of small beds enclosed by hedges – some rectangular, others more elaborate – are laid out in nine groups separated by gravel walks. Each group is internally symmetrical, and has at its center a decorative pillar. Within each bed are the vegetables, and many of these, such as cabbages of contrasting colors, are used as much for decoration as for their value as food. At intervals, the flowery outer margins of the groups of beds are punctuated by fruit trees grown in containers, their arrangement again being completely symmetrical. Trellised arbors and fountains complete the scene, making a vegetable garden that owes as much to architecture as to gardening.

· DECORATIVE VEGETABLE GROWING ·

The few grand-scale *potagers* remaining today are living reminders that growing food need not always be a purely utilitarian business. Although most of today's gardens are on a trifling scale compared with the grounds of country houses and châteaux, growing vegetables in a decorative way can be very successful on a small scale, and is rapidly becoming one of the rediscoveries of twentieth-century gardening.

The essence of the decorative vegetable garden lies in creating a permanent ornamental structure, one that remains while the yearly cycle of sowing, transplanting and harvesting goes on within it. This can be produced in a number of ways. Clipped hedges, even as little as 1 foot (30 cm) in height, provide shelter for young plants as well as define the beds. The garden's structure can also be created by paths, laid out in

an ornamental network that defines the beds. Both these techniques have been used at Barnsley House in Gloucestershire, one of the most celebrated of decorative vegetable gardens. Here, a geometrical pattern has been created by a network of intersecting brick and stone paths. The spaces left between the paths, which may be circular, rectangular or diamond-shaped, are planted not with vegetables of a single type but often with a mixture of vegetables and flowers. Low borders of herbs such as lavender and arches of fruit trees and climbers combine to give the vegetables all the interest and color of a flower garden.

Trelliswork *(see p.166–7)* is also an effective way of providing further decoration in a formal vegetable garden. It is striking simply because it is unexpected, especially when it is used in something as geometrical as an obelisk to support climbing beans. Pots, urns, cisterns and other containers all add interest. Like trelliswork, these are normally only seen in the flower garden, and their presence half-hidden among such prosaic plants as cabbages further surprises anyone who stumbles on them.

Vegetables themselves have tremendous visual potential, which often goes unexploited. Foliage can be extremely diverse – variegated cabbages, brilliant red ruby chard, curly kale and asparagus are worth growing for their appearance alone. For stateliness, nothing can match the globe artichoke, while the Jerusalem artichoke can be used to produce a floral screen topped with flowers in high summer. When flowers such as nasturtiums and marigolds are also planted among the beds, the effect is a fascinating combination of color and succulence.

· THE KITCHEN GARDEN ·

Kitchen gardens, as their name suggests, were designed to supply the culinary needs of country houses. The classic kitchen garden lies within a rectangle of high, protecting walls, and is laid out on a cruciform plan, with two alleys that split the garden in quarters and meet in the center, where some feature – a sundial perhaps – decorates the scene. Sometimes the plan was adapted to suit the space available. George Washington's kitchen garden at Mount Vernon, for example, which was created in 1786, is shaped like a flatiron, tapering to a point at one end. In some kitchen gardens, the house itself provided one of the walls, leaving just three sides free-standing.

The alleys of a kitchen garden are often hedged with fruit trees – apples, plums and pears – and these often have packed herbaceous borders at their feet. Around the entire garden, a perimeter path allows access to narrower beds

(see p.166–7)

THE GARDENER AS DRAFTSMAN
The essence of the formal vegetable garden, which reached its height of perfection in the grand potager, was an elaborate and intricate design planted with impeccable precision. To achieve this the gardener needed a line, which was his equivalent of the draftsman's ruler and set-square. These lines were wound on beautifully crafted reels made of wood or iron and were often equipped with long spikes that were driven into the ground.

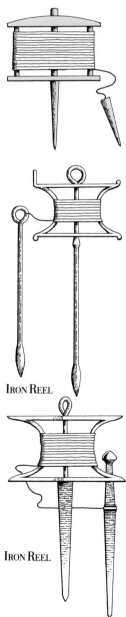

WOODEN REEL

IRON REEL

IRON REEL

THE FORMAL VEGETABLE GARDEN

C REATING A FORMAL VEGETABLE GARDEN IS A QUESTION of striking a balance between productivity and visual appeal. While some plants are grown purely for their decorative value, the emphasis is still very much on providing food.

The garden shown on these pages features a number of small beds intersected by paths. This allows good access for cultivation and weeding, and ensures that the beds themselves do not become compacted by being walked upon. The overall structure of the garden must be strong so that harvesting does not spoil the decorative effect. Here, permanent features such as hedges, espalier fruit trees and arches provide a basic framework for the garden in which the work of the seasons can be carried out.

NASTURTIUM AND RUNNER BEANS
Two climbers with brightly colored flowers, nasturtiums and runner beans, make an appealing and productive combination when grown over an arch.

GOOSEBERRY STANDARD
By cutting away its lowest branches, a gooseberry bush can be encouraged to develop into a standard, providing a vertical feature in the garden. Staking is needed to prevent the trunk from bending under the weight of the crown and fruit.

BLACK CURRANTS
Two black currant bushes flank the gooseberry. They should be pruned every winter to maintain their compact shape.

LAVENDER
A border of lavender provides a flush of scented flowers in late summer. A compact variety such as the English lavender Lavandula angustifolia *'Munstead' is most suitable in this position. The plants should be pruned back every year.*

ORNAMENTAL CABBAGES
Also known as "flowering cabbages," these plants are both edible and highly decorative. Their leaves are colored in various mixtures of purple, pink, cream and green, and have frilled edges.

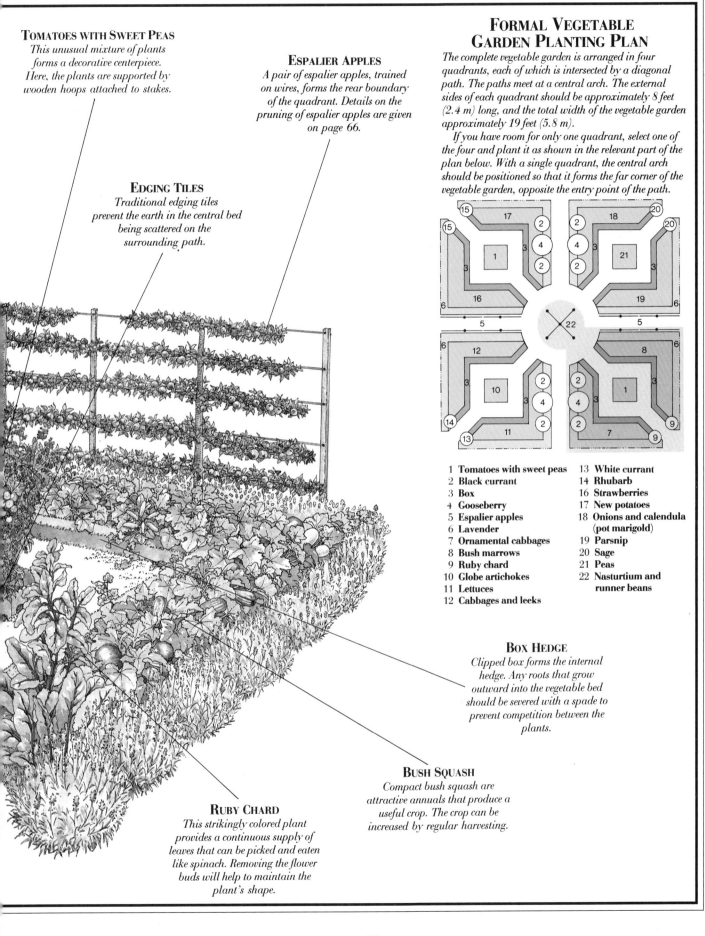

TOMATOES WITH SWEET PEAS
This unusual mixture of plants forms a decorative centerpiece. Here, the plants are supported by wooden hoops attached to stakes.

ESPALIER APPLES
A pair of espalier apples, trained on wires, forms the rear boundary of the quadrant. Details on the pruning of espalier apples are given on page 66.

EDGING TILES
Traditional edging tiles prevent the earth in the central bed being scattered on the surrounding path.

FORMAL VEGETABLE GARDEN PLANTING PLAN

The complete vegetable garden is arranged in four quadrants, each of which is intersected by a diagonal path. The paths meet at a central arch. The external sides of each quadrant should be approximately 8 feet (2.4 m) long, and the total width of the vegetable garden approximately 19 feet (5.8 m).

If you have room for only one quadrant, select one of the four and plant it as shown in the relevant part of the plan below. With a single quadrant, the central arch should be positioned so that it forms the far corner of the vegetable garden, opposite the entry point of the path.

1 Tomatoes with sweet peas	13 White currant
2 Black currant	14 Rhubarb
3 Box	16 Strawberries
4 Gooseberry	17 New potatoes
5 Espalier apples	18 Onions and calendula
6 Lavender	(pot marigold)
7 Ornamental cabbages	19 Parsnip
8 Bush marrows	20 Sage
9 Ruby chard	21 Peas
10 Globe artichokes	22 Nasturtium and
11 Lettuces	runner beans
12 Cabbages and leeks	

BOX HEDGE
Clipped box forms the internal hedge. Any roots that grow outward into the vegetable bed should be severed with a spade to prevent competition between the plants.

BUSH SQUASH
Compact bush squash are attractive annuals that produce a useful crop. The crop can be increased by regular harvesting.

RUBY CHARD
This strikingly colored plant provides a continuous supply of leaves that can be picked and eaten like spinach. Removing the flower buds will help to maintain the plant's shape.

NATURAL HEAT

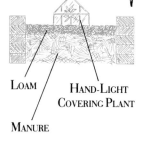

A hot bed consisted of a mound of manure that released heat as it decomposed. The bed was covered either with a glazed frame, or with hand-lights over individual plants. A freshly charged bed was capable of producing a considerable amount of heat. Its temperature would be monitored with the aid of a long-stemmed thermometer that was plunged into the fermenting mass.

LOAM   HAND-LIGHT COVERING PLANT

MANURE

SPROUTING SEA KALE

FORCED TO PERFECTION

A heavy terracotta sea kale or rhubarb forcer cuts out all light, encouraging the plant it covers to produce long stems. A removable lid at the top of the forcer allows the crop to be inspected.

against the walls. Over the blooms and through the fruit tree trunks there are glimpses of abundant fruit and vegetable beds.

The list of vegetables that were grown in a well-maintained kitchen garden reads like a nurseryman's catalogue. In most kitchen gardens, new potatoes would be raised as a delicacy, the main crop often being consigned to a less favored spot. The root vegetables would include turnips, carrots, Jerusalem artichokes, celeriac, giant salsify, beets and rutabagas. Of leaf vegetables, there would be summer cabbages, cauliflower, kohlrabi, broccoli and Brussels sprouts. Every kitchen garden would feature onions and leeks, and as well as these there would be dwarf, broad and runner beans, peas, lettuce, horseradish, black currants, rhubarb, sorrel, scorzonera, parsley, marjoram, basil and green fennel.

The beds between the perimeter path and the walls would be set aside for yet more fruit, herbs and flowers for cutting. They would include rows of raspberries, arranged by variety in order of maturation, and also gooseberries and red currants. Nearest to the kitchen would be the herbs that were most in demand, which included sage, copper fennel (used for flower arrangements as well as cooking), dill, anise, oregano, angelica, tansy, chervil, mints, lovage and chives.

· PLANTS FROM THE PAST ·

Through the centuries, the plants grown in vegetable gardens have changed in accordance with the prevailing tastes and introductions from abroad. A sixteenth-century gardener would find much that was unfamiliar in a modern garden,

RHUBARB FORCER

SEA KALE FORCER

and even in a nineteenth-century kitchen garden he would perhaps be surprised to find some once popular plants missing.

Growing some of these period plants adds a fascinating touch to a vegetable garden. A border of such historical vegetables could include two members of the cabbage family — salad rocket and sea kale — both of which are today infrequently seen in cultivation. Salad rocket, which was grown for its leaves, fell from favor before the nineteenth century. Sea kale, which produces succulent leaf-stems, was still in cultivation in the early 1900s, but today has vanished in most areas. To be thoroughly authentic, sea kale should be blanched by growing it inside a pottery forcer. These objects, which resemble chimney pots, were common in Victorian gardens, where they were also used for forcing rhubarb. Unfortunately, due to their fragile nature, not many survive intact today.

In Europe, sixteenth-century gardeners also made much use of Good King Henry, a woodland plant whose leaves were eaten boiled, and rock samphire, a cliff plant whose fleshy and rather salty leaves were eaten pickled. These were both cultivated and collected in the wild. Collecting samphire was a precarious and dangerous business. In *King Lear*, Shakespeare describes it as a "dreadful trade" — one that no doubt caused many fatalities in the pursuit of savory foods for jaded palates.

· BELL-JARS AND HAND-LIGHTS ·

In the eighteenth century, when gardeners wished to protect individual plants or small sections of a row of a crop early or late in the season, they would cover them with *bell-jars*. These rather unwieldy objects were made of thick glass. A knob at the top of the bell, also made of glass, enabled it to be carried around. As ironwork became cheaper, bell-jars were later replaced by *hand-lights*, which were like miniature greenhouses, made of many small panes of glass set in an iron frame.

A problem with confining any plant in a closed space is that, without ventilation, the air heats up rapidly on warm days, causing wilting and encouraging fungal diseases. Bell-jars suffered from the problem that, as most were fashioned from a single piece of glass, they could only be ventilated by being propped slightly to create a gap between the jar and the ground. Hand-lights were an improvement in this respect, because most had ventilating panes, or tops that could be removed to allow air to flow in and out.

Both bell-jars and hand-lights are highly decorative and embellish any garden, but, because they break easily, they are hard to find.

Nowadays, plastic sheeting drawn over tunnel frames can be used to do the same job. It is cheap, convenient and easy to use, but only someone with defective vision could see it as anything but ugly. While appreciating its value, old gardeners with a regard for the aesthetic appeal of a well-tended garden would no doubt have regretted having to use it.

· THE HOT BED ·

As long ago as the sixteenth century, gardeners realized that, in the process of fermenting, animal manure generates large quantities of heat. Knowing that plants progress more quickly when their roots are warm, they used the heat to warm soil into which they transplanted seedlings in spring. This produced early crops, craved after a long winter on a restricted diet.

In the gardens of cottages or farmhouses, manure was often simply piled into a large heap and covered with a scattering of soil. Seedlings of pumpkins and marrows would be planted on the heap, where they would grow to prodigious sizes, nourished by the pile's heat and fertility.

In larger gardens, the heat was often harnessed by building *hot beds*. Instead of being an open pile, a hot bed was contained in a frame, usually made of timber or brick. This acted as an insulator, keeping the heat where it was wanted.

A substantial pile of manure would be forked into the bottom of the frame and then covered with a thick layer of good loam. The seedlings would be planted in the loam, and would be protected by a hand-light, or a sloping glass roof. The hand-lights or glass could be removed to prevent overheating on sunny days. In the most sophisticated hot beds, removable panels at the bottom of the frame allowed fresh manure to be shovelled in when the original supply had fully fermented and begun to cool down.

HAND-LIGHTS
Hand-lights were the predecessors of today's cloches, creating ideal conditions for the growth of young plants. Their frames were made of iron, zinc or copper, with small panes of glass being fixed in position with putty or metal strips. In some hand-lights, the individual panels of glass were bolted together, allowing the light to be dismantled for storage.

BELL-JARS
Beautiful but somewhat impractical, bell-jars (below) preceded the hand-light and fulfilled the same function. Bell-jars were much used in France, where there was a thriving glass industry.

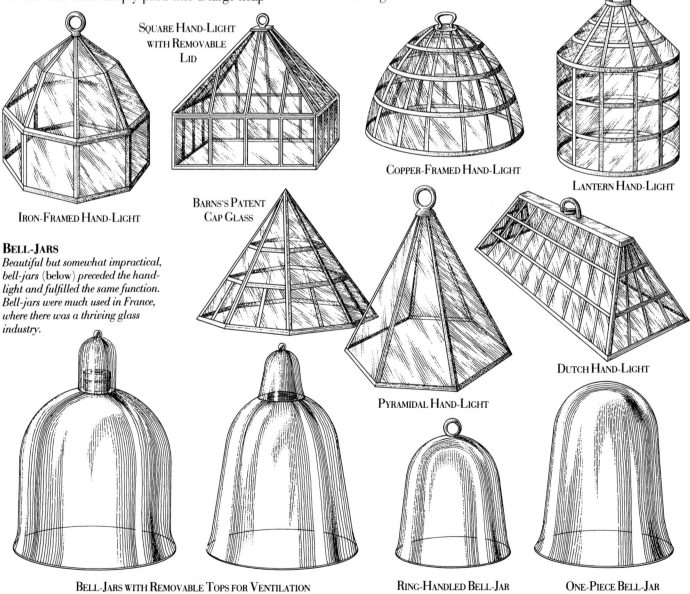

IRON-FRAMED HAND-LIGHT

SQUARE HAND-LIGHT WITH REMOVABLE LID

COPPER-FRAMED HAND-LIGHT

LANTERN HAND-LIGHT

BARNS'S PATENT CAP GLASS

PYRAMIDAL HAND-LIGHT

DUTCH HAND-LIGHT

BELL-JARS WITH REMOVABLE TOPS FOR VENTILATION

RING-HANDLED BELL-JAR

ONE-PIECE BELL-JAR

Hot beds made excellent starting nurseries for a wide range of salad and vegetable crops, or for rooting tree, shrub and flower cuttings. They were especially favored for growing memorable marrows, melons and squashes.

To build a hot bed today, you would need not only a keen interest in garden history, but also access to huge supplies of fresh manure and understanding neighbors. In theory, smell would only be a problem before the bed was covered over, or while it was "recharged," but neither could be guaranteed!

A much easier option is electric heating cable, which is buried in the soil inside a frame. This enables the temperature to be controlled very precisely. Today's frames are usually made from corrosion-resistant aluminum alloy, rather than wood as they were originally. The more expensive models are still glazed, but cheaper and more robust varieties are usually clad in rigid polycarbonate sheet. This does have the advantage that it is transparent to all the useful wavelengths of light, unlike glass, which tends to filter some of them, blocking their warmth.

VERTICAL VEGETABLES
At Barnsley House, simple metal arches (opposite) *transform the vegetable garden, providing an opportunity to show off the much-undervalued flowers of runner beans. Even a squash* (left) *becomes a point of attraction when allowed to trail over an arch rather than along the ground.*

FLOWERS AND FRUIT
Sweet peas and tomatoes (below) *make a pleasing combination when grown together. This imaginative planting makes the best use of the supporting sticks that the tomatoes require.*

GROWING CLASSIC PEARS

P EAR CULTIVATION IS AN ANCIENT ART, AND OVER THE generations, fruit growers have produced over a thousand cultivars of this much valued fruit. The ancestry of the garden pear remains clouded. A number of wild species exist, and it is likely that six or more feature in the garden pear's pedigree.

Pear fruits fall into five main classes according to shape. The oldest varieties are the *rounded* pears, which have much in common with the wild species. *Bergamot* pears have a rounded base with straight-sloping sides, while *conical* pears are more tapered. *Waisted* pears, as their name suggests, have a clearly defined waist, while *calebasse* pears are characterized by their length. If you buy a pear tree in Europe, it will usually be grafted onto quince rootstock, which produces a dwarf tree that fruits early. In North America, a specially developed pear rootstock will have been used. These provide the hardiness necessary for the trees to survive the continent's harsh winters. When planting pears, it is important to ensure that they are either self-fertile or, if not, that a nearby pollinator is available. Some varieties have specific pollinators. One of the pollinators of 'Doyenné du Comice', for example, is 'Glou Morceau'.

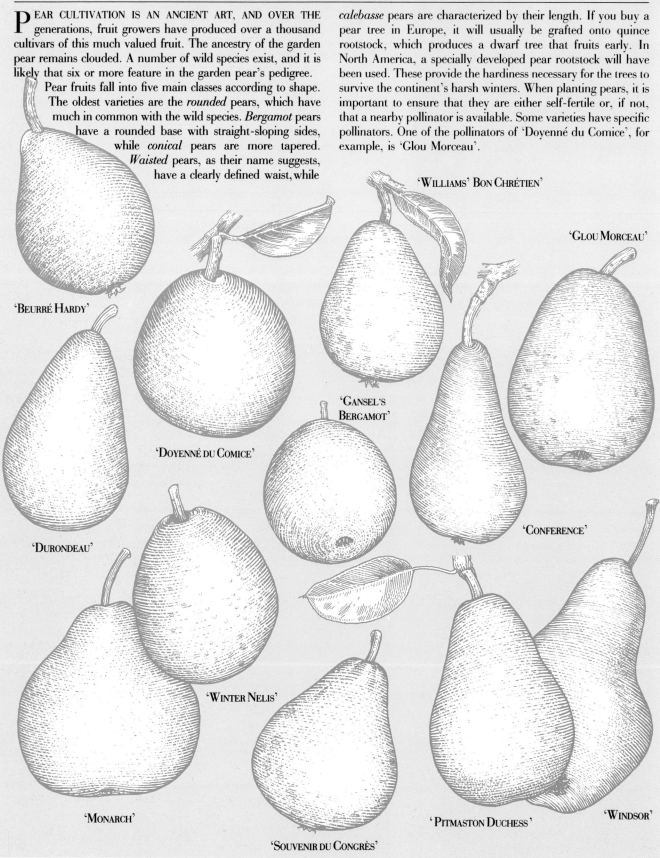

'BEURRÉ HARDY'

'WILLIAMS' BON CHRÉTIEN'

'GLOU MORCEAU'

'GANSEL'S BERGAMOT'

'DOYENNÉ DU COMICE'

'DURONDEAU'

'CONFERENCE'

'WINTER NELIS'

'MONARCH'

'PITMASTON DUCHESS'

'WINDSOR'

'SOUVENIR DU CONGRÈS'

· MAINTAINING THE SOIL ·

In the oldest kitchen gardens, the soil was worked for so many years that it often extended to a considerable depth — far below the extent even of the trenching that was used every year to improve its fertility.

Above ground, great attention was paid to weeding. From the moment the seedlings emerged, hoeing became a priority. Initially it was carried out to *single* salad crops such as lettuce and beets. In this process, a practiced gardener would throw the blade of his hoe at a clump of seedlings and, in a single deft movement, cut away all but the strongest-looking individuals. He would repeat the operation and then, with a few quick sweeps across the row, would remove all the surplus plants between. The whole garden would then be patrolled regularly and even the finest wisps of emerging weed seedlings would be uprooted before their first true leaves had fully opened.

Victorian gardeners could afford to thin out so many seedlings because seed, for the most part, was free, being saved from previous crops.

· THE ART OF GROWING FRUIT ·

Unlike vegetables, fruit trees have always been accepted as a decorative feature in gardens. They combine both beauty and utility — the charm of their blossom enlivens a garden in early spring, while branches weighed down by fruit make an appetizing sight in autumn.

The history of tree or "top" fruit — apples, pears, plums, peaches, and so on — is often well documented. One reason for this lies in the way fruit trees are cultivated. For centuries, they have been propagated by grafting, which produces young trees with exactly the same characteristics as their parent. Once a good variety has been identified, it can be spread by grafting throughout its long life, giving it ample time to become established, described and remembered.

Although fruit growing goes back to Roman times, the 1880s probably mark the time when fruit growing reached a peak of perfection. By then, centuries of traditional cultivation techniques had been handed down, but they had also been tempered by an increasing understanding of the science of growing food. Countless varieties of the different fruits had been created for different tastes, soils and climates.

· THE HISTORY OF THE PEAR ·

The documented history of one of the most important tree fruits — the pear — goes back many centuries. The ninth-century French king Charlemagne ordered pears to be grown because

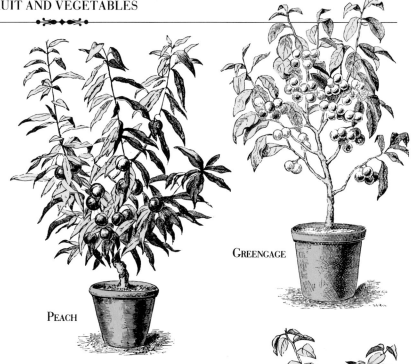

GREENGAGE

PEACH

they were so nutritious, but his appreciation only echoed that of the Romans who had regularly enjoyed them and grew them wherever they governed Europe.

As with roses, the gardens of France were the great center of pear cultivation. Eleanor of Provence, the wife of King Henry III of England, insisted on taking the pear variety 'Caillhou' from France to plant in gardens at Westminster and the Tower of London. The French were also highly influential in developing the skills of grafting trees to produce improved crops. Like the wild crab apple, the wild pear is a tree that can grow to an inconvenient height. Le Gendre, a parish priest in Henoville in 1660, wrote a book about fruit growing that extolled the virtues of grafting pears onto quince rootstocks. This reduced their size, making them more suitable for intensive planting, and also improved their fruit and made them crop sooner. Formerly pears had been grown on their own roots, or as grafts onto natural rootstocks such as crab apple, hawthorn or blackthorn. These all led to large and tall trees, which were difficult to harvest, and, in the case of blackthorn, to very gritty and disagreeable fruit.

· IN SEARCH OF EXCELLENCE ·

Although French pear varieties were considered supreme in Europe for centuries, French growers were not alone in trying out novelties. Stair, an English schoolmaster, raised a new pear in 1770 that is still widely grown throughout the world because it is particularly good when cooked. Stair gave it the name 'Stair's Pear', but in parts of Europe it became better known as 'Williams' Bon Chrétien' or 'Williams' after the man who

PEAR

POTTED FRUIT
Today's dwarfing rootstocks make the growing of pears, apples and other fruit trees in pots a practical possibility even where space is in short supply. To produce an early crop, the pots should be overwintered outside in a sheltered position and then brought indoors in early spring to flower. After fruiting, they should then be returned outside.

CREATIVE FRUIT CULTIVATION

ALTHOUGH MANY TRADITIONAL FRUIT TREE SHAPES ARE HIGHLY DECORATIVE, MOST HAVE VERY practical origins. Without pruning, a free-standing tree will produce large amounts of small fruit, much of which develops in clusters on high branches. A shaped tree, on the other hand, produces less fruit, but the size, quality and accessibility is greatly improved, so that far less is wasted. Many of the traditional tree shapes shown here were devised in the eighteenth and nineteenth centuries and were the products of a great deal of experimentation by fruit growers. With time and patience, they can be reproduced in a garden today.

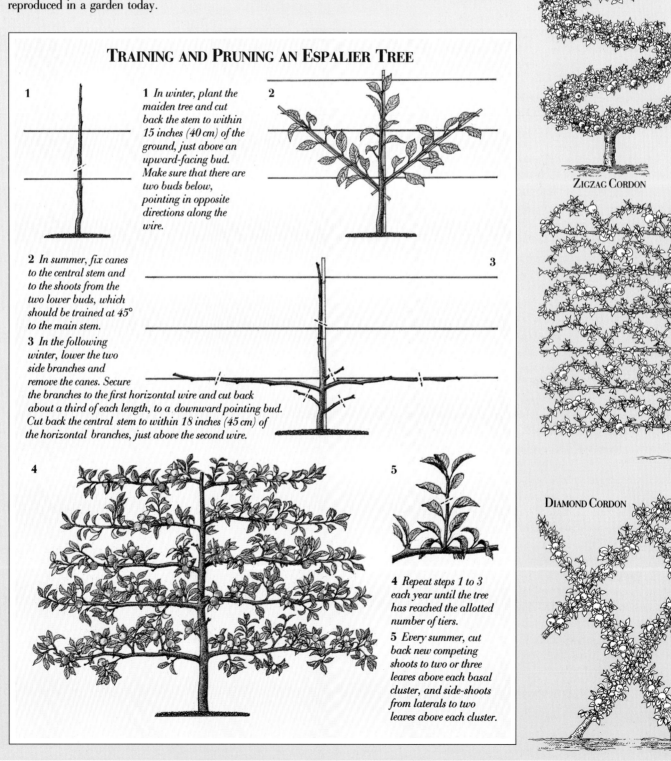

TRAINING AND PRUNING AN ESPALIER TREE

1 *In winter, plant the maiden tree and cut back the stem to within 15 inches (40 cm) of the ground, just above an upward-facing bud. Make sure that there are two buds below, pointing in opposite directions along the wire.*

2 *In summer, fix canes to the central stem and to the shoots from the two lower buds, which should be trained at 45° to the main stem.*

3 *In the following winter, lower the two side branches and remove the canes. Secure the branches to the first horizontal wire and cut back about a third of each length, to a downward pointing bud. Cut back the central stem to within 18 inches (45 cm) of the horizontal branches, just above the second wire.*

4 *Repeat steps 1 to 3 each year until the tree has reached the allotted number of tiers.*

5 *Every summer, cut back new competing shoots to two or three leaves above each basal cluster, and side-shoots from laterals to two leaves above each cluster.*

ZIGZAG CORDON

DIAMOND CORDON

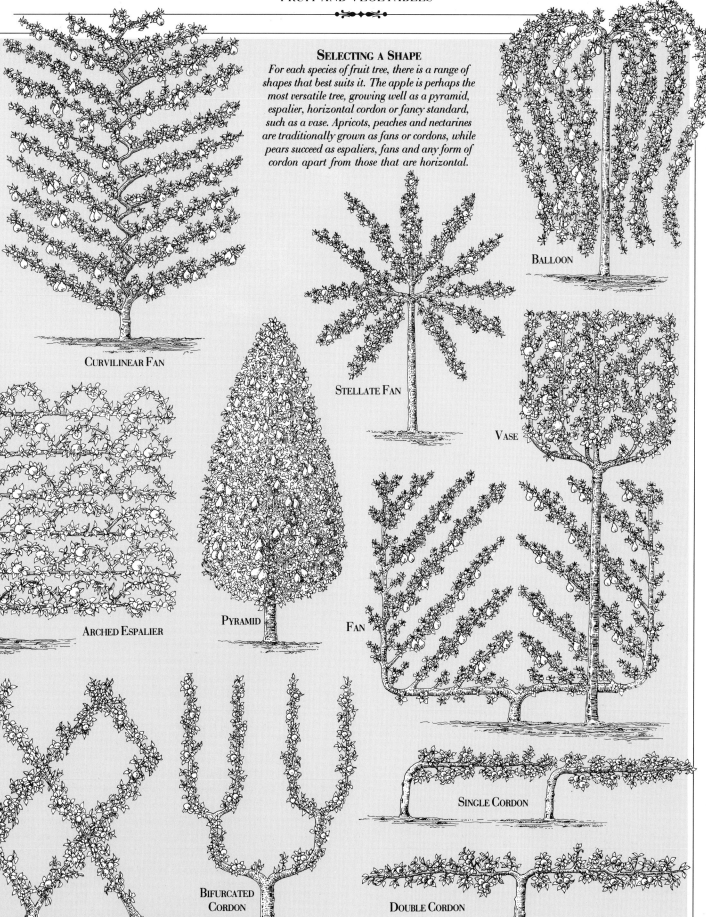

SELECTING A SHAPE

For each species of fruit tree, there is a range of shapes that best suits it. The apple is perhaps the most versatile tree, growing well as a pyramid, espalier, horizontal cordon or fancy standard, such as a vase. Apricots, peaches and nectarines are traditionally grown as fans or cordons, while pears succeed as espaliers, fans and any form of cordon apart from those that are horizontal.

CURVILINEAR FAN

BALLOON

STELLATE FAN

VASE

ARCHED ESPALIER

PYRAMID

FAN

BIFURCATED CORDON

DOUBLE CORDON

SINGLE CORDON

PRUNERS AND GATHERERS

WITHOUT THE BENEFIT OF DWARFING ROOTSTOCKS FRUIT TREES once grew to considerable heights. Long-handled pruners, known as *averruncators*, were essential to check and shape the growth of these vigorous trees. The fruit borne on high branches was reached with the aid of long-handled fruit gatherers. It was important that the fruit was brought to the ground without bruising, as any damage would increase the likelihood of decay setting in during winter storage.

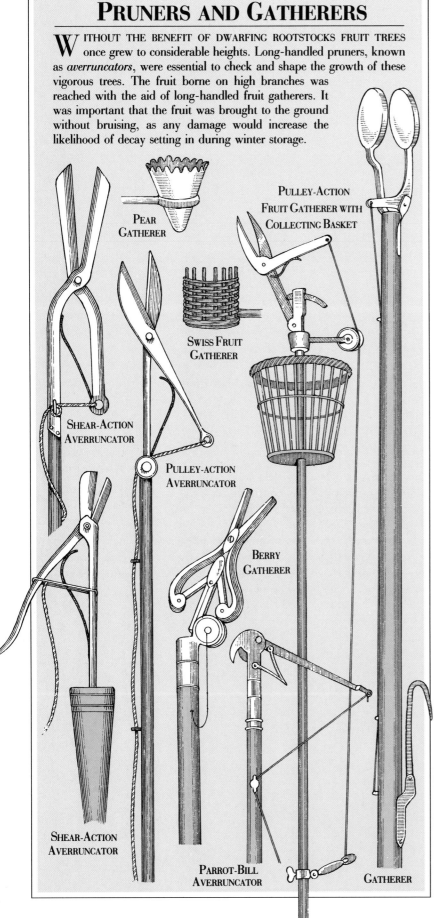

PEAR GATHERER

PULLEY-ACTION FRUIT GATHERER WITH COLLECTING BASKET

SWISS FRUIT GATHERER

SHEAR-ACTION AVERRUNCATOR

PULLEY-ACTION AVERRUNCATOR

BERRY GATHERER

SHEAR-ACTION AVERRUNCATOR

PARROT-BILL AVERRUNCATOR

GATHERER

had been responsible for its cultivation. 'Bon Chrétien' is a description of a type of pear – a class rather than a simple variety.

Pear cultivation was also influenced by growers in North America. In 1799, Enoch Bartlett bought an estate at Roxbury, Massachusetts, on which 'Williams' pears had previously been planted. Finding them good, he propagated them and not being aware of their name, he sold then as 'Bartlett' pears. These soon became very popular and are grown widely today in California for canning.

Perhaps the greatest of all pears, however, is 'Doyenné du Comice'. This emerged from trials in the Loire Valley near Angers and first bore fruit in 1849. A year later, grafting wood was taken from it and sent to other parts of France and America. It was brought to Britain in 1858 and has been a firm favorite ever since. It has been rivaled for popularity by 'Passacrassana' from Italy and France and 'Conference', which since the turn of this century has been one of the most widely planted of all pears. 'Conference' was introduced in 1885 and was an immediate success. It, like 'Comice' and 'Williams', has remained popular because it keeps so well, and for such time, in cool stores.

· PRUNING AND PEST CONTROL ·

In old orchards and gardens, one of the time-consuming chores of growing fruit was the winter pruning – cutting back the fruit-bearing spurs from the main branches to leave only one or two of the fatter buds. Winter washing, using a knapsack sprayer, was a backbreaking but necessary task. The winter wash was applied to the trees when their bark was still damp in the early spring. The tar oil emulsion streamed white down the trees and then left them black and oily and reeking of phenols when the water had evaporated. The treatment cleaned all the moss from the trees and at the same time killed the overwintering pests and their eggs to reduce summer infestations.

Today, selective pesticides for fruit trees are much easier to apply than this. Whether or not you actually use them depends on the severity of the pests, and your feelings about using chemicals close to your food.

Keeping weeds at bay, to prevent them from competing with the trees, used to involve endless hoeing. In a modern garden, trees will do quite well if surrounded by mown grass. One practice that will repay you is the traditional summer pruning. This curbs excessive growth, lets more light into the canopy and helps ripen the fruit. While carrying out this task, which is relatively easy on all but the tall old standard fruit trees, the fruit can also be thinned. This involves taking off immature fruit to leave the rest well separated so that they will ripen into large specimens.

In order to protect the ripening fruit in the autumn against birds and wasps, French fruit-growers would wrap the unblemished fruit in thin white paper bags. They festooned rows of trees, and the paper served to break up the sunlight to make the fruit ripen more slowly and evenly, producing the best flavor.

If you grow fruit trees today, you are unlikely to have the time to wrap your fruit individually. A nylon net, colored green to make it unobtrusive, may not keeps the wasps at bay, but it will act as a barrier to birds.

· SHAPING FRUIT TREES ·

Winter is the time for pruning to shape fruit trees. There is an almost unlimited number of traditional ways of doing this, and which you select depends very much on how much time you can devote to developing and maintaining the desired shape.

One popular and decorative technique is espalier training along wires strung between posts or set against walls. As the laterals extend, they can be curved down towards the ground and held in place as swags to encourage earlier fruit-bud production. Training on wires or against walls can be as simple as making a splay of branches from a low crown, or it can be used to make the branches into highly decorative contortions of great complexity.

Planted with their leading stems sloping and tied into wire, fruit trees can be formed into cordon hedges. If they are set further apart and upright and kept below 7 feet (2 m), the lateral branches from a single erect main stem can be pruned to form slightly conical columns known as dwarf pyramids.

When less densely planted, as free-standing trees between which other crops are sometimes grown, they can developed as bushes, half-standards with a foot or two (30–60 cm) of bare main stem, or full-scale standard trees. These are all formed by pruning to enable plenty of air and light to penetrate to the canopy and to increase the maximum size of its fruit-bearing "skirt."

In more decorative situations, fruit trees can be developed into low espaliers to form the margins of vegetable plots in kitchen gardens. The trees can be shaped by training over frames to make tunnels. The growing points of trees on either side of the tunnel are either intertwined when they meet, or they can be grafted together. In this case, each combined plant is fed by two roots, which send all their sap to the fruit-bearing lateral branches.

In the past, pruning and training often developed into artistic topiary work *(see pp. 94–105)*. Sometimes the trees were left with single bare trunks and their canopies shaped into balls. Alternatively, several stems could be allowed to develop into a low crown and fixed as they grew to form a circle of erect frame bars, the whole resembling a candelabra.

· TECHNIQUES FOR TRAINING ·

Today pears, apples, plums, greengages, figs and cherries can all be obtained on what is known as a *dwarfing stock*, which greatly restricts the height that the mature trees reach. They are often initially pruned, so that they can be grown into all shapes from fans on walls to free-standing bushes.

The young shoots of espaliered trees are usually tied to lateral wires with garden twine. But as traditional espalier makers have always known, it is better to train young shoots by tying them to thin bamboo canes fixed to the wires. Tying them directly to the wires can fracture young stems and destroy the whole balance of the plant.

Training wires used to be attached to walls using iron wedges driven into the surface whose projecting ends were pierced to take up the wire. These days, quicker and more secure supports can be made by using screw eyes held by plastic plugs. These are pushed into holes in the wall drilled with a masonry bit.

If you are keen to experiment with this kind of creative cultivation, you need not confine yourself solely to tree fruit. Currants can be successfully trained into fans, either growing against walls or free-standing, in which case the fan is supported by a hoop of bent wood. Dense bushes, such as gooseberries and black currants, can be pruned to make hedges that combine decoration with an easily picked crop.

WATER ON WHEELS
Before the advent of the high-pressure garden hosepipe, fruit and vegetables were watered with the aid of water carts or barrows. Some were simply mobile reservoirs, but the "garden engine" was a more sophisticated device that featured a long-handled pump. It was used to force water out of a nozzle, and its fine spray would water rows of young plants without damaging them.

GARDEN ENGINE

WATER CART

LAWNS

The origin of the grass lawn — Flowery meads —
Medieval lawn maintenance — Mowing by machine
— The striped lawn arrives — The ultimate turf —
Modern materials for period paths

T HE PRINTS AND PAINTINGS OF JOLLY EIGHTEENTH-CENTURY SCENES
showing lawns being mown by hand have about as much semblance
of reality as do postcards of modern holiday resorts. Cutting grass with a
scythe may look a very congenial activity, but as anyone who has used one
will know, it is an instrument that provokes as much pain as pleasure.
There may be no sensation or sound more satisfying than that of wafer-thin
honed steel slicing through the grass stems on a dewy morning, but there is
also no sensation quite like the ache that the scythe can produce.

Before the invention of the lawnmower, cutting the grass of large lawns
was very much a team effort. Men splayed out in an echelon formation
would cut neighboring swathes through the grass, while women would
carry out the equally burdensome role of tidying up. The clippings were
raked together, massed in woven willow baskets and then barrowed away.
Children were no doubt called in to help as well, and it is easy to imagine
their shouts adding to the gossiping of the adults and the swish of the
scythes as the team went about its work.

Although eighteenth-century mowers used equipment only slightly more
refined than that used by the Romans centuries before them, the results
they produced were probably much more satisfactory than might be
thought. The reason for this is that, awkward though the scythe may be to
use, in experienced hands it is a superbly effective tool. Even today, a good
operator can cut a dense stand of grass fairly evenly down to 1¼ inches
(3 cm), which is as good as most power mowers. So, while they were

ARTISTRY IN GRASS
The severe geometrical appearance of a striped grass walk complements formal masonry in
the garden at Buscot in Oxfordshire.

PLANTED SEATS AND BENCHES

T URF SEATS AND BENCHES ARE VERY OLD GARDEN FEATURES, DATING back at least to medieval times. They are not often seen today, having largely been supplanted by garden furniture of wood and stone. One reason for this is undoubtedly that, like all plants, grass gives off water vapor, making a turf seat feel damp even on the driest of days. However, despite this practical disadvantage, planted seats and benches have great decorative value, and add an interesting period note to any garden. Grass is not the only plant suitable for this living furniture. Scented seats can be created by planting mat-forming herbs in the place of grass. The three herbs shown here are all low-growing plants that will tolerate occasional clipping, making them ideal for a seat's surface.

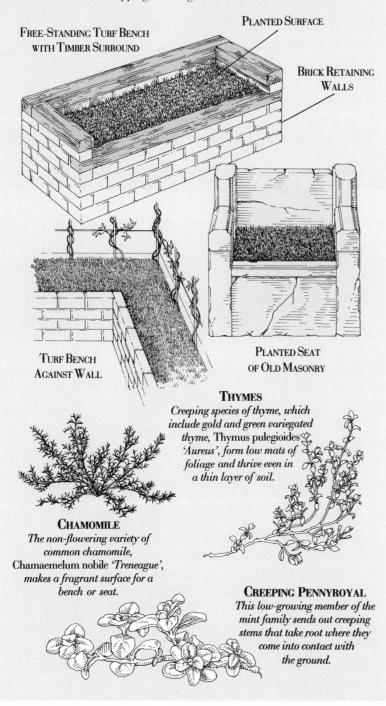

FREE-STANDING TURF BENCH WITH TIMBER SURROUND

PLANTED SURFACE

BRICK RETAINING WALLS

TURF BENCH AGAINST WALL

PLANTED SEAT OF OLD MASONRY

THYMES
Creeping species of thyme, which include gold and green variegated thyme, Thymus pulegioides 'Aureus', form low mats of foliage and thrive even in a thin layer of soil.

CHAMOMILE
The non-flowering variety of common chamomile, Chamaemelum nobile 'Treneague', makes a fragrant surface for a bench or seat.

CREEPING PENNYROYAL
This low-growing member of the mint family sends out creeping stems that take root where they come into contact with the ground.

hardly emerald tablets like today's golf greens, many eighteenth-century lawns may have looked as well trimmed as those found today in modern suburban gardens.

Once the grass had been cut, the clippings were gathered with wide, wooden-pronged rakes, while moss and dead grass, which lay deeper in the turf, was dragged out with metal rakes. These had thicker teeth than those of today because their iron was weaker and less flexible than ours.

Regular mowing and raking would have suppressed or exhausted many of the deeper-rooted perennial weeds, and also most of the annuals. Plants like thistles, whose leafy rosettes seem to sink deeper and deeper into the turf the more they are mown, were uprooted using long-handled tools known as *spudding forks*, which were specially made for this job.

· PLANTING FOR CONTRAST ·

The continuing popularity of the lawn as a garden feature dates back more than two thousand years. Pliny the Younger, in describing the Apennine garden left to him by his uncle, mentions a large flat "lawn" area planted with acanthus. We cannot be too sure to which plant he was referring, but it must have been one that provided a uniform expanse of green in much the same way as grass.

Pliny's lawn, although very different in composition to today's close-mown turf, served the same purpose. It provided a visually calm area that contrasted strikingly with the bright colors and upright form of the other garden plants. Like a modern lawn, it filled a need for a bland and soothing prospect, something that was cool and open.

This visual contrast and coolness seems to have a very strong appeal in gardening. To some extent, all gardening depends on contrast. The historian John Harvey has suggested that to gardeners in northern Europe, the lawn has acted as a substitute for the stretches of water favored in the south, where Arab influence was strongest.

· THE ORIGIN OF THE GRASS LAWN ·

As Pliny's records reveal, early lawns were not always made of grass. The Romans certainly experimented with other plants that would withstand trimming, and it seems probable that they were familiar with chamomile as a substitute for grass. Chamomile is a plant that seems almost to thrive on abuse, and it will prosper on poor, sandy soils and remain green and attractive during periods of drought. Certainly, the art of making chamomile lawns was well known in medieval times and it is a tradition that has never quite died out over the centuries.

By the twelfth century, contemporary manuscripts suggest that lawns made of grass had become essential features in the gardens of northern Europe. In England, for example, a cloistered garden that included a lawn was made at Windsor in 1196 for Henry III. Completely enclosed gardens like this copied those of monasteries, and it is fairly safe to assume that they featured lawns because, in monastic gardens, these were already an established tradition. Over six hundred years ago, a notable German monk, Albert Count of Bollstadt, observed that "the sight is in no way so pleasantly refreshed as by fine and close grass kept short."

· FLOWERY MEADS ·

Although grass gradually gained acceptance as the ideal lawn material, early grass lawns were quite different in composition to those of today. Before the advent of selective lawn weedkillers, lawns were more like herb-filled meadows than sleek green carpets. According to the historian Teresa McLean, "medieval lawns, unlike modern ones, were luxuriously long, and full of

A MEAD IN FLOWER
Seen at the height of its glory in early summer, a "flowery mead" is a deep carpet of blooms. The grasses, clovers and buttercups are given a chance to flower before the summer cut.

SCYTHING A BANK
Whether on level ground or on a bank (left), a skilled gardener can produce the smoothest of surfaces with a scythe. However, scything is not an operation that can be hurried. Not only is it hard work, but the scythe needs constant sharpening with a whetstone to produce a clean cut.

A REVOLUTION IN MOWING

THE DEVELOPMENT OF THE MECHANICAL lawnmower transformed both the activity of mowing and the lawn's appearance. The first machine, designed by Edwin Beard Budding, was manufactured in England in 1830. Over the next fifty years, many more designs using the cylinder blade were patented in England and America. The "Excelsior" mowers – both horse-drawn and hand-pushed varieties – were American models, and were suitable for use even on lawn tennis courts. The "Coventry" machine from England was lighter to use, while Ransome's "New Automaton" lawnmower was possibly the best design of the period. By the turn of the century, steam-powered and gasoline-driven mowers were being manufactured for heavy-duty work.

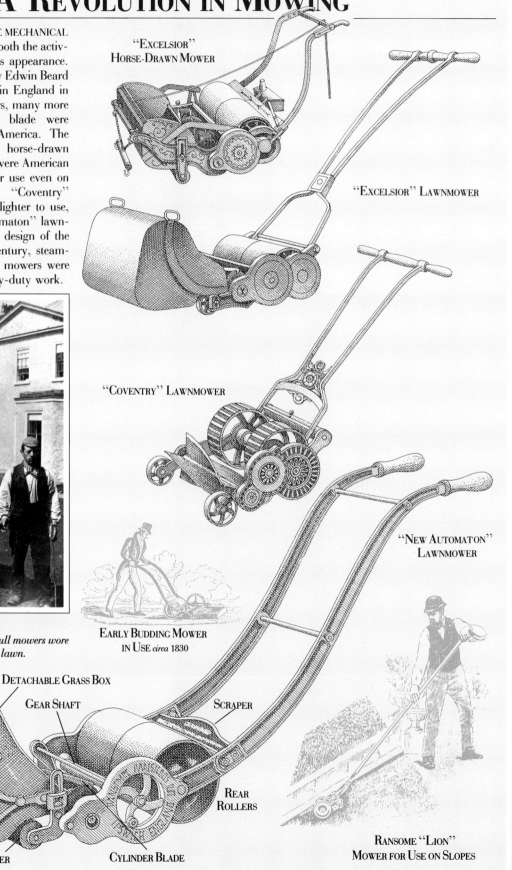

"EXCELSIOR" HORSE-DRAWN MOWER

"EXCELSIOR" LAWNMOWER

"COVENTRY" LAWNMOWER

"NEW AUTOMATON" LAWNMOWER

EARLY BUDDING MOWER IN USE *circa* 1830

RANSOME "LION" MOWER FOR USE ON SLOPES

DETACHABLE GRASS BOX

GEAR SHAFT

SCRAPER

REAR ROLLERS

ADJUSTABLE FRONT ROLLER

CYLINDER BLADE

DONKEY-POWERED MOWER
The donkeys and ponies used to pull mowers wore special leather boots to protect the lawn.

flowers and herbs. They were fragrant carpets to be walked, danced, sat and lain upon.'' Far from being dominated by just a few selected species of grasses, these ''flowery meads'' were a glorious mixture of plants, in many ways similar to the wild flower meadows (*see p.129*) of today's wildlife gardens.

Flowery meads seem to have been common-place throughout the fourteenth century. Paintings of the period show flowers growing in turf at both ground level and on the top of earth seats and surrounding earth-filled walls. The plants most frequently portrayed were daisies of various types, including *Bellis perennis*, which was considered a symbol of purity and discreet charm, together with periwinkle, several different kinds of violets and primroses.

Conservationists aside, there are many gardeners today who consider any lawn plants, other than grasses, to be weeds. But centuries ago, wild flowers were greatly admired. In the *Decameron*, for example, Boccaccio glowingly describes ''a meadow plot of green grass, powdered with a thousand flowers.'' In his day, grass simply never grew on its own.

· MEDIEVAL LAWN MAINTENANCE ·

Any gardener today who has had experience of laying a lawn with turf would be familiar with most of the techniques used in medieval times. In 1320, a certain ''Adam the Gardener'' is recorded as having laid a lawn with 3,300 turfs at the Palace of Westminster. Unlike most modern gardeners, he stripped the turf himself, and to do this he would have used a turfing spade very similar to the ones used by Victorian gardeners in preparing their beds and borders (*see p.20*).

Lawns would also have been sown by seed. This would be broadcast – or thrown by hand so that it covered the ground in an even layer – just as it often is today. By the eighteenth century, this process could be speeded by the use of the *seed fiddle*, a hand-held device originally designed for planting grain seed in fields. A bow like that in a fiddle was drawn backwards and forwards to turn a spindle that scattered the grain over the ground.

The method of cutting turf to replace damaged areas in a lawn has changed little over the years. Sections would be cut out and patched in, although perhaps not with the precision seen today. Modern turf intended for lawns comes from fields that are sprayed to eradicate weeds. In former times, meadow turfs would bring with them their own wild flowers, which would be left to flourish.

Not everything that developed on the turfs was so welcome. In 1387, there is a record of a man

being employed to remove moss from a lawn. Then, as now, gardeners knew that if left unchecked, it would dry out and disappear in the summer to leave unsightly bald patches.

· MOWING BY MACHINE ·

Two early nineteenth-century engineers can be thanked for removing much of the hard work involved in keeping a lawn tidy. Their ingenuity must have been ecstatically welcomed by estate workers who, by that time, had begun to suffer the added indignity of working on their knees with hand clippers to obtain a tighter finish on the turf near the house.

In 1809, the American Robert McCormick invented a horse-drawn reaper, which transmitted power from the land wheels to a reciprocating cutter bar. Designed initially to cut cereals, it was soon in use for cutting grass around the house. But the real demise of the scythe and hand clipper came when an English engineer, Edwin Beard Budding, invented the first cylinder mower and patented it with his partner, John Ferrabee, in 1830.

Budding's invention was an adaptation of the rotary cutters used to remove nap from the surface of cloth in a wool mill. Gears powered by pushing a roller over the ground were used to transmit power to a rotating horizontal shaft supporting three interspersed helical blades. As they turned, the blades swept very close to a straight and rigid base plate, guillotining the grass stalks, which they had trapped and carried with them.

· THE STRIPED LAWN ARRIVES ·

The lawnmower appeared at a time of booming economic growth in Europe and North America

THE POWERED MOWER
The first powered mowers were heavy machines operated by steam. It was only when the gasoline engine was developed that powered mowers became light enough for use in smaller gardens.

·VERGE·CUTTERS

MᶜINTOSH'S CUTTER

CUTTING AN EDGE
Grass spreads rapidly by sending out lateral shoots that take root. Although this characteristic enables grass to create a hardwearing lawn, it also allows it to spread into borders and paths. Edge cutters are used to keep the grass in check. In the past, their blades were either pushed down to cut through the advancing grass, or pulled along to slice through it.

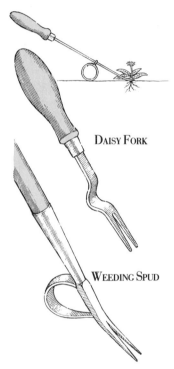

DAISY FORK

WEEDING SPUD

A LEVER FOR WEEDS
Spudding forks were used for grubbing out deep-rooted weeds such as dandelions. Leverage was improved by including an iron loop or curve that was forced against the ground when the implement was used.

and this was one reason for its phenomenal success. Where surburban houses with quite large gardens sprang up to house newly prosperous merchants and professional people, no garden was without its lawn mimicking those of the great houses.

Budding's hand-pushed model was ideal for mowing these lawns quickly and it was soon appreciated that it could cut more closely and evenly while rolling the lawn at the same time. Within just twenty years of the mechanical lawnmower's invention, regularly trimmed lawns were at the height of fashion. In the middle of the nineteenth century, the author Anthony Trollope wrote of one lawn that it was "as smooth, as level and as much like velvet as grass has ever yet been made to look," thanks to the mechanical mower.

The striped washboard effect produced by Budding's mowers soon became, as it remains for many, the symbol of a well-kept garden. It was not long before horse-drawn versions of machines operating on the same principle were being manufactured with the increased capacity to cope with the much larger lawns of those with country houses.

Mechanized mowing was so easy compared to scything that it could be carried out frequently, and this had a great impact on the character of lawns. Gradually, all but the most persistent flowering plants were mown out of existence, as were many of the coarser grasses. Victorian gardeners discovered that mowing stimulated the grass plants to *tiller* or send out lateral shoots which then took root. This produced a thick mat of grass that left little room for weeds. The grass plants could tolerate regular mowing because only a small percentage of their total leaf area was removed with each clip.

After years of mowing to this type of regime, the fine grasses became so tightly packed that they resembled the shorn pile of a high-quality carpet. Any alien growth, such as that of wild flowers, was anathema. The Victorians did not care if the ancients saw the daisy as a symbol of purity: to them it was a weed, something to be mown down and rooted out.

· TOWARDS A SLEEK SURFACE ·

With the ability to achieve a finer finish, gardeners' aspirations grew. The flawless became the mode. Instead of being content with roughly leveled lawns mown out of former meadow, the gardener sowed species of selected grass strains on plumb-flat, pipe-drained soil. Regimes of cutting and heavy rolling were adhered to with an earnestness that tended towards fanaticism. The result was such a smooth surface that the idea of blemishing it with hoof marks was unthinkable. The ponies and horses drawing the heavier mowers had to be fitted with specially designed, flat-bottomed leather boots to avoid damaging the grass.

The ability to produce such a smooth sward was ultimately responsible for substantially

ROLLED TO PERFECTION

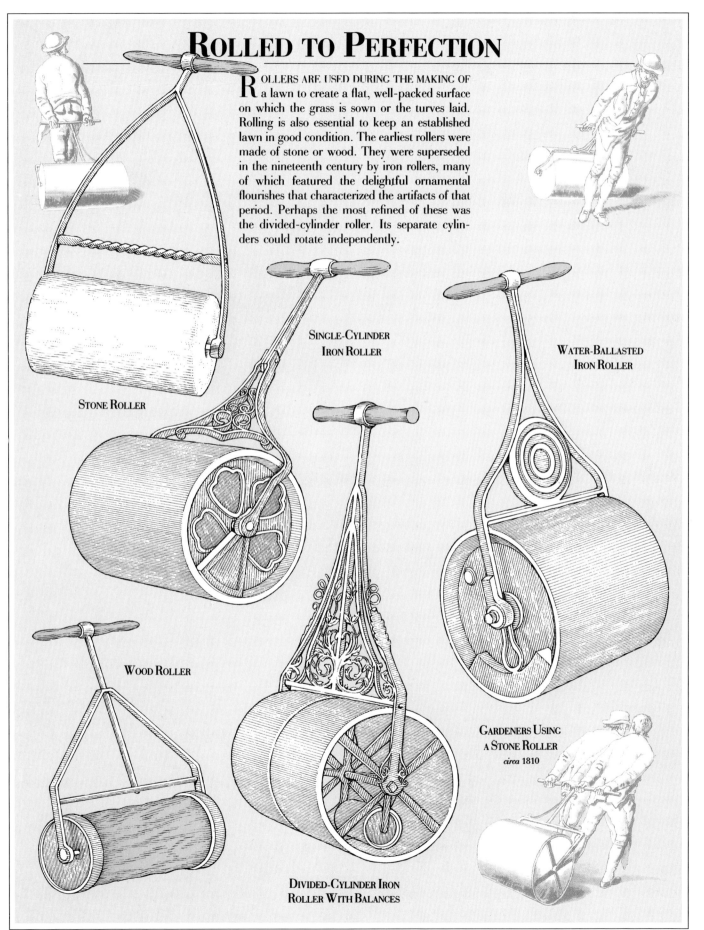

R OLLERS ARE USED DURING THE MAKING OF a lawn to create a flat, well-packed surface on which the grass is sown or the turves laid. Rolling is also essential to keep an established lawn in good condition. The earliest rollers were made of stone or wood. They were superseded in the nineteenth century by iron rollers, many of which featured the delightful ornamental flourishes that characterized the artifacts of that period. Perhaps the most refined of these was the divided-cylinder roller. Its separate cylinders could rotate independently.

SINGLE-CYLINDER
IRON ROLLER

WATER-BALLASTED
IRON ROLLER

STONE ROLLER

WOOD ROLLER

GARDENERS USING
A STONE ROLLER
circa 1810

DIVIDED-CYLINDER IRON
ROLLER WITH BALANCES

GARDEN SHEARS

THE EARLIEST GARDEN SHEARS WERE OF THE SINGLE-handed sprung type, originally used for shearing sheep. Single-handed shears require considerable strength in the wrist, and their short blades restrict their use to inaccessible corners and under shrubs. Scissor-action shears were a more recent invention. The two blades were usually straight, but in some models, they had a convex or concave curve. This ensured that they always met closely at the cutting point, giving a clean cut. Verge cutters were designed to enable the gardener to trim the edge of lawns without having to kneel down. The wheeled verge cutter could be pushed along, taking the weight off the operator's arms. The fact that this and the "grass cutting machine" subsequently vanished strongly suggests that neither worked well enough to recommend them to gardeners.

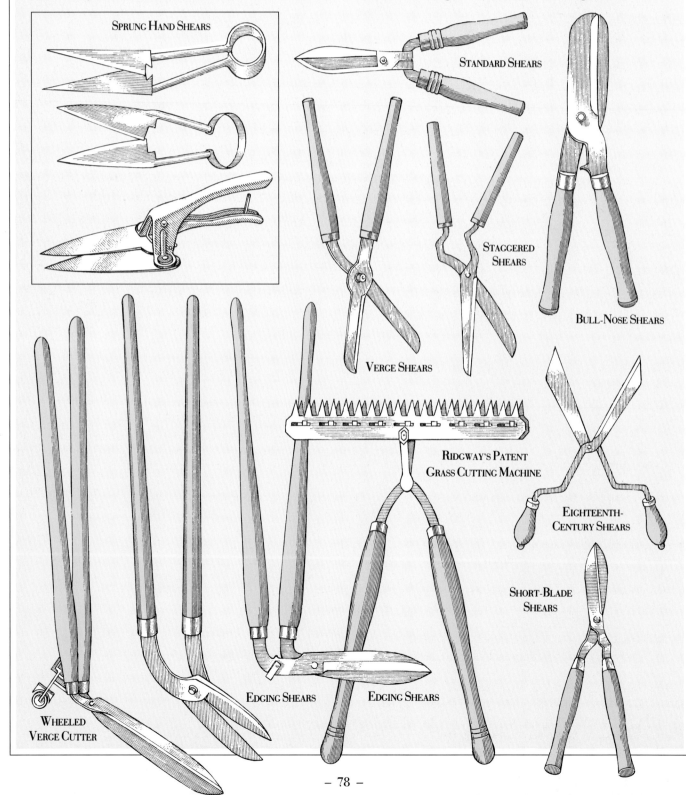

SPRUNG HAND SHEARS

STANDARD SHEARS

STAGGERED SHEARS

BULL-NOSE SHEARS

VERGE SHEARS

RIDGWAY'S PATENT GRASS CUTTING MACHINE

EIGHTEENTH-CENTURY SHEARS

SHORT-BLADE SHEARS

EDGING SHEARS

EDGING SHEARS

WHEELED VERGE CUTTER

changing the character of games like croquet, golf and bowls and it permitted the development of lawn tennis later in the century. It was sports like lawn tennis that helped to turn lawn management into a science for which diplomas were, and indeed still are, awarded. Laying lawns became much more complex. Deep foundation layers of products like furnace ash or the crushed clinker from iron- or glassworks were laid above piped drains. Above this would be a blend of various grades of sand and a thick topping of rich but permeable loam. It was only when this final layer was put down that grass would be seeded or turf laid.

The object of all these layers was the perfect drainage of a rich soil of good moisture-retentive capacity. This would then promote the greatest gardening anomaly – the maximum growth of plants destined to be cut frequently to reduce their size.

This seemingly odd goal arose because our Victorian ancestors soon realized that to obtain tight, thick and springy – but truly even – lawn that would tolerate heavy foot traffic, the twice-weekly cutting that allows balls to run true, *and*

which would recover quickly after being damaged, the grass must grow strongly.

Mowing was supported by a whole ritual of further treatments. The topsoil was regularly forked to improve both aeration and drainage. High-phosphate autumn feeds encouraged grass root development during the dormant season, while in spring, nitrogen was applied to boost spring growth. In early spring, heavy raking pulled out dead matter and moss, and lime was scattered over the lawn to adjust the soil's acidity. Any small bumps were flattened by frequent rolling, and sand and seed mixtures were used to fill hollows. Above all, watering was mandatory, with automatic sprinklers becoming a common feature in many gardens.

· THE ULTIMATE TURF ·

In their growing obsession with the perfect lawn, the gardeners of Victorian Britain adopted what became one of gardening's strangest commodities. It was known as *sea-washed turf*. This was grass that grew at the seashore and which was washed by sea water during exceptionally high tides. Two areas of England where naturally

A CLEAN SWEEP
No doubt spurred on by the presence of the photographer, these two gardeners are engaged in the nineteenth-century ritual of sweeping away worm casts. To do this, they are using besoms, *brooms made of birch twigs tied together.*

GROOMING A LAWN

GROOMING A LAWN
Before selective herbicides became available, gardeners used a selection of rakes, scythes and scrapers to deal with any blemishes that disfigured their otherwise perfect lawns. Daisies were universally deplored, and came in for particularly harsh treatment. The daisy rake *was used to tear off their flowers, while the* daisy scythe *had a two-edged blade that sliced through the offending plants as it was swung from side to side.*

DAISY RAKE

LAWN RAKE

DAISY SCYTHE

SCRAPING RAKE
FOR REMOVING
WORM CASTS

occurring sea-washed turf was exceptionally abundant were in the north at Silloth on the Cumbrian coast and at the head of Morecambe Bay in Lancashire. These are both areas where, instead of eroding the land, the sea builds it up. Silt is thrown up into banks along the coast which initially emerge as islands but eventually coalesce with the shore. The banks are close-grazed by sheep. Their fastidious grazing habits, together with the cultivating effect of their hooves, and the fact that they fertilize the silt, all helps to produce an exquisitely fine sward.

Sea-washed turf was used in the past to lay the finest golf and bowling greens. Its reputation was so high that unscrupulous merchants would often offer ordinary mown turf to the undiscriminating town gardener as "sea-washed turf" and demand a high price for it.

These days, conservationists are understandably not anxious to see these seaside pastures exploited commercially. There is less need for the turf as high-quality substitutes are available at turf farms, and so the sheep graze on their immaculate lawns without interruption.

· LIFE BELOW GRASS ·

Today's conservationists might well take an equally dim view of the traditional pest control that kept a lawn free from blemishes.

In 1344, there is a record of a molecatcher being paid four shillings to catch moles that were making a lawn untidy. That was a lot of money in those days, so clearly his services were in demand. The molecatcher would be adept at setting a sprung trap or at patiently watching for the unusual trembling of plants which betrayed moles' underground mining activities. Then, thrusting the blade of a spade deep into the earth behind the mole to trap it in its tunnel, he would have dug it out with a second spade and quickly killed it. It would be several hundred years before the use of poisons displaced his ancient skills.

Although they are actually invaluable aerators of the soil, earthworms too were often condemned as vermin — indeed, the very word vermin stems from the Latin for worm. In damp weather especially, worms eject casts of soil, forming heaps which are visible in the grass. In a formal garden at the turn of the last century, this was not to be tolerated.

The usual remedy for such disfigurements was a vigorous brushing with a birch broom. However, a chance observation by an intelligent wharf owner in the East End of London offered another solution to this problem which was rapidly accepted after the First World War. He noticed that where some sacks had recently been standing, there were thick layers of dead worms.

They had been attracted to the mowrah nut meal which the sacks contained, and in feeding on the fragments had somehow been poisoned.

Mowrah nut meal, mixed with bran, was soon on sale as a worm killer. However, although it killed worms most effectively, it left them dead on the lawn's surface in a glutinous mass. On golfcourses and the lawns of large houses, greenskeepers and gardeners were faced with the job of cleaning up the decomposing remains with shovels and stiff brooms.

Eventually labor became too expensive for this procedure, and although other chemicals were developed which killed the worms but left them below the surface, most gardeners came to realize that worms were more useful alive than dead. Today bad attacks of real pests such as leather-jackets — the larvae of daddy-longlegs flies, which eat grass roots — can now be controlled with soil insecticides spread on to the surface and watered into the ground.

· PATHS AND PAVING ·

Because even the toughest grass can be worn away by being walked on, lawns are often crossed and bounded by paths. The materials used to provide the surfaces for paths have changed as building techniques have become more sophisticated. The earliest surfaced paths were made of coarse grit, fine river gravel, large beach pebbles, rock fragments from quarrying or crushed sea shells. Apart from their practicality and ease of laying, these materials have a pleasing natural appearance and attractive texture which has helped to maintain their popularity. Their relatively subdued colors also make it easy to integrate them into a wide variety of garden schemes.

A disadvantage of loose materials which would have been discovered early in the history of gardening is that they tend to scatter unless confined in some way. Traditionally, this was achieved by setting them in wide and shallow trenches excavated into the lawn, or by sinking timber edging planks or logs into the ground. But in more pretentious gardens more permanent materials like stone slabs, bricks or lengths of slate were used instead of timber. The Victorians were especially keen on edging tiles, which were placed on end along the sides of a path.

· BRICK AND STONE PATHS ·

By the sixteenth century, garden designers were using well-laid paths to emphasize the geometry of formal gardens. Bricks were becoming widely used for building houses, and they were also used for making paths. Many paths from that time are still in use today, complete with original bricks.

Bricks have the advantage that they are easy to lay in a series of patterns which helps to increase the interest of the path's surface. They can also be combined well with other materials such as pebbles or cut flints set in mortar, to offer even more sophisticated effects.

As brick became commonplace in northern Europe and began to replace wattle-and-daub infill in timber-framed buildings, wealthy land-owners began to demand something better and built their homes in more expensive cut stone. This, in turn, led to a much greater use of matching stone slabs for topping garden paths. Since the feeling of quality flags impart to a path is so obvious, it is easy to understand why they are still the material of preference for owners of stone houses.

Crazy paving, with irregular fragments of real stone, enabled Victorian gardeners and those after them to obtain some of the quality offered by stone slabs more cheaply. There were other early alternatives: worn grinding wheels or mill wheels were sometimes set into grit surfaces, or used as stepping stone paths set out across lawns.

· MODERN MATERIALS FOR PERIOD PATHS ·

The development of concrete as a building material during the last century has given gardeners a path-making material that is so easy to lay that it is often difficult to resist. However, concrete on its own is rarely an asset to any garden. Gardeners have tried many techniques to avoid the rather raw look of newly made concrete, some more successful than others.

In the early years of this century, grit and gravel was rolled into the upper surface of the concrete before it set, or it was used to hold patterns of pebbles of different sizes and colors. A simpler solution favoured by suburban gardeners in the 1930s was to include colored stains in the water used to mix the concrete. These produced rather garish effects initially, but the intensity of the color soon faded after exposure to sunlight.

Fortunately, gardeners today do not have to resort to this sort of disguise. Since the 1950s, great progress has been made in cement technology, and nowadays it is possible to obtain fairly convincing cement-based simulated stone slabs or setts of intriguing shapes. These can be laid in a variety of patterns and, after weathering, blend in well with traditional garden features.

Bark chippings make another useful surfacing material for paths. Apart from making a very satisfactory mulch for suppressing weeds, they can also be used to top informal paths in wilder areas of the garden.

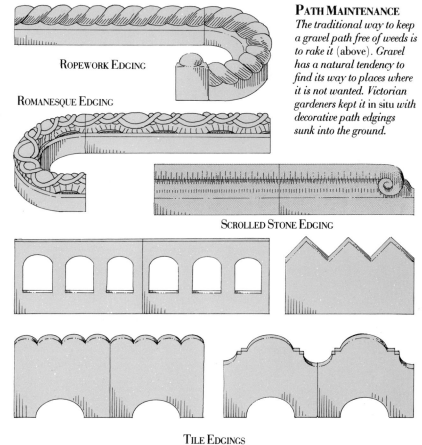

ROPEWORK EDGING

ROMANESQUE EDGING

SCROLLED STONE EDGING

TILE EDGINGS

PATH MAINTENANCE
The traditional way to keep a gravel path free of weeds is to rake it (above). *Gravel has a natural tendency to find its way to places where it is not wanted. Victorian gardeners kept it* in situ *with decorative path edgings sunk into the ground.*

THE WALLED GARDEN

Building in brick — The versatility of stone — A special climate — The walled town garden — Decorating a small walled garden — Staging an entrance — Gateways and arches — Planting a walled garden

B Y LIMITING THE VIEW AND MUFFLING ANY SOUNDS FROM OUTSIDE, walls create a unique sense of privacy and privilege. The plants that grow within the confines of a walled garden appreciate a climate that is moderated by the presence of so much stone or brick. They are shielded from the worst effects of strong winds, and they are also bathed in the heat that is accumulated by the walls throughout the day and then slowly released at night.

In medieval times walls were used primarily for defense, rather than for pleasure. But as the need to provide impregnable barriers declined, the mason's and bricklayer's arts were transferred to the garden. Walled

SANCTUARY IN STONE
Roses and clematises scramble over simple iron arches within the walled garden at Pusey House in Oxfordshire.

SERPENTINE WALL

A serpentine or crinkle-crankle wall (right) has great strength, because its corrugations prevent any lateral movement. The curves also increase the length of wall available for growing plants.

BRICKLAYING BONDS

Bricklaying, as many enthusiastic amateurs have discovered, can be a highly creative occupation. Part of the art of laying a brick wall lies in selecting a suitable bond – a characteristic arrangement of bricks (below) designed to ensure that the mass binds together without any lines of weakness. Over the centuries, many distinctive bonds have developed in different regions.

FLEMISH GARDEN BOND

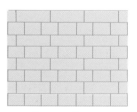

FLEMISH BOND

HEADER BOND

STRETCHER BOND

ENGLISH BOND

DUTCH BOND

MONK BOND

ENGLISH GARDEN BOND

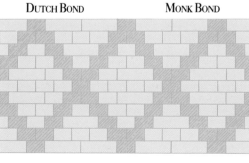

DIAPER BOND

gardens, both for leisure and for growing food, became almost a necessity and were sometimes created on a truly grand scale.

Few private individuals today can afford anything like the expense that was borne in previous centuries in creating such garden sanctuaries. But the accumulated experience of gardening in and around walls is still relevant to us because many of today's gardens – whether they surround houses in the country or back on to those in towns – have walls within them.

· BUILDING IN BRICK ·

Although the traditional materials for garden walls can be summed up under two headings – stone and brick – a great variety of effects can be obtained with each of them. There is a world of difference between a simple wall of plain brick and one that includes panels and buttresses, or between a dry-stone wall and one made of cut stone that has been jointed and mortared.

Today brick is usually the cheapest material for building walls, and it can be very satisfactory if properly used. Second-hand bricks – if you can get them – are ideal for garden walls, where their less-than-new appearance will help the wall to blend in with its surroundings. In the eighteenth and nineteenth centuries, much use was made of patterns composed of different kinds of bricks. Glazed bricks, which have a slightly glossy surface, can be very effective if used sparingly among ordinary bricks.

A brick wall should be set on a concrete foundation, and a damp-proof course consisting either of non-porous brick or impermeable plastic membrane will help to maintain it in good order. A further continuous damp-proof membrane should be set in a thick sandwich of mortar capping the bricks just below the coping. This will prevent any water that may penetrate the joints in the coping from seeping down into the wall which would cause it to crack when the water expands on freezing.

Both the color of mortar and the way it is finished at the joints make important contributions to the appearance of a wall. Strong contrasts in color between the bricks and mortar are best avoided. In old walls, mortar was generally applied so that it lay flush with the surface of the bricks. The recessed appearance of old, weathered mortar looks appealing, but the effect is hard to mimic in a new wall. If mortar is scraped out deeply the result often looks thoroughly modern.

A soundly built brick wall will stand up very well to high winds if it is reinforced by building piers at intervals along its length. For the very ambitious, there is another structural variation worth trying. This is the *serpentine* wall, which, as its name suggests, follows a sinuous path across the ground. The curves give it great resistance to toppling, so it needs no buttressing of any kind. It is worth noting that serpentine walls do take up a considerable amount of space, and so only a short length can be fitted into a small garden.

· THE VERSATILITY OF STONE ·

A brick wall always has an element of regularity by virtue of the way it is put together. A stone wall, on the other hand, can be as formal or irregular as you wish, provided of course that you have access to the raw materials.

The most imposing of stone walls, those made of *ashlar*, or stone that has been "dressed" or cut into flat-sided blocks that are mortared together, are rarely built in gardens today. Cut stone is expensive, and has largely been supplanted by brick or simulated stone. A dry-stone wall, however, is a different matter.

The raw materials used in a dry-stone wall – rough, uncut stones – are relatively inexpensive provided that they can be obtained nearby. The dry-stone wall has no mortar, and the length of

THE WEATHERPROOF WALL

THE SIDES OF A WELL-BUILT GARDEN WALL SHOULD STAND ANY amount of rain without suffering damage, but the same cannot be said for the top if it is left unprotected. To be durable, a coping is needed to prevent water from penetrating the wall, as this can weaken the mortar and cause damage, especially if followed by frost. In the past, walls were sometimes equipped with additional weatherproofing to protect fruit trees. At its simplest, this protection consisted of a wide roof-like coping that threw rain off the wall. In glazed walls, removable panels of glass allowed complete protection from the elements. Heat from sunlight that was reflected back by the wall would be blocked by the glass, raising the temperature within and encouraging fruit to ripen.

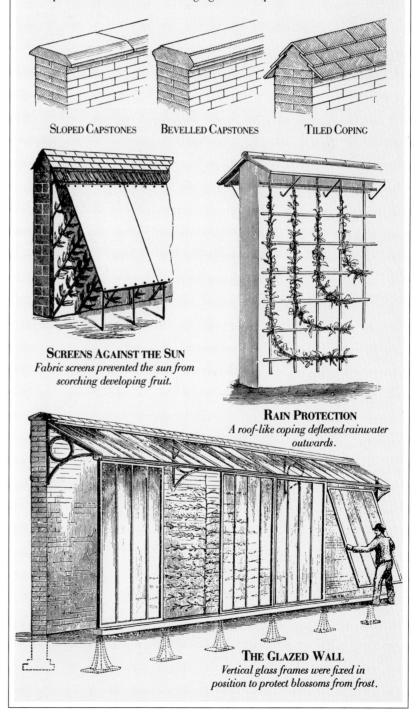

SLOPED CAPSTONES   BEVELLED CAPSTONES   TILED COPING

SCREENS AGAINST THE SUN
Fabric screens prevented the sun from scorching developing fruit.

RAIN PROTECTION
A roof-like coping deflected rainwater outwards.

THE GLAZED WALL
Vertical glass frames were fixed in position to protect blossoms from frost.

Given time, a dry-stone wall acquires a considerable amount of plant life. However, the process can be a slow one, and those who want faster results can speed it up by applying a home-made "fertilizer," for example, very dilute yogurt or compost steeped in water. The minerals in the fluid will encourage the growth of mosses and lichen that give the wall a weathered and time-encrusted appearance.

Flowering plants can be introduced by the simple expedient of sowing seeds among the wall's crevices. As nature so frequently demonstrates, some plants, such as red valerian and wallflower, can thrive in the most improbable wall-top locations. All that is needed is a reliable source of moisture and sufficient minerals to permit growth.

Brick walls and newly mortared stone walls are harder for plants to colonize, and therefore take longer to age. Again, an application of fertilizer will help. The luxuriant vegetation of really old brick walls appears when the mortar starts to crumble. In a new wall, plants can be grown in built-in pockets just large enough to hold a handful of soil.

· A SPECIAL CLIMATE ·

Once a wall has been built, it starts to affect the climate around it by altering the way the sun's warmth reaches the ground. At the foot of the sunny side, the average soil temperature increases, while on the shaded side it falls.

The gardeners of previous eras made great use of this effect. In northern Europe, walled gardens were used to coax fruit from plants of warmer climes, such as figs and peaches. In some gardens, the heating effect of walls was exaggerated by building walls within walls. At Trengwainton in Cornwall, the walled garden contains beds that are themselves walled and also banked, so that they receive the maximum amount of heat by directly facing the sun.

Sometimes walls can provide too much heat. In *The Natural History of Selborne*, the celebrated naturalist Gilbert White records how, in the particularly hot summer of 1781, his wall-grown peaches and nectarines were "scalded" by the sun – this in the usually mild climate of southern England.

During winter additional heat was often used in walled gardens. In the eighteenth and nineteenth centuries, many garden walls contained flues for fires, which allowed them to be heated. Glass roofs and frames were fitted to the walls in winter to protect the tender plants.

In a damp climate, the shaded side of a garden wall is an ideal place for growing moisture-loving plants. In Victorian times, this

COLOR AND CONTRAST
Old red brick (top) *has a characteristic warmth that creates a special atmosphere in a walled garden. By contrast, the stone blocks of a granite wall* (above) *are somber and dark. Here, they act as a perfect foil for the light green foliage of wisteria and the brilliant flowers of a crinum.*

BEDS AND NICHES
Raised beds surrounding a niche (opposite) *bring smaller plants closer to the eye, increasing their impact. This walled garden at Snowshill Manor in Gloucestershire is made of Cotswold stone, the material being used both in the walls and in the paths.*

time it holds together depends entirely on the skill of the builder in locking its stones together. A foundation of large, flat slabs is first laid down, and then the wall is built up with the best stones forming two faces that slope slightly towards each other, on either side of a central infilling of smaller rubble stone. If correctly constructed, with "stretchers" or "throughstones" at intervals connecting the two faces, a dry-stone wall should last for decades or centuries.

· SPEEDING THE AGING PROCESS ·

Part of the charm of truly old garden walls lies in structural imperfections such as bows, bulges and haphazard buttresses, and also in the scatterings of plants that grow out between the bricks or stones. It is obviously not a good idea to "age" a wall by building in structural imperfections, but plants can be encouraged to take root on most stone walls without too much difficulty.

CLOTHED BY A CLEMATIS

A vigorous clematis (above) *makes an ideal wall plant. It will anchor itself to wires by means of tenacious, twining leaf-stalks, and will produce a brilliant display of flowers every year.*

would have been a spot for growing ferns — plants which were particularly treasured during this period. The shade at the foot of a wall also make a good place to grow clematises, which prefer cool roots.

Near to any wall, air circulation is much reduced. On the whole, plants benefit from this, especially because it protects their developing buds. However, there is one notable exception that often comes as an unpleasant surprise to the uninitiated. Despite the best efforts of breeders, many roses suffer badly in these conditions, developing mildew from spores that settle on their foliage in the still air. Aided by the warmth, mildew attacks some rambling roses with great rapacity. The same varieties, when grown on a more airy support such as a tree or trellis, will often be quite unaffected.

· THE WALLED TOWN GARDEN ·

Town houses offer many opportunities for wall gardening. A small garden enclosed by a boundary wall, or the sunken courtyard outside a ground-level apartment, are both ideal locations for "vertical gardening," which makes the best possible use of the limited space available.

In a town house garden or courtyard, the conditions for plant growth are often surprisingly good. The walls provide excellent shelter from the wind, and the proximity of heated houses often increases the air temperature significantly

WALLED GARDEN PLANTING PLAN

1 **Clematis**
  Clematis armandii
2 **Poet's jasmine**
  Jasminum officinale
3 **Clematis**
  Clematis macropetala
4 **Climbing hydrangea**
  Hydrangea petiolaris
5 **Clematis**
  Clematis alpina
6 **Clematis**
  Clematis montana
7 **Osmarea**
  Osmanthus × burkwoodii
8 **Plantain lily**
  Hosta sieboldiana 'Elegans'
9 **Orris root**
  Iris pallida 'Argentea Variegata'
10 **Plantain lily**
  Hosta 'Thomas Hogg'
11 **Drumstick primrose**
  Primula denticulata
12 **Camellia**
  Camellia japonica
13 **Sweet violet**
  Viola odorata
14 **Lily of the valley**
  Convallaria majalis
15 **Hen and chickens**
  Jovibarba sobolifera
16 **Bird's-eye primrose**
  Primula farinosa
17 **Fatshedera**
  × Fatshedera lizei
18 **Tulip**
  Tulipa 'White Triumphator' and
  Forget-me-not
  Myosotis sylvatica

CLEMATIS
Clematis alpina
Early-flowering clematis with semi-closed flowers; blue, pink and white varieties available

OSMAREA
Osmanthus × burkwoodii
Evergreen shrub with deep green leaves; flowers in clusters

TULIP
Tulipa 'White Triumphator'
and
FORGET-ME-NOT
Myosotis sylvatica

PLANTAIN LILY
Hosta sieboldiana 'Elegans'

PLANTING A WALLED COURTYARD GARDEN

COURTYARDS AND SMALL TOWN GARDENS BELOW STREET LEVEL PRESENT several challenges to the gardener. Lack of light is foremost among them, while lack of space and a good planting medium often add further complications. The walled garden shown here overcomes the problem of shade by using plants that thrive in the absence of direct sunlight. It also makes the fullest use of vertical surfaces and reflected light. The walls are clad in trellis panels, and the mixture of deciduous and evergreen climbers ensures a changing pattern of foliage and flowers throughout the year, with the persistent tufted seed-heads of the clematises adding a point of interest during winter months. The garden's non-climbing plants are mostly grown in containers, scattered on either side of a waterspout and basin. The arrangement of pots can be changed as the seasons progress, preventing the garden from becoming static. The central mirror acts as the garden's focal point.

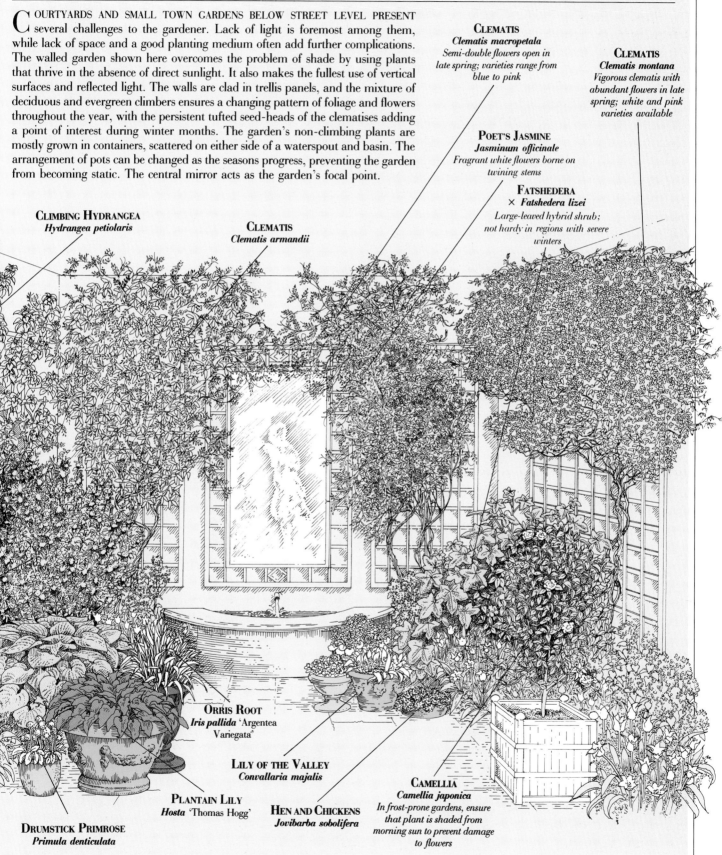

CLEMATIS
Clematis macropetala
Semi-double flowers open in late spring; varieties range from blue to pink

CLEMATIS
Clematis montana
Vigorous clematis with abundant flowers in late spring; white and pink varieties available

POET'S JASMINE
Jasminum officinale
Fragrant white flowers borne on twining stems

FATSHEDERA
× *Fatshedera lizei*
Large-leaved hybrid shrub; not hardy in regions with severe winters

CLIMBING HYDRANGEA
Hydrangea petiolaris

CLEMATIS
Clematis armandii

ORRIS ROOT
Iris pallida 'Argentea Variegata'

LILY OF THE VALLEY
Convallaria majalis

PLANTAIN LILY
Hosta 'Thomas Hogg'

HEN AND CHICKENS
Jovibarba sobolifera

CAMELLIA
Camellia japonica
In frost-prone gardens, ensure that plant is shaded from morning sun to prevent damage to flowers

DRUMSTICK PRIMROSE
Primula denticulata

in winter. Plants in such situations often look unhealthy, and it is easy to imagine that this is somehow due to the harshness of the town environment. However, much of this ill-health is due simply to neglect. Plants in town gardens, if properly cared for, not only thrive but often look more resplendent than those in the country, such is the contrast that they make with the walls and buildings around them.

Establishing a formal framework helps to give a town walled garden a feeling of unity. Trellis-work is useful here, and makes a good support for clematises and roses. Regular pruning is needed to ensure that the flowers appear low enough to be appreciated, rather than disappearing upwards and out of sight.

In a paved garden, plants in containers make an attractive feature. In the past, most fruit trees grew too vigorously to be grown in pots or boxes. Today, apples, pears and other tree fruit are available grafted on to ultra-dwarfing rootstocks, which restrict their upward growth. Trees like this can be espaliered in the tiniest garden – provided that light is sufficient – making delightful miniature features. Potted fuchsias and camellias also thrive in this situation.

· DECORATING A SMALL WALLED GARDEN ·

Water makes a charming focal point in a small walled garden. In a very dark courtyard, a small formal pool with a mirrored bottom will reflect light, giving a more airy feel to the garden. Wall fountains, consisting of a gentle trickle of water issuing from a spout, perhaps incorporated in a piece of statuary, gives a distinctly period flavor.

Walled gardens in the past often had alcoves, niches and even sunken seats. In the oldest walled gardens, some of these niches were used for housing old straw beehives, or *skeps* as they were called. At Edzell Castle in Scotland there is an extraordinarily elaborate example of a wall that is punctuated with these features. It not only has recesses for bee skeps but also has plaques featuring sculpture, and, crowning the top of the wall, elaborate stone canopies at intervals. While something as flamboyant as this would look quite out of place in a garden today, recesses for pots or small pieces of statuary are easily incorporated while a wall is being built. It is much easier to include such features at this stage than to attempt to excavate them later.

The ground enclosed in a rectangular walled garden is an ideal place for some of the decorative features described on pages 171–185. In the Lady Emily Garden at Pusey House in Oxfordshire, there is a sundial – shown at the beginning of this chapter – mounted on a decorative column below a central arch. It is the sort of feature that seems an essential ingredient in any walled courtyard, reminding you that the charm of any great garden is timeless.

· STAGING AN ENTRANCE ·

Few garden experiences are as evocative as that moment of first entry through a door in a wall into what lies behind. Strangely, the value of gates and entrances is often overlooked in today's gardens. This is a pity, because the very presence of a gate or door does much to arouse curiosity about what lies behind it.

A heavy, solid door gives an incomparable feeling of privacy. Doors of well-weathered wood, equipped with iron or bronze latches and hinges, have been popular since people first became interested in ornamental gardening. So too have decorative grilles, which provide some privacy without limiting vision. They have been used as a substitute for solid doors since the Chinese first devised them in the Bronze Age.

Doors, gates and their surrounds usually follow the architectural styles that prevail during the period in which they are made. Some styles have been repeated throughout history. The "moon gate," for example, is a popular feature in walled gardens. This design, a completely circular aperture in a solid wall, was invented by Chinese garden designers several millennia ago. It was used again when *chinoiserie* was in vogue in the eighteenth century, and it has been used by many twentieth-century designers in schemes with an oriental flavor.

· GATEWAYS AND ARCHES ·

We have relatively little detailed evidence of what garden doors or their surrounds and arches looked like much before the fourteenth century. But from that time onwards there are plenty of illustrations to consult.

As domestic architecture and garden designs became more ambitious from the Middle Ages to the present, the entrances and exits from walled gardens, and indeed from gardens as a whole, also became increasingly sophisticated. Gateposts changed from being simple vertical timbers to much more elaborate structures made out of brick or stone. Eventually they evolved into highly decorative pillars, which were either panelled or carried refined relief carving. They could be topped with finials that might be as simple as a perfect stone sphere or as complicated as an equestrian statue.

Gateways experienced a similar metamorphosis. In some gardens, this culminated in great screens of wonderfully convoluted wrought iron, which were some of the finest products of the

FROM POSTS TO PILLARS
Early gateposts had little in the way of decoration, but as they gave way to brick and masonry pillars, increasingly elaborate finials began to appear. The taste for geometric styles such as ball finials alternated with that for more figurative designs, such as the ones shown here.

FRUIT BASKET

FLUTED URN

PINEAPPLE

OPEN INVITATION
The decoration of gateways and entrances often defines the degree of formality of what lies beyond them. Brick piers with ball finials (top left) make a dignified support for wrought-iron gates leading into a rose garden, while pillars topped by elaborate carved finials (top right) frame another formal entrance. A stone surround (bottom left) gives a feeling of solidity, while a traditional wooden door set in a brick wall (bottom right) is simple, unpretentious and inviting.

PLANTED SEAT
Stately plants such as the taller hydrangeas (right) can be grown up a wall to create a mass of foliage surrounding a seat.

THE DECORATED WALL
With the exception of niches and statuary, the majority of wall decoration (below) tends to be relief work, meaning that it projects from the wall rather than being recessed into it. Relief decoration, such as sundials, brackets and wall pots, can be added to an already existing wall without any structural work being needed. Recessed niches and alcoves can be incorporated in a new wall as it is built. Excavating them in an existing wall is only practical if the wall is deep enough to withstand the weakening this produces.

metalworker's art. These were used not only to stamp a feeling of grandeur on entrances. They punctuated axes and were used to mark divisions between areas of garden or, if they straddled the end of broad alleys, between the garden and the landscape beyond.

Even in an open type of garden design, visitors feel more comfortable when offered the sense of enclosure conveyed by such highly decorative exits to the landscape. It is a feeling that visitors can experience on the river margins of Hampton Court Palace, or, in a more rural setting, at Hidcote in Gloucestershire. Here fine ironwork at the end of a long vista marks the separation between a highly contrived garden landscape and the rolling Cotswold countryside beyond.

· TRADITIONAL DOORS FOR THE MODERN GARDEN ·

As the scale of walled gardens has reduced in the twentieth century, so too has the need for such wide and highly decorative gateways. Nevertheless, the role of entrances and exits has not altered, and they remain important decorative features in our gardens.

For solid walls, simple tongue-and-groove cross-braced pine doors, fitted with iron latches, make satisfactory substitutes for more costly versions in woods such as oak or elm. With the

WALL-MOUNTED SUNDIAL

LION MASK

FOUNTAIN

BRACKET

OVAL NICHE

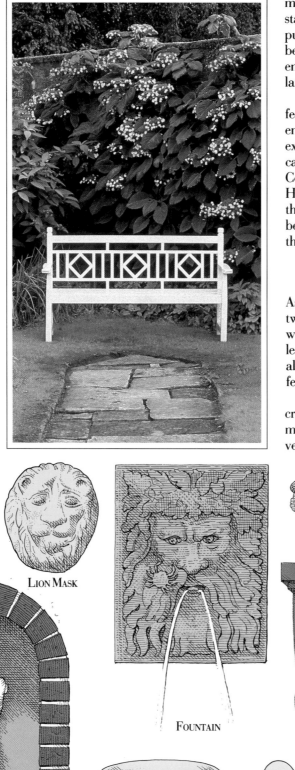

NICHE WITH STATUE

WALL POTS

revival of the art of carpentry, attractive hand-made wooden gates and archways can be bought in both traditional and more contemporary styles. They are usually more expensive than mass-produced models, but this additional cost is easily justified by the superior quality of both their design and their manufacture.

Cast aluminum is now frequently offered as a substitute for wrought iron. Many have designs reminiscent of Victorian ironwork, but there are also cast alloy gates from Japan with traditional oriental patterns that, to Western eyes, are quite unfamiliar. Although some of these designs are quite elaborate, they are in a new idiom and can be used to great effect to embellish gardens around modern houses.

· PLANTING A WALLED GARDEN ·

Choosing plants for a larger walled garden — either a new one or one that is being restored — can be a difficult matter, because the choice is so great. The Lady Emily Garden at Pusey House shows what can be done within four walls that encompass a fair amount of ground.

The planting in this walled paradise is confined to ornamental plants. With a single entrance midway along its southern wall, its two main diagonal walkways are paved with regularly cut old flagstones laid in an informal pattern. These hard surfaces provide access to the garden in all weathers and need less maintenance than turf paths.

Away from the walls themselves, the walkways intersect at a central arch, each arm of which supports a climbing rose paired with a clematis. The pairs are *Clematis* 'Perle d'Azur' with the rose 'Parade', *Clematis* 'The President' with the rose 'Cupid', *Clematis* 'Gypsy Queen' with the rose 'Pink Perpétue' and *Clematis* 'Mrs. Cholmondeley' with the rose 'Lady Waterlow'.

The arch makes a high point that balances well with a domed gazebo set in the angle between two walls. A circular rose bed surrounds the arch and is divided into quadrants by intersecting paths. It supports the prolific repeat-flowering rose 'Violinista Costa', which is spectacular despite having an unfortunate tendency to develop mildew in some situations.

Between the circular rose bed and the perimeter track there are eight irregularly shaped beds separated by paved paths and four narrower cross-tracks. These contain a wide variety of perennial herbaceous plants arranged to flower in sequence through the season. Notable among them are peony, iris, scented tobacco, hyssop, heliotrope, *Platycodon*, phlox, bush honeysuckles, asters, eryngium, clumps of hardy geranium and also stately alstroemeria.

· PLANTING IN SHADE AND SUN ·

As is appropriate, the great glory in the Lady Emily Garden is the walls themselves, and they are notable because the gardeners who planted them overcame the problem of satisfactorily cladding the north- and east-facing walls in an English garden, which are always the most difficult to handle.

The plants that have prospered best on those bleaker surfaces include carefully selected honeysuckles, roses and clematises. The honeysuckle *Lonicera fragrantissima*, which is partially evergreen, produces fragrant cream flowers in late winter and bright red berries in spring. The early Dutch honeysuckle *Lonicera periclymenum* 'Belgica' whose reddish flowers eventually fade to yellow, covers the walls with its blooms in spring and early summer and often again in late summer. Three roses are grown that resist disease well against a wall. 'Zéphirine Drouhin' has fragrant carmine blooms throughout a long season, while 'Handel' has beautiful pink blooms edged with cream. 'Veilchenblau', which has large clusters of small, purplish-violet flowers with white centers, is in bloom in mid summer, and presents an interesting spectacle as the flowers change color as they fade.

Clematises, being plants of the woodland understory in the wild, fare well in the shade of the high garden walls. At Pusey House, the velvety purple flowers of *Clematis* 'Royal Velours' appear in late summer, at about the same time as the other variety grown, *Clematis* 'Comtesse de Bouchaud', which has large, soft rose-pink flowers.

At the foot of the shaded walls are hydrangeas, plants that enjoy the cool and calm conditions. At Pusey, *Hydrangea aspera villosa* produces masses of large, lilac-blue lacecap flowers in late summer. Also present is a spectacular species hydrangea well worth growing in a garden that has sufficient space. This is *Hydrangea sargentiana*, which has velvety leaves and bluish lacecap flowers.

On warmer walls, gardeners are never stuck for a choice of beautiful subjects to plant. If the climate is mild enough, this is the place to grow tender species like the yellow-flowered mimosas, which create a Mediterranean look.

Such magnificent plants as *Magnolia soulangeana* 'Alba Superba', which produces majestic, white, strongly scented flowers in mid spring before its bright green leaves emerge, also glory in such favored positions, as do members of the ceanothus family, such as *Ceanothus impressus*, which has deep blue flowers in spring and small-leaved evergreen foliage.

TOPIARY

· *Labyrinths, mazes and knots — Grand topiary —*
Living embroidery — Emblems and whimsies — Shapes
from the Orient — Topiary plants and techniques
— A problem of growth

Vienna is full of marvels to admire and delights to enjoy, but perhaps the most enchanting experience is one that is frequently missed by tourists. It is not drinking rough green wine in the Vienna woods, or gasping in wonder before the Brueghels in the city's galleries, or even feasting on the delicious *Sachertorte*. It is watching the gardeners at the Schönbrunn Palace, aloft on their platforms, clipping the topiary tunnels much as they have done every year since the tunnels were formed in the eighteenth century.

Schönbrunn's tunnels are not some light-hearted fantasy. They are heavyweight living structures, each one formed by two widely separated towering hedges of linden, which have been fashioned so that their upper branches meet, forming a huge vaulted ceiling as impressive as any Roman basilica. The platform from which the gardeners work is mobile and motorized. It can be raised or lowered as required, and it supports an outrigging of round, arched frames to guide the clippers' shears. When it is being used, the keen gardeners among the city's population dash for the tram out to Schönbrunn and watch the operation, which is so precisely carried out that when the gardeners have finished, they leave the inner surface of the leafy vault as smooth as a well-mown lawn.

Schönbrunn and its gardeners are modern practitioners of an art which began at least five thousand years ago, probably at the hands of vine growers in the Caspian region. To be productive, the grapevine demands

A QUESTION OF SCALE
Although always impressive on a grand scale, topiary lends itself just as well to more intimate treatment, as this courtyard topiary garden demonstrates.

CREATING A KNOT GARDEN

URING THE HEYDAY OF KNOT GARDENING IN the sixteenth century, garden designers vied with each other to produce knots of ever increasing complexity. Some of these were recorded in books, but it is likely that many more existed only on the ground, to vanish once the craze for knot gardening had passed.

The design shown here is typical of the period. It uses three traditional knot garden plants – lavender cotton, wall germander and box – each of which has foliage of a different color. The combination of color contrast and careful clipping produces the illusion that the hedges weave over and under each other where they meet, rather than simply butting up against each other.

The knot garden shown here has sides 14 feet (4.25 m) long, and the hedges are 9 inches (23 cm) wide. The young plants should be grown about 6 inches (15 cm) apart. Pinching out the developing shoots will encourage the bushy growth needed to form a miniature hedge.

■ **LAVENDER COTTON**
Santolina chamaecyparissus

□ **WALL GERMANDER**
Teucrium chamaedrys

■ **BOX**
Buxus sempervirens or
B. sempervirens 'Suffruticosa'

MARKING OUT THE DESIGN

Marking out is an exercise that calls for some patience. Care taken at this stage will be amply repaid in years to come. The basic tools needed are a supply of wooden pegs and a ball of good, non-stretching string. The design can be scratched into the ground, but a more refined technique makes use of sand trickled out of a bottle. The first set of lines to be marked out is the square outer frame. Next comes the center point, which is located by crossing diagonal lines. Finally come the lines that make up the knot itself. The curves are marked by pegging a line to a fixed point.

WALL GERMANDER

This shrubby evergreen plant is a relative of the mints. It has deep green, oval leaves and, if allowed to, will produce flowers carried on spikes.

COMMON BOX

Common box is an evergreen tree with small dark green glossy leaves. The dwarf variety Buxus sempervirens *'Suffruticosa' requires less pruning but takes longer to become established.*

GRAVEL

Traditional knots often featured gravel of different colors to accentuate the design.

LAVENDER COTTON

An evergreen member of the daisy family, lavender cotton has finely divided leaves that are covered with silvery felt. Unclipped plants produce masses of small yellow flowers.

considerable attention. It needs to be pruned back to its trunk or main stems every autumn, and the following season's new shoots must be further pruned, then tied securely to supports.

Centuries of experience with the crop showed that it seemed to prosper best when treated in different ways in different regions. As a result, there were almost as many ways of pruning and training vines are there were areas in which they would grow. Many of these ways survive today. In parts of the Middle East, for example, each vine is annually pruned back to a short stump from which several shoots are allowed to emerge and straggle over the ground. In the Bordeaux region, new shoots are trained along wires suspended between posts. In the Po valley in Italy, they are initially pruned to form tall trunks from which the lateral shoots are led along wires between trees such as willows and alders.

The experience gained with vines must have taught early gardeners that many woody plants could be cut and formed at will without losing their capacity to flower and fruit. It cannot have been long before the more innovative and curious among them began exploiting this property to create clipped hedges, which were a useful alternative to masonry walls. They would, no doubt, also have experimented with the purely decorative shaping of plants, and at this point the art of topiary, as we know it today, was born.

· LABYRINTHS, MAZES AND KNOTS ·

There is some evidence to suggest that the Persians were making pleached hedges, in which the lateral branches of rows of trees were intertwined, before the Greek conquest in the third century BC. Certainly, compelling shrubs to adopt forms of man's choosing was an established practice in Roman gardens by the first century AD.

During the Dark Ages, the skills of the topiarist were kept alive in monastic cloisters. This was a time of religious fervor, in which disciplinary exercises were used to demonstrate faith and keep worldly matters at bay. Baffling penitential labyrinths and mazes were created in monastery grounds, frustrating and humbling the walker, and thereby teaching patience and persistence. The tracks in these constructions were often bordered by tightly clipped hedges of box, shrubby germander, myrtle or thyme. Unlike later mazes, which had tall screening hedges, the hedges of earlier mazes were quite low. This in itself was a test of self-discipline, because the monk or young man aspiring to knightly status could see his way out – or could easily have stepped over the hedge to escape. He was obliged to resist that shameful temptation.

CHANGING WITH THE SEASONS
Hornbeam is a tree that is very tolerant of pruning, and can therefore be made to adopt a wide variety of shapes. In winter, the hornbeam tunnel at Hidcote in Gloucestershire (above) is a tangle of intriguing stems clad in bright bark. In summer (left), it forms a dense tunnel luring the eye along its length. Hornbeam tunnels like this are formed by winter pruning then tying the sappy new growth to a metal framework.

TOPIARY IN CONTAINERS

Box was a favorite topiary plant as far back as Roman times. One of its advantages is that it is fairly drought-resistant, and as a result thrives when grown in containers. The trimmed box bush above has been planted in a zinc pot.

Low hedges, similar to those used in early mazes, were planted as borders around medieval herb gardens. The experience in growing and clipping them must have been useful when, in the fourteenth and fifteenth centuries, gardeners succumbed to the craze for making knot gardens. At first, lines of hedging were grown to make simple geometric patterns. Often two separate species such as box and germander were used to trace separate lines of the pattern. They were clipped in such a way that when the lines intersected, it appeared that the plants in one line passed below those of the other as do strings or ribbons when a knot is formed.

Initially, the ground between the hedges form-ing the knots was covered with colored gravels and grit to form patterns. But later these spaces came to be planted – sometimes with solid blocks of a strongly contrasting color, like the paler green of rue, the silvery greens of lavender and santolina, or the richer dark green of rosemary. To enhance the feeling of contrast, the packed filler plants were kept shorter than the boundary hedges and clipped perfectly flat like lawns.

· GRAND TOPIARY ·

Little by little, as tastes became more sophisti-cated, the simple knot gardens evolved into something grander and more complex. Other features, such as shrubs clipped into perfect

spheres or combinations of geometric shapes, were introduced. In some places, like the Castello Balduino at Montalto di Pavia in Italy, whole gardens containing little else but precisely arranged and clipped topiary were created.

It is thought that the extraordinary solid geometry at Montalto was first shaped in the sixteenth century. But topiary in that era was not confined to the geometric. In England, in the Hampton Court of Henry VIII's time, there was figurative and *stilt* hedging, in which shrubs were pruned to reveal their trunks. There are plenty of monastery gardens shown in Italian Renaissance paintings in which features like topiary archways and tunnels were prominent.

As early as 1632, the gates of the Oxford Botanic Garden were guarded by a pair of statuesque topiary giants.

A popular sixteenth-century form of topiary was to use evergreens like yew to create "walks" – double lines of carefully clipped hedge with a passageway between surfaced with lawn, paving or gravel. Frequently quite extensive and arranged around three sides of a rectangle, they provided places of shady exercise and doubtless the opportunity for discreet rendezvous or secret plotting. It is not hard to imagine that in crowded households, where the risk of being overheard was always very high, these walks served a variety of private purposes. A good example of

TERRACED TOPIARY
Very striking effects can be produced by creating low hedges of box, set in gravel, and punctuating them with vertically trimmed trees and shrubs. This sunken topiary garden is at the Bishop's Palace at Albi, in France. It is composed chiefly of box, and was laid out at the end of the seventeenth century. In today's gardens, the gravel can be laid over black plastic sheeting, which does away with the need for weeding between the hedges.

CLIPPING A CHESSPIECE

FORMER PLACED IN POSITION OVER YOUNG PLANT

PLANT GROWING THROUGH FORMER

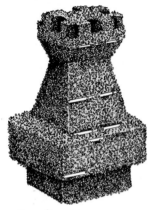

FINAL SHAPE WITH HIDDEN FORMER

Complicated shapes such as chesspieces are traditionally produced with the aid of a former – a frame that defines the final shape of the work. Flexible young stems can be attached to the former, or the former can simply be used as a guide when clipping and pruning. Formers are traditionally made of wood, which rots away when the topiary plant has reached maturity. Today, they are also made out of strip metal, or, on a domestic scale, heavy-gauge wire. Wire mesh is particularly useful for creating topiary animals.

Formers have a two-fold value. As well as helping to ensure the correct shape, they also allow the design to be appreciated long before it is fully grown.

such a walk, which is said to have been planted by the gardener and botanist John Tradescant the Elder, can still be seen today at Cranbourne Manor near Salisbury.

· LIVING EMBROIDERY ·

By the mid-seventeenth century, the simple knot garden had evolved into designs as complex as those of embroidered cloth. In fact, many of them were drawn up by artists whose main occupation was embroidery design. A garden of this type became known as a *parterre de broderie*. Unlike the simple knots that were designed to be viewed from the ground, these parterres were made to be seen from first-floor rooms or terraces. They often included such features as water in basins as well as gravel and plants. One of the most notable of these designs, the work of André le Nôtre, can still be seen at Vaux-le-Vicomte in France.

A similarly impressive parterre was made at St Germain outside the château in which Louis XIV was born. However, the only topiary that remains is the enormous pleached hedge lining the terrace overlooking the Seine. Le Nôtre made Louis a magnificent parterre at Versailles which still attracts millions of visitors each year.

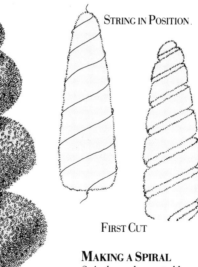

STRING IN POSITION

FIRST CUT

MAKING A SPIRAL

Spirals can be created by cutting a helical channel into the foliage of a tree. Fine-leaved evergreens such as yew are best for this purpose. The cut is first marked with a length of string wound evenly around the tree. Using the string as a guide, a shallow first cut is then made. The string can then be removed, and the cut extended until it reaches the trunk. When this has been done, the remaining foliage can then be clipped to give a rounded finish.

JUG

BALL AND CYLINDER

CROWN ON PILLAR

SQUIRREL

CAPPED SPIRE

PYRAMID

SHAPING TRADITIONAL TOPIARY

T RADITIONAL TOPIARY DESIGNS – WHETHER FORMAL OR frolicsome – have developed over many centuries. When choosing a design, it is important to remember that they do differ very much in the amount of maintenance they require. A straight-sided architectural shape, such as a pyramid, takes little time to trim. Designs that have a number of curved surfaces, such as those featuring crowns and animals, require much more work with the trimmers or clippers. Perhaps the most time-consuming of all designs are those with closely spaced tiers. When these are young, clipping has to be supplemented by bud-rubbing, a springtime task that prevents unwanted stem buds from shooting and producing foliage on areas intended to be bare.

CAKESTAND

CAPPED MUSHROOM

FRENCH POT

SCULPTED SPHERE

CAPPED POST

DANCING BEAR

TIERED DOVE

STILTED POST

CLOSED SPIRAL

BIRD ON CROWN AND BALL

forms, they became more significant when it was realized that, as at Packwood House for example, they were visual metaphors for Christ and his apostles. Chessmen in topiary set out on a chessboard have always proved attractive to garden visitors because they can attempt to solve the problems posed by the position of the pieces remaining on the board.

With the accession of William of Orange to the English throne in 1688, Dutch style came to dominate English topiary gardens. It was at this period that topiary began to appear in American gardens. Some examples still survive in towns like Williamsburg, and in parts of Virginia, Maryland and Massachusetts.

In the early eighteenth century, when a freer, more romantic and naturalistic notion of garden design emerged, there was a strong reaction in Britain to the artificiality of topiary. Influential men like the politician and gardener Horace Walpole railed against "trees cut into grotesque forms." Until garden designs again became more formal, in the middle of the nineteenth century, topiary fell from grace – officially at least.

However, just as there have always been cottage gardens, even when flowers were out of fashion, there has always been topiary. Whether it was in vogue or not, there were, and still are, plenty of gardeners who would seize their clippers or secateurs when prompted by the hint of a fanciful shape in a tree or shrub. Frequently, this sort of improvization leads to a disastrous mess, but it can also produce the most whimsical green sculpture – overproud roosters, dancing pigs, battle-scarred men of war or lovesick poets. Doubtless many such fantasies, produced from long-lived yew in the period when topiary was out of fashion, are still being preserved today.

Since its readoption to garnish Victorian formal garden schemes, topiary has continued to wax and wane in popularity. The pleached hornbeam hedges at Dumbarton Oaks in Washington and the stilted hedges created by Lawrence Johnston at Hidcote in Gloucestershire are good early twentieth-century examples of the art. The prices asked, at garden centers today, for box plants formed into pyramids and spheres certainly suggest that topiary is in the process of a revival.

· SHAPES FROM THE ORIENT ·

It is interesting to note that while mazes were being clipped into shape in medieval European gardens, gardeners were creating something similar to these mazes in Japan. In Zen Buddhist temples, the awkward paths of stepping stones across the patterned gravel of courtyard gardens symbolized the difficult route through life. They

PRESERVING A SHAPE
Even simple topiary (above) *needs regular clipping to maintain its shape. Geometrical topiary, as seen in this pillar at Cliveden in Buckinghamshire* (opposite), *can be kept in shape and allowed to grow at the same time. More complex designs, such as the peacock seen in the background, present problems, because their shape can be lost if the trees or shrubs that produce them are allowed to expand.*

In the hands of thoughtful gardeners, the parterre became more than just a decorative feature. At Villandry, near Tours in the Loire valley, a giant parterre was made, in which hundreds of yards of box hedges were woven into intricate symbolic patterns. These can be viewed from a raised terrace and visitors can still enjoy unraveling the puzzles that they present.

· EMBLEMS AND WHIMSIES ·

Seventeenth-century thinkers took great pleasure from emblematic gardens of all types. In Britain, well-grown yews planted in meaningful groups were clipped into shapes like cylinders and pyramids. Attractive when viewed as simple

CHOOSING TOPIARY PLANTS

NOT ALL TREES MAKE SUCCESSFUL SUBJECTS FOR TOPIARY. SOME cannot tolerate severe cutting, eventually losing their vigor. Others grow much too quickly, or produce foliage that is too open to allow any impression of shape. The trees shown below suffer from none of these drawbacks. They are generally slow-growing and densely leaved, and will respond to trimming by producing new shoots each year.

EVERGREEN

YEW *Taxus* **spp.**
Slow-growing conifers with dense foliage; very tolerant of clipping. Will grow on most soil types. Common yew, T. baccata, is one of the oldest of topiary plants.

BOX *Buxus* **spp.**
Slow-growing trees with glossy green or variegated foliage. Excellent for low hedging. A number of cultivated varieties are available.

HOLLY *Ilex* **spp.**
Stout trees with large, glossy and often prickly leaves, ideal for simple shapes. Common holly, I. aquifolium, is available in many ornamental forms.

PINE *Pinus* **spp.**
Conifers with long needles produced in bunches. Many species of pine can be "cloud pruned" to exaggerate natural asymmetry.

BAY *Laurus nobilis*
A small tree with aromatic leaves; sensitive to frost especially when young. Traditionally trimmed into "mop-headed" shape.

ARBORVITAE *Thuja* **spp.**
North American conifers with spreading, scale-like aromatic leaves. Useful for simple shapes and hedging. Leaves green or yellow.

DECIDUOUS

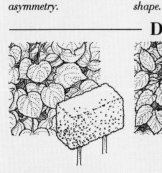

LINDEN *Tilia* **spp.**
Handsome trees with light green, heart-shaped leaves and attractive winter wood. Stout trunks make linden excellent for stilt hedges.

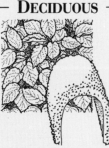

HORNBEAM *Carpinus* **spp.**
Slow-growing, small-leaved tree that produces a dense canopy. Very tolerant of clipping and pollarding; good for tunnels and arbors.

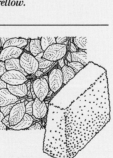

BEECH *Fagus* **spp.**
Potentially large trees with oval leaves, translucent when young. If trimmed for hedging, dead leaves are retained throughout winter.

too were designed to impose discipline, making the monks pause frequently and contemplate features in the garden from many angles, while pondering great philosophical problems. While thus preoccupied, they must have become aware of the tortured shapes into which the trees and shrubs in the garden had been formed by training and pruning.

The trees in Japanese gardens often had their leading stem removed when they were quite young. This led to them developing asymmetrically until they had achieved a new and satisfying balance. By cutting out major side-branches, the gardeners made the remaining foliage appear as distinct and separate layers reminiscent of floating clouds.

Although to western eyes trees treated like this may appear unnatural, in a country raked by typhoons they seem quite normal because few mature trees in nature remain intact. While Japanese gardeners continue to practice this traditional form of topiary, it is also becoming popular in the West. Several American landscape gardeners have modified the "floating cloud" approach, to produce very decorative and original tree forms. When grown in pots, such trees are well suited to even the smallest gardens.

· TOPIARY PLANTS AND TECHNIQUES ·

The plants traditionally chosen for topiary work are those evergreens that best tolerate clipping and which are capable of budding from the mature wood revealed in that operation. In warmer places, species like Italian cypress have always been a first choice, while elsewhere common laurel, box, holly, yew and *Viburnum tinus* have often been favored for larger works. Some pines can be used where less symmetrical shapes are needed. Small box, shrubby germander, myrtle, lavender and rosemary have always been favorites for lower features.

Not all topiary species are evergreens. Linden, hornbeam, beech and chestnut frequently appear in tall worked hedges. However, the two types of plants — evergreens and deciduous trees and shrubs — are traditionally treated in different ways. Evergreens are pruned in late spring, because this allows plenty of time for new growth to ripen before potentially damaging winter frosts arrive, although vigorous species may require a light trimming later. Major work on deciduous species is carried out in the dormant season. Being faster growing, they nearly always require at least one and sometimes two further clippings in the summer.

Complicated and geometric shapes are traditionally produced with the aid of *formers* — wooden, wire or strip metal frames which define the final shape of the work. Flexible young stems can be attached to these formers or they can simply be used as guides when clipping and pruning.

Several firms now supply ready-made formers, which can be selected from illustrated catalogues or examined at garden centers. As ever, it is the obelisks and pyramids or the formers for chesspieces that are proving to be the most popular.

· A PROBLEM OF GROWTH ·

Although would-be topiarists can draw on many different plants for their work, they are often in something of a quandary when it comes to making a selection. On the one hand, there are fast-growing plants that enable shapes to be created as soon as possible, but which demand frequent maintenance. On the other hand, there are plants that grow slowly, but which, when shaped by many years of careful clipping and training, require only an occasional light trim to keep them true to form. In the past, impatient gardeners often chose the former approach, causing endless problems for those who have inherited their work.

If you wish to edge some beds with low box hedges, you face a difficult decision. To plant a 12-inch (30-cm) high hedge do you choose the quicker-growing box *Buxus sempervirens*, which will, if allowed, make a small tree reaching 20 feet (6 m), or do you opt for *Buxus sempervirens* 'Suffruticosa', which grows almost imperceptibly slowly, and which tends to remain dwarf? The question is complicated by economic overtones. Because it grows only slowly, it takes a nursery-man a long time to raise 'Suffruticosa' to a saleable size. This variety is therefore very expensive, particularly as many are needed to obtain a satisfactory hedge within any gardener's lifetime; *B. sempervirens* is much less costly.

One way in which seventeenth- and eighteenth-century gardeners overcame this problem was to plant slower-growing subjects, destined to become important feature hedges, inside wooden frameworks. Their dimensions defined the ultimate shape and size of the hedge, allowing impatient clients the opportunity to get some idea of the way their gardens would look when the hedge was mature. Meanwhile, the frames acted as useful guides to the gardeners charged with looking after the hedge as it developed. They only had to clip away the stems of the hedge plants that escaped from the confines of the frame to ensure the correct shape. By the time the wooden framework had finally rotted away, the hedge plants would have grown to their ultimate thickness and height.

AT THE WORKFACE
Before the invention of the electric trimmer, topiary had to be kept in shape using hand shears. This made the cutting process both long and arduous. Trees like these mature yews would need trimming at least once a year, and considerable care would be needed in cutting them. One difficulty with clipping a substantial tree was that the topiarist was too close to the work to see how the shape was developing. To produce a smooth and symmetrical finish, he would have to climb down at intervals to inspect the work from the ground.

PARALLEL-
HANDLED SHEARS

SPLAY-HANDLED SHEARS

TOPIARY TOOLS
Although the Victorians showed great ingenuity in designing new garden tools, sometimes their enthusiasm for new gadgets ran away with them. One example of this was the patent hedge-trimmer, seen above in the hands of a gentleman gardener. The scene suggests that the trimmer was a wonderful labor-saving device. In practice, it would have put an immense strain on the forearms and shoulders, making a few minutes' work with it quite enough for most people. Simple shears were, and still are, the most effective manual clippers.

ARBORS & RETREATS

The origin of the arbor — Renaissance retreats —
Pergolas — Gazebos — Romantic retreats — Traditional
summerhouse design — Inside the Victorian summerhouse
Modern retreats — Leafy bowers

Secrecy and surprise are two of the most powerful effects that can be produced by good garden design. A garden that reveals itself at a glance may have enormous grandeur and spectacle, but it may well leave the visitor feeling that there is nothing to be gained by walking through it. On the other hand, a garden that only slowly yields its secrets excites the curiosity and maintains interest.

Arbors and retreats are garden structures that are designed to bring a feeling of intimacy and secrecy into a garden. As gardening has developed, they have taken an extraordinary range of forms. From their early beginnings as simple shelters designed to offer protection from sun or wind, they have developed into elaborate structures that have ranged from the thoroughly practical to the completely fanciful.

Arbors are essentially semi-enclosed structures that usually support plants, or have plants arranged around them. The fact that they are exceptionally ancient garden features was borne out by the work of the

WATERSIDE TEMPLE
With its simple classical lines, this Doric temple at Barnsley House in Gloucestershire is a triumphant example of a graceful garden building in a sympathetic setting.

nineteenth-century archeologist Charles Chipiez. While working on excavations in Egypt, Chipiez created a detailed perspective view of the villa and garden of a high official in the court of the Egyptian king Amenhotep III, who lived between 1411 and 1375 BC. The garden lay within a high-walled compound, and it included wide and shady vine-clad trellises, under which the air would be cooler and the light less harsh. Screening trees, planted against the walls, provided shelter on days when dust-laden wind blew in from the desert.

Two rectangular arbors offered views over rectangular ornamental ponds. According to Chipiez's reconstruction, they would have had open sides and would have been topped by canopies, providing shady seating from which the garden could be enjoyed.

The villa itself had a feature that was to reappear in many forms in subsequent centuries. This took the form of an open-sided awning, suspended from poles on the house roof. It not only reduced the temperature indoors, but – like gazebos many centuries later – also offered a high viewpoint from which much of the garden and the landscape beyond could be seen.

· THE VILLA AND ITS ATRIUM ·

In a sense, the atrium of a Roman house in holiday resorts like Pompeii was like a large arbor. Most of them were surrounded by deep and shady colonnades, upon which plants were trained, and they were backed by solid walls. No matter what the time of day, or how gusty the wind, there would always be somewhere shady or calm to sit and enjoy the splashing of the atrium's central fountain. Several Roman sources suggest that, like the Egyptians, they built vine-clad trellis arbors, both at ground level and on flat roofs.

The Romans seem to have invented the ultimate of retreats – grottos and structures known as *nymphaea*. These were originally underground rooms below the house. They retained their cool air and were decorated with frescoes of garden scenes, to prevent the people using them from feeling too hemmed in. Later, the Romans made insulated structures on the surface using tufa – a soft volcanic rock – lined with stucco.

· RENAISSANCE RETREATS ·

During the Renaissance, Italian garden designers built grottos and nymphaea of great architectural refinement and often massive interior dimensions. They often built impressive alcoves in walls to provide shelter and shade and a feeling of intimacy for seats. They also reproduced, some-times on an even grander scale, Roman features like colonnades, high belvederes or viewing turrets and wide loggias, frequently linking them with water features so that they would benefit by their cooling and soothing effect.

As gardens became more refined, topiary was used instead of masonry to provide intimate enclosures in which to locate seats. It did not take long for Italian Renaissance ideas to influence garden design both farther north and west. In the *Book of Hours* of Isabella of Portugal, which dates from 1480, King René of Anjou is seen writing in his garden house, which is depicted as a room with a vaulted ceiling with a paved floor and completely open to the garden at one end.

At the height of the Renaissance, but farther north at Versailles, *treillage (see pp.176–7)* and masonry were frequently combined in arbors.

· PERGOLAS ·

Pergolas are an extended form of arbor. As well as making attractive screens and useful supports for climbing plants, foliage-clad pergolas offer welcome relief from hot sunshine. They can do more as well. The fragrant air and more subdued light beneath a well-clad pergola affects the senses, so that on leaving the leafy shade, a garden seems larger and brighter than before.

Throughout gardening history there seem to have been almost as many ways of making pergolas as there have been plants that can be trained to grow and ramble over them. In simple designs, straight timbers span lines of square-sectioned timber posts. But columns of round timber, brick, stone, rubble set in plaster or metal tubes have all been used to support rails of equally diverse character.

No matter what materials are use to make the basic pergola, they are nearly always supplemented by a lighter roof. This provides more attachment points for climbers. When the gaps between the vertical columns are also filled by something for climbers to grasp, the whole pergola becomes a green tunnel. Trellis panels, light timber sheeting cut to form arcading, or even just patterned wire strands can all provide lateral support and increase the sense of intimacy and enclosure.

Variants in the design of pergolas include those that are free-standing and those that consist of several parallel rows supporting an open roof structure that carries the stems of really vigorous climbers and vines.

· GAZEBOS ·

When many great houses were built or expanded in England during the sixteenth and seventeenth centuries, garden designers made glazed and

PERIOD PERGOLAS

M URALS AT POMPEII SHOW THAT PERCOLAS HAVE BEEN popular at least since Roman times. In the past they were often built on a grandiose scale – some Renaissance pergolas, for example, were even long enough for horses to be given a daily gallop in their shade. The pergola's long history gives a large choice of shape and materials that are suitable for a traditional garden. At its simplest, a pergola can be little more than a double row of wooden posts supporting a slatted roof. More ambitious is the trelliswork pergola. This consists of square-sectioned upright posts that support the roof timbers and trellis panels, which can be bought ready-made. To make the structure as durable as possible, the timbers should be treated with a preservative. Constructing a pergola with brick piers calls for more skill because the piers, which should be at least 7 feet (2.15 m) high, must be exactly vertical. An alternative to brick is rough-hewn stone, which gives a softer appearance more appropriate in an informal garden.

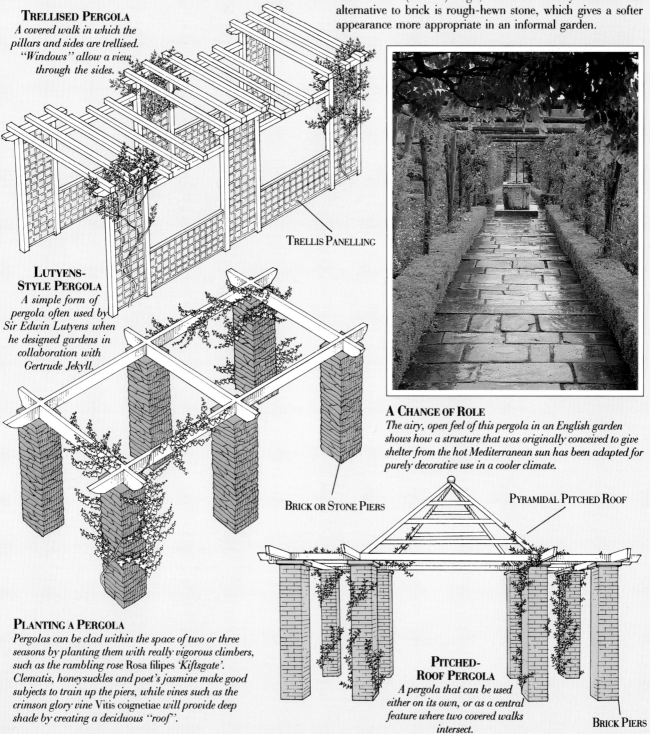

TRELLISED PERGOLA
A covered walk in which the pillars and sides are trellised. "Windows" allow a view through the sides.

TRELLIS PANELLING

LUTYENS-STYLE PERGOLA
A simple form of pergola often used by Sir Edwin Lutyens when he designed gardens in collaboration with Gertrude Jekyll.

A CHANGE OF ROLE
The airy, open feel of this pergola in an English garden shows how a structure that was originally conceived to give shelter from the hot Mediterranean sun has been adapted for purely decorative use in a cooler climate.

BRICK OR STONE PIERS

PYRAMIDAL PITCHED ROOF

PLANTING A PERGOLA
Pergolas can be clad within the space of two or three seasons by planting them with really vigorous climbers, such as the rambling rose Rosa filipes *'Kiftsgate'. Clematis, honeysuckles and poet's jasmine make good subjects to train up the piers, while vines such as the crimson glory vine* Vitis coignetiae *will provide deep shade by creating a deciduous "roof".*

PITCHED-ROOF PERGOLA
A pergola that can be used either on its own, or as a central feature where two covered walks intersect.

BRICK PIERS

GARDEN ARBORS

WOODEN ARBORS WERE ORIGINALLY MADE for use in festivals and pageants, and, rather like today's marquees, they were dismantled once the event was over. It was perhaps inevitable that some garden owners, having seen how much these temporary structures improved the appearance of their grounds, allowed them to remain rather than having them packed away. Arbors intended specifically for growing roses became popular in the eighteenth and nineteenth centuries. It was then that the production of robust iron wire enabled designers to create structures that were strong enough to support plants, yet light and open enough to admit their perfume.

Today, reproduction wirework arbors can be bought in kit form, and assembled in just the same way as their Victorian counterparts. Wooden arbors are also becoming increasingly popular. A simple booth-like arbor can be made with treated timber and trellis panels, while arbors that feature more elaborate architecture can be bought ready for assembly.

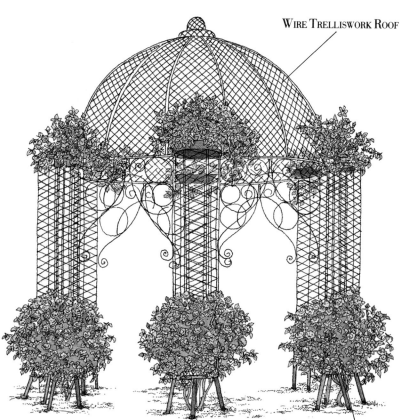

WIRE TRELLISWORK ROOF

PLANTS IN CONTAINERS

VICTORIAN WIREWORK ARBOR
The pillared wirework arbor satisfied the Victorian desire for ornament without falling into the trap of becoming over-ponderous. Decoration was provided by climbing roses or plants in tubs and troughs.

ITALIAN ARBOR
Italian arbors tended to be grand and robust, framed with thick ironwork. The architectural motifs would echo those of the house in whose grounds the arbor stood.

FRENCH TIMBER ARBOR
Trelliswork lends this arbor a feeling of intimacy while at the same time giving support for climbing roses.

enclosed retreats that were more appropriate to gardens in a chillier climate.

One product of their work was the gazebo – said to mean, in dog Latin, "I will gaze." Gazebos were usually small buildings located high on the house or at the end of a raised terrace. They acted both as refuges and eye-catchers, and they also offered visitors the choicer long views to be seen outside the garden boundary. Because their windows and doors could be thrown open or kept tightly shut, they were serviceable in all weathers.

Despite their often simple lines, architects took considerable pains over these buildings, and the results were often exquisite. Gazebos were often square-sided or octagonal, with steeply pitched roofs clad in tile or stone slabs, crowned by some decorative device such as a stone sphere.

Traditional gazebos often overlooked high walls, sometimes being built in at a corner. Although most were of stone, gazebos were also built of wood. The raised gazebo has rather fallen from favor in modern times because, with the exception of rural gardens in agreeable landscapes, most of today's gardeners prefer to look inwards at their gardens rather than outwards at the buildings that surround them.

· ROMANTIC RETREATS ·

While structures like arbors, gazebos and pergolas usually had serious intent, the same cannot always be said of some of the retreats to be found in gardens of the romantic period.

During the eighteenth century, garden designers often stationed eye-catching features in the vistas they were creating. These structures, which ranged from temples to "hermit's cells", took a host of intriguing forms. On the very occasional English day when the sun became intolerable, Gothic pavilions, Turkish tents, temples to Bacchus and canopied bridges undoubtedly offered moments of relief, as did simpler seats in shady places among the trees en route.

By this time, the chief justification for making these retreats was often the capacity to amaze or amuse, rather than their ability to provide comfort. Indeed, their too-frequent use would have threatened the illusion that the romantic garden designers worked so hard to create.

· THE VICTORIANS ESCAPE OUTDOORS ·

Ironically, it was the stuffy Victorians in England who developed the making of intimate garden structures into a high art. Although we are beginning to realize that their era was less prudish than was formerly thought, it is difficult to imagine exactly why Victorian parents should have felt safe in creating such ideal venues for

RETREAT WITH STYLE
The curved roof line of this gazebo at Hidcote Manor in Gloucestershire (above) echoes an architectural style of French origin. In placing great emphasis on garden buildings and structure, Hidcote's American creator, Lawrence Johnston, perfected a modern interpretation of traditional gardening that has since gained a great following.

A WONDER IN WIRE
Victorian rose temples were flamboyant structures of great architectural pretension. The temple shown here, which was delivered ready for assembly and painted in two shades of green, cost $75, a considerable sum in the late nineteenth century.

SUMMERHOUSES, GAZEBOS AND PAVILIONS

W HETHER TO CHILDREN OR ADULTS, THE APPEAL OF A MINIATURE house, remote from the cares and constraints of everyday life and set in the midst of a tranquil garden, is universal. In cool climates, these homes-away-from-home have practical advantages as well, for they offer shelter from the elements, a place where the magnificence of the garden can be enjoyed whatever the weather. The design of these garden buildings has provided architects with unrivaled opportunities for whimsy and experimentation. The styles seen in traditional summerhouses, gazebos and pavilions reflect influences not only from the distant past, but also from distant shores. Some of these traditional buildings are difficult or impossible for the amateur to reproduce today, because they call for skills in masonry or joinery that are the province of the craftsman. Others, especially rustic summerhouses can be made by anyone familiar with basic woodwork.

CHINESE FLOATING PAVILION

GOTHIC SUMMERHOUSE

TUDOR GAZEBO

HEXAGONAL PAVILION

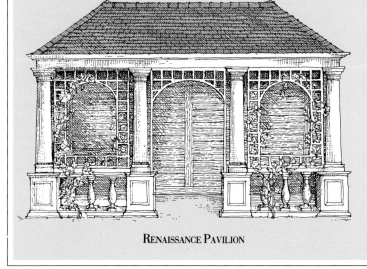

RENAISSANCE PAVILION

CLASSICAL SUMMERHOUSE

BELL-ROOFED PAVILION

TRELLISED PAVILION

HEXAGONAL SUMMERHOUSE

RUSTIC SUMMERHOUSE

CURTAINED ARBOR

OPEN PAVILION

ORIEL GAZEBO

CHINOISERIE GAZEBO

PILLARED PAVILION

THE RUSTIC SUMMERHOUSE

EW FASHIONS IN GARDEN BUILDING AND ORNAMENT GAIN such a powerful hold on the popular imagination as did rustic work in the nineteenth century. Spurred on by a spate of instructive books and broadsheets, Victorian gardeners vied with each other to create fantastical structures out of logs, twisted branches and varnished wood, and manufacturers of chairs, pots and other objects echoed the style in their own products. Making garden rustic work can be an enjoyable exercise, principally because there are no rules to follow save one, which is the more eccentric the better. The summerhouse shown here is a typical rustic retreat. The walls are made of stout poles or the trunks of sapling conifers, sawn in two and machined so that their edges are parallel. These are arranged with their bark outermost, forming the walls and supporting the roof timbers. The .trellis-like decoration is made of sawn branches, apple or pine being ideal for this.

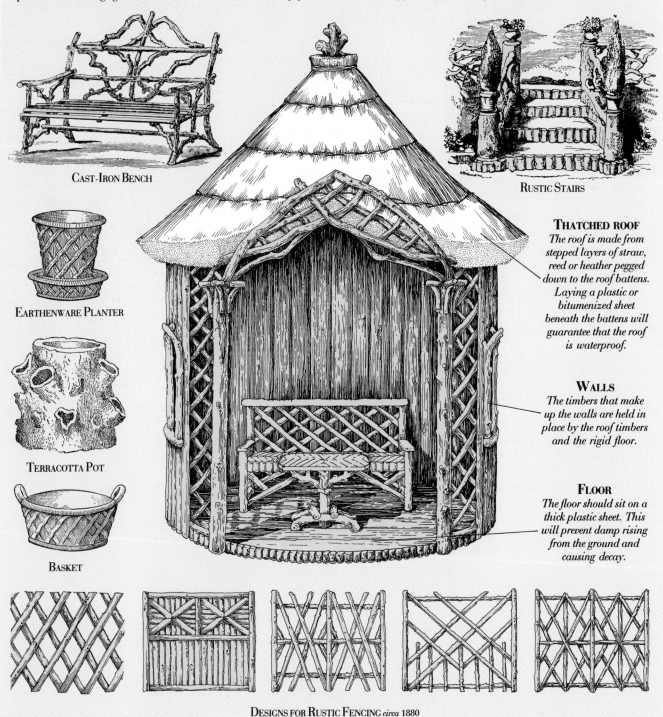

CAST-IRON BENCH

EARTHENWARE PLANTER

TERRACOTTA POT

BASKET

RUSTIC STAIRS

THATCHED ROOF
The roof is made from stepped layers of straw, reed or heather pegged down to the roof battens. Laying a plastic or bitumenized sheet beneath the battens will guarantee that the roof is waterproof.

WALLS
The timbers that make up the walls are held in place by the roof timbers and the rigid floor.

FLOOR
The floor should sit on a thick plastic sheet. This will prevent damp rising from the ground and causing decay.

DESIGNS FOR RUSTIC FENCING *circa 1880*

assignations in their gardens. Was it because they believed that their children were paragons? Or was it because the father of the house may have had designs on certain members of his staff?

Whatever the real reason for building their shelters and summerhouses, the Victorians ostensibly erected them to provide shelter. This could be to counter chilly breezes, to protect pale and delicate skin from the dreaded effects of the sun, or just to provide suitable conditions for taking tea.

To be roomy enough to be useful, these buildings became important garden features that could also be used to lure the eye along vistas. They had to be attractive and discreetly sited, and were often the destination of a walk out into the garden which, when reached, offered charming views. The house itself would not feature in that scene because the designer of the retreat deliberately tried to create a feeling of idyllic isolation and escape from the realities of everyday life that the house itself inevitably represented.

· AN EXPLOSION OF STYLES ·

The Victorians were not noted for their restraint in experimenting with architectural styles, and whatever inhibitions they may have had in building houses were completely abandoned when it came to buildings for the garden.

Some of the least eccentric shelters, mock cottages and summerhouses were built in local stone and roofed in the same material. Many of them have survived to this day. Less expensive, but, if well built, equally popular, were brick structures roofed with slate or slightly porous clay tiles, which quickly acquired an enchanting softening of moss.

However, it was in the use of timber that the Victorians were at their most inventive. Styles varied from those of a frontiersman's cabin in crude logs to the tea-room of a Chinese emperor, the rondavel of an African tribal chief to a Swiss mountain chalet. There were chunky, squared timber frames infilled with soft mortar, different patterns of regional weatherboarding and, above all, a host of fantasies in what was known as "rustic work".

Rustic work was constructed out of branches with their bark either stripped or left intact, which were selected for peculiarities in their shape. At its best, rustic work in the form of steps and garden furniture looked very tasteful. At its most excessive, a neo-Gothic garden building, with its tangle of branches and low thatching, lurking in the corner of a garden like some extraordinary aberration of nature, looked as though the branches used in its construction might at any moment burst into leaf.

Because they did not have the problem of making doors fit to exclude drafts, doorways provided designers with unbridled opportunities to let their imaginations run riot. Victorian garden retreats were entered through circular moon gates, Moghul arches, the erect jawbones of whales or between Egyptian tomb stelae and clinker-built fishing boats standing on their sterns. Taste varied from the exquisite to the comically vulgar. Many of them were saved from total absurdity only by thatchers who made their attractive and workmanlike roofs of heather, reed or long wheat straw.

· TRADITIONAL ·
· SUMMERHOUSE DESIGN ·

Since the soil of most northern gardens was often damp, the floors of summerhouses had to be set well above it and often insulated. To supplement the builders' provisions and counteract the cold striking upwards, summerhouse owners often used mats made from sensible materials like woven sisal or straw, which could easily be shaken free of soil brought in from the garden. The most ambitious summerhouses also had verandahs as well as inside accommodation.

SHELTER WITHIN A WALL
A seat converts any sheltered space into a retreat against the elements. Here at Scotney Castle in Kent a bench is protected by the masonry of a deep wall.

TOPIARY ARBORS
The dense foliage of evergreen trees makes an effective windproof shelter around a seat. In the past, topiary arbors were usually made of clipped yew, but they can also be formed from faster-growing deciduous trees such as elms. The trees are planted around a seat, and those on the lateral margins are clipped so that their branches join to form the canopy.

All these requirements added up to fairly complicated building specifications that became more and more sophisticated as the nineteenth century progressed and garden owners competed with each other for the provision of luxury.

With the development of factory building techniques, many companies entered the market to supply summerhouses. They seem to have had little difficulty in persuading people of quite modest means that their gardens would be incomplete without one.

As the enthusiasm for mechanism and gadgetry grew, garden buildings, too, became objects of innovation. The most notable and persistent among them was mounting the whole structure of a summerhouse on a turntable base that allowed the views to be changed, or the disposition altered at will to offer better shelter from the wind or shade from the sun.

These rotating summerhouses were usually sited in more open areas of the garden where full advantage could be taken of their ability to be turned. It is fascinating to imagine the scene as the gentlemen of the house pushed the creaking structure with all their might, while inside, grave elderly ladies were revolved along with the furnishings and the tea-trays.

· INSIDE THE VICTORIAN SUMMERHOUSE ·

While references to the role of summerhouses in fictitious romances are numerous, no one can be quite sure how many good books have been composed in them when they served as quiet studies away from the house. Mark Twain, for example, wrote most of *The Adventures of Tom Sawyer* in the summerhouse of a garden in upper

New York State. However, what is more certain is that at a time when strict conformity to order and habit conferred respectability, the summerhouse, like the conservatory, was a liberating feature in the Victorian garden.

Normally, reading was an activity confined to the nursery or the schoolroom when young; the library, study or drawing-room when adult. Taking tea, with its ritual accompaniments of toast and honey, crumpets and gentleman's relish, tissue-thin cress sandwiches, scones with clotted cream and raspberry jam, was a ceremony that usually took place in the parlor. Therefore in the *belle époque*, when nothing resembling a "dinette" or a "breakfast bar" had been invented, merely reading a book or taking tea in a summerhouse had something akin to heresy about it and it induced an exciting sense of mischief. This was amplified because the weather in those northern regions where summerhouses were most frequently built was only rarely kind enough to make using them a pleasure.

But even when the decision to use the summerhouse had been taken, the ripple of anticipation of a more relaxed feast in the garden was mitigated by the fact that a large element of ceremony still had to be preserved. Flawless, well-starched linen would cover the table. Genteel cutlery and crockery would be used and a maid in a pinafore and cap would ensure suitably deferential service.

To stage such a tea party, a summerhouse had, in many ways, to be designed to resemble a parlor. It had to be large enough to seat up to eight people in some comfort. So that they could all enjoy the garden view, it had to have large windows on most of its sides. In very hot weather it had to be suitably ventilated, which meant that the windows had to be capable of being opened to create a through draft. Adjustable roof-ventilation was often provided to allow rising heat to escape. Under adverse conditions on windy days the summerhouse had to be suitably snug. Apart from the main table and chairs, there also had to be shelf space for such paraphernalia as kettles heated by spirit lamps to provide hot water to replenish the tea pots. By modern standards, tea in the Victorian summerhouse was hardly a spontaneous affair.

· MODERN RETREATS ·

Until the 1950s, ambitious gardeners tended to design and decorate arbors and retreats in accordance with the styles of past eras, altering their scale to suit the smaller size of most of their gardens. Thatched summerhouses were popular for many years after the heyday of the Victorian garden came to a close, although few are built today. Rustic work has never achieved anything like its former hold over popular taste, although it has its charm in the right setting. Given a supply of wood and some imagination, it is well within the abilities of the average gardener.

There was a period when more functionalist architecture finally had an effect upon garden design. New shapes were given to the archways of pergolas and loggia roofs, which were made from modules of materials like precast concrete.

However, modern interpretations of the structures so enjoyed by the Victorians are becoming steadily more popular. Although durable plastic has been responsible for introducing some of the grossest horrors to our gardens, it should not be universally shunned. Several firms are now able to supply extremely attractive simulations of pretty Gothic summerhouses, which present a convincing likeness to some of the best of the earlier timber structures. They are strong and have the advantage that they never need to be painted or treated against wood rot.

· LEAFY BOWERS ·

One charming Victorian feature that remains popular today is the bower. Bowers seem to have been a feature since the earliest days of pleasure gardening. They consist of a seat that is surrounded, or even sometimes half-smothered, by plants. The seat can be portable or permanent, and the plants growing around it may be deciduous or evergreen.

Climbers like ivies, clematis or roses make excellent cover for a bower, although trees such as yew or box were also used in the past. Rapid growers such as cypresses also found their way into the garden as shade for bowers. Since they are more rigid than climbers, they were simply planted to form an alcove, with those on the lateral margins of the seat being clipped so that their lateral branches formed a canopy.

Alcove bowers, of the kind that feature shrubs or trees, take longer to establish. One short cut that can be taken is to place a seat in an alcove that has been clipped into an already existing hedge. If the hedge on either side of the seat is then allowed to grow outwards a little, it gives the bower the seclusion that makes it so attractive.

For the really ambitious, there is a third possibility, which consists of training and clipping trees to produce a truncated topiary tunnel, enclosing the seat on three sides. This takes much longer to establish than the other two methods, but the finished bower is a striking structure. When planted with deciduous trees, such as hornbeam, the light outside is beautifully screened by the translucent green leaves, giving dappled shade that plays around the seat.

CREATING A VICTORIAN BOWER

BOWERS ENVELOPED IN CLIMBING PLANTS ARE ATTRACTIVE YET simple to create. For rapid results, the climbers can be grown over a frame of wood or metal that forms the backing, sides and roof to the bower. Metal frames can be bought ready-made, while wooden frames are easily constructed from bark-clad poles, or timber that has been treated with a preservative to prevent decay. The plants will quickly climb up and through the support without the need for training, effectively masking it. They will also envelop the air in their scent, especially in the evening. If the frame surrounds an ornamental seat, for example one made out of painted cast-iron, the effect can be quite out of proportion to the amount of effort needed to create it.

CLIMBING ROSE
'Gloire de Dijon'
Yellow flowers with a slight pink flush borne on vigorous stems

POET'S JASMINE
Jasminum officinale
A deliciously perfumed climber; not suitable for areas with severe winters

IVY
Hedera canariensis
'Variegata'
Pinching out leading shoots encourages bushy growth

CLEMATIS
Clematis montana
'Grandiflora'
A large-flowered variety of this vigorous clematis

THE WILDERNESS GARDEN

Nature tactfully adorned — Wild scenes in the Gothic garden — An end to sophistication — The landscape movement — The wild garden — The new American garden — Managing a wild flower meadow

◆◆◆◆

IT COULD BE SAID THAT THERE IS SOMETHING ALMOST INSOLENT ABOUT the concept of introducing an area of wilderness within the confines of a garden. By definition, a garden is an area set aside and separated from the wild by walks, fences or other barriers. It is a place where plants either useful or pleasing can be grown, protected from animals and screened from the worst of the weather.

That was an arrangement which, with few exceptions, seemed to satisfy most gardeners until well into the seventeenth century. People were still quite thinly scattered and there was no shortage of land. With plenty of genuine wilderness, or at least forest and unplowed unfenced meadowland

INTO THE UNKNOWN
Informality is the most important feature of a wilderness garden. Nature should appear to be in control, with nothing seeming to be contrived or deliberately planted.

– 119 –

all around, there was little need to create an artificial imitation in the gardens of the day.

At this time, ambitious gardening was a privilege of the few and the rich. They frequently used it as a form of display. Like their gorgeous clothes, their gardens were symbols of wealth and power. Such a highly mannered and over-dressed society needed highly decorative and stagey gardens. Their requirements were met by pleasure grounds with wide and flawlessly groomed alleys, giving enough room for visitors in voluminous skirts to pass while taking the air. Not for them narrow muddy tracks that might spoil delicate shoes, or intrusive brambles that could snag fine silken hose.

· SLIPPING THE KNOT ·

From the late fifteenth century and all through the sixteenth, designers became increasingly adept at making well-ordered gardens for their princely patrons. They appeared first in Italy, and later, as Renaissance ideas spread, in France, northern Europe and Britain.

Gardens like these were little more than highly decorative strolling grounds studded with urns, statues and fountains, and they became progressively grander and grander in scale. In the immediate region of the great house the simpler knot garden of earlier periods was magnified into extensive parterres with patterning as intricate as that of any tapestry. They were made to provoke an increasing sense of wonder, and to be explored, not simply admired during a brief overview. They frequently extended over ranks of wide-stepped terraces. Even the park beyond was managed symmetrically, being divided by broad alleys between blocks of trees to impose a formal and decorative order on the whole vista.

But by the end of the sixteenth century a new class of patron had begun to emerge. Populations were increasing, trade, industry and towns were growing, and the beneficiaries of this greater wealth now formed a much more numerous middle class. They could not afford palaces like Versailles or Hampton Court but they did build fine mansions. While initially they had their garden designers mimic the formal spreads of their monarchs, with their knotted hedges and perfect symmetry, they soon tired of such constricting formality. Full of originality and confidence, they aspired to something different.

· NATURE TACTFULLY ADORNED ·

As early as 1625, in his prescription for an ideal Jacobean garden, Francis Bacon suggested the inclusion of "a heath or wilderness." He described it as being "nature imitated and tactfully adorned," and that neat summary remains about as good a definition of a wilderness garden as you could hope to find.

Although Bacon's notions were soon taken up by influential English landowners like William Russell, the first Duke of Bedford, at Woburn Abbey, some traditions died hard. High Renaissance men liked to impose order on nature and it was a habit they were reluctant to abandon completely. The change took time.

At Woburn in the 1660s the main garden was divided into two distinct halves by a broad central alley. On one side there were geometrical beds, in the previous formal style, while the other half was devoted to a wilderness. This consisted of blocks of trees and shrubs separated by an elaborate series of alleys.

· A WILDERNESS FOR ROYALTY ·

By the 1680s, making wildernesses had become commonplace. It was an activity that received royal approval when Christopher Wren designed a huge wilderness for William and Mary at Hampton Court. But even there some of the former taste for formality and the Dutch love of restraint was evident. Despite nature apparently having the upper hand, the blocks of thickly planted trees and shrubs were symmetrically cut through by two wide intersecting alleys.

These rather tame wildernesses had a lot in common with the continental *bosquet*. This was a block of trees divided by complicated patterns of intersecting paths. The bosquet, in its turn, seems to have been derived from an earlier Italian fashion for planting *boscos*. These were solid groves of evergreens, designed to provide refuge from the hot sun. They relied on the variety of the trees' trunks and branches when seen in subdued light for their main attraction.

Early wilderness-makers borrowed ideas from some of the continental bosquets. They included curving labyrinthine blind alleys leading to open glades of lawn that were surrounded by trees. These sometimes included features such as ponds or fountains, to be viewed by visitors before they were obliged to retrace their steps.

· WILD SCENES IN THE GOTHIC GARDEN ·

When the craze for wildernesses arrived in Scotland in the early 1700s, one man at least was not impressed. "They are too formal and stiff," complained Thomas Hamilton, Earl of Haddington. "Were I to plant a wilderness there would be nothing in it but evergreens, flowering trees and bright yellow-barked willow."

Hamilton would undoubtedly have been happier if he had visited the garden created by the Digby family at Sherborne in Dorset. When the writer Alexander Pope saw this garden in 1724 it was fully mature, so its main planting must have taken place at least fifty to sixty years previously.

To Pope, the great beauty of the garden lay in its irregularity. The ground on which it was made undulated with sudden rises and falls, twists and turns, offering frequent unexpected views of the surrounding landscape. "The views about it are let in," as Pope phrased it.

In the more formal area close to and in front of the house, there was a triangular area filled with "the best kind of cherry trees." The house was set in a natural amphitheater with tracts of woodland, which rose to its rim penetrated by shady winding walks. These led to a rustic stonework "hermit's seat" and then to some fine and ambitious simulated ruins beneath the canopy of vast old trees, "which makes the whole part inexpressibly aweful and solemn."

In saying this Pope, as a lover of the Gothic romantic movement, was being fulsome in his praise. By "aweful" he meant full of awe – the capacity to provoke fear and amazement, and by "solemn," ponderous and commanding respect and reverence. The place satisfied the same desire in early eighteenth-century man to face the intimidating and mysterious as earlier man had betrayed when creating myths and magic.

· AN END TO SOPHISTICATION ·

The style of the garden at Sherborne would certainly have been well in accord with the ideas of Batty Langley, whose *New Principles of Gardening*, published in 1728, was to become a seminal gardening tutor for several decades. He hated formal topiary and parterres, and encouraged a move towards a truly Arcadian approach to garden design, in which meandering paths

and the wilderness would play a major role. By the second half of the eighteenth century the ideas of two outstanding thinkers, Thomas Paine and Jean-Jacques Rousseau, had permeated all aspects of life including garden design. Their pleas for an end to over-sophistication undoubtedly helped to reduce the taste for formal garden plans. When, for example, Dr John Fothergill started making an important Botanical Garden at East Ham in 1762, the design was anything but formal. Apart from building a vast greenhouse 260 feet (80 m) long to accommodate exotic species from abroad which were not winter-hardy, he made all the rest of his garden

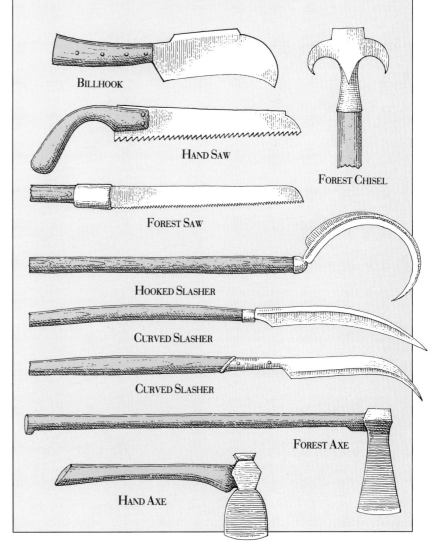

TOOLS FOR TAMING NATURE

I N THE SEVENTEENTH CENTURY, A GREAT DEAL OF WORK WAS EXPENDED in fashioning "wildernesses" out of woods and uncultivated land. Hand tools such as billhooks were used to clear the undergrowth to make paths, while saws, axes and long-handled slashers were needed to cut down trees and lop branches. The forest chisel was used to split or *rive* large branches into more manageable and useful sections. All these forestry tools were made of soft iron which required constant sharpening to keep its edge.

BILLHOOK

FOREST CHISEL

HAND SAW

FOREST SAW

HOOKED SLASHER

CURVED SLASHER

CURVED SLASHER

FOREST AXE

HAND AXE

STATUES IN A LANDSCAPE

I N FORMAL GARDENS, STATUES ARE PROMINENT ORNAMENTS THAT ARE designed to be seen from some distance. But in a wilderness garden, a statue can be used in a quite different way so that it evokes a feeling of decay and neglect. The art in this deception lies in careful siting, so that the statue is concealed until the last moment, when the visitor stumbles upon it quite unexpectedly. Growing plants close to a statue, rather than keeping them clear as is the usual practice, accentuates the feeling that nature has taken the upper hand.

REFLECTED IN A POOL

Statues are traditional features in water gardens where formality is the keynote. However, a formal statue placed in the very informal surroundings of a woodland pool (above) produces an altogether different impression. The combination of stone and water shaded by trees conveys a "fruitful melancholy".

CONTROLLED NEGLECT

Simply letting plants grow around statues creates a feeling of wildness. This statue in a meadow area (above) is surrounded by lank, unmown grass, which contrasts strongly with the much more familiar practice of placing statues in closely-cropped lawns. A Chinese urn half-hidden by trees and shrubs (right) looks not only wild and neglected, but also encourages the visitor to wander further.

into one vast wilderness. To do this, he used thickets of well-established trees and shrubs. The hope was that these would provide protection for those exotics which might become winter-hardy if they were sheltered until they had become naturalized. Of formally arranged beds and paths, there was no sign.

· THE LANDSCAPE MOVEMENT ·

By the time Fothergill began his Botanical Garden, "Capability" Brown was establishing himself as a major landscape architect by transforming the gardens of many of England's great houses. In a sense what he prescribed was close to Bacon's notion of "nature imitated and tactfully adorned," but in most cases Brown's adorning was somewhat less than tactful.

No matter what the topography of the site, Brown moved prodigious quantities of earth to create gently undulating tree-girded slopes and long views over ambitious water features which, he felt, typified the best in Britain's landscapes. By banishing all suggestion that the land had in any way been gardened, he offered the ultimate man-made wilderness, and a total escape from the constraints of formalism.

With hindsight, many of Brown's creations seem bland. However, at the time, his uniquely English landscaped parks proved enormously popular with landowners. One reason for this was that their tailor-made slopes and separated copses were ideal for hunting and shooting, a great recommendation in the days when these were the main leisure pursuits of those with land and money.

For about fifty years, Brown and his imitators transformed their patrons' estates. They wiped out what they considered frivolous intrusions: temples, grottos, labyrinths, mazes, topiary work, mounts, gazebos, exotic species of trees, beds of flowering plants and deliberately created wildernesses concealing "ruins" had no place in the landscape, and were all swept away.

· GARDENING NATURALLY ·

By the 1820s, when plant explorers were beginning to send back newly discovered species of plants in great numbers, formality had returned in gardening. In England, the well-to-do in their suburban villas competed with each other to be the first to grow novelties from abroad. Many of the plants were herbaceous annuals or biennials of relatively small stature, and they found their way into massed arrangements in well-groomed formal beds. Through the middle years of the century the designs for these carpet beds became increasingly convoluted as the Victorians indulged their taste for rigid and over-ponderous decoration provided by plants of garish color. Inevitably, there was a reaction from this tedious formality. It came with the wider acceptance of herbaceous borders, in which annuals and biennials were used in a freer way, and with the writings of the plantsman William Robinson.

During the 1860s, Robinson worked for several years in the Royal Horticultural Society's garden in Regent's Park. Here, among other things, he was in charge of the Society's wild flower collection. He found their raggle-taggle habits, when growing and seeding together in lank grassy swards, more charming than anything produced by the perfection-seeking gardeners making carpet beds in the surrounding public parks, and he set about preaching these ideas to the public.

· THE WILD GARDEN ·

In his bestselling book *The Wild Garden* published in 1870, Robinson wrote that "the idea of the wild garden is placing plants of other countries as hardy as our hardiest wild flowers in places where they will flourish without further cost or care." One of the illustrations in the book exemplified what he meant: it showed a charming clump of double Chinese peonies set in grass

and left to grow without interference. Robinson was quick to make use of any plant that could survive without persistent cossetting and encouragement. Shrubs like rhododendrons and magnolias, for example, which had reached Europe from China and the Himalayas, were ideal for his purposes. Once established, they required little maintenance and could form sizeable shrubberies or small copses where space allowed. Robinson suggested planting herbaceous plants among and around them. These could eventually be allowed to fend for themselves.

In a period when garden labor was becoming expensive, anything that reduced the need for maintenance appealed to the parsimonious Victorians. However, many of them must have been disappointed in their adoption of Robinson's ideas. As many recent aspirants to wild gardening have discovered, getting plants to establish themselves in the wild is not always easy. Given the right circumstances, plants like lupines, montbretia, day lilies and irises seem to naturalize very readily and are able to overcome competition. But the list of plants that are likely to succeed under such circumstances is quite short, and the soil and position must be exactly right. Nevertheless, Robinson was respected and influential

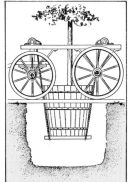

INSTANT GARDENING
No wilderness garden would be complete without its trees, and in the past impatient landowners went to great lengths to have mature trees moved to create "natural" vistas. In Capability Brown's time, trees were carried on wagons to create instant copses. The sapling transporter (above) was a later device used by Victorian gardeners to move small trees. A wooden jacket was fastened around the tree's roots, and then the tree was winched above ground to be slung between the wheels of a small carriage. The Barron Tree Transporter (left) was on a much grander scale, and was capable of lifting mature trees.

PLANTING A VICTORIAN WILD GARDEN

SIBERIAN SQUILLS GROWING ALONGSIDE BLUEBELLS

WILD GARDENING, AS IT WAS KNOWN IN VICTOrian times, was a phenomenon that for a while enjoyed tremendous popularity. The wildness referred not so much to the plants, which included cultivated varieties as well as true wild flowers, but to the way in which they were allowed to grow.

The chief proponent of wild gardening, William Robinson, advocated the use of plants whose inherent vigor allowed them to hold their own when planted in a garden meadow or woodland. His list of suitable plants included species collected from all over the world, and it was undoubtedly on the generous side: many would have failed without the assistance of frequent weeding. However, the idea behind wild gardening is still a valid one, and much pleasure can be gained from experimenting with plants that can be grown very informally and largely left to themselves.

One particularly successful way to do this is to grow bulbs and hardy perennials in rough grass. Victorian wild gardeners grew lupines and peonies in this way. The edge of shrubberies and copses was used for growing taller plants such as umbellifers and meadow rues, which appear year after year and require only a superficial trim in winter to remove their dead stems.

A wild garden not only needs less maintenance than an orthodox border, it also creates an unusual spectacle every year as plants appear apparently without intervention from the gardener, blooming freely before fading away and setting seed.

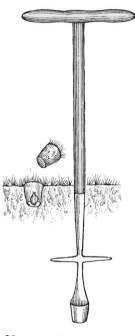

COLUMBINES AND HARDY
GERANIUMS GROWING IN A
GARDEN MEADOW

DOUBLE CRIMSON PEONIES
GROWING IN SCATTERED GROUPS IN GRASS

A WILD GARDEN MEADOW

*This photograph (left) taken at the turn of the last
century, shows a meadow area in the wild garden at
Crowsley Manor in Oxfordshire. It was planted in
accordance with the ideas put forward by William
Robinson, and Robinson himself described this scene as
"the most brilliant effect I have ever seen in any
garden." Large clumps of pale-flowered lupines were
interspersed with perennial poppies, while around
them more delicate flowers bloomed among the grass
stems. A meadow area like this makes an interesting
change from more customary ways of growing flowers.*

PLANTS FOR A WILD GARDEN MEADOW

LUPINE *Lupinus polyphyllus* 'Albus'
*Short-lived pale-flowered lupine that can be propagated
by cuttings taken from near the base of the stem*

ORIENTAL POPPY *Papaver orientale*
*Robust perennial with large orange flowers and finely
divided leaves*

COLUMBINE *Aquilegia × hybrida*
*Vigorous perennial with spurred petals; hybrids are
mixtures of blue, yellow, red and white*

GERANIUM *Geranium pratense*
*Easily grown tall perennial with long flowering
period; different color varieties available*

PEONY *Paeonia officinalis*
*Very long-lived perennial with bowl-shaped flowers.
'Rubra Plena' is a good crimson double variety*

and experiments with his notion of the wild
garden were widespread.

· WOODLAND GARDENING ·

Gertrude Jekyll was the other great figure who
helped foster the Victorian idea of the wild
garden. However, she had little interest in it as a
way of saving labor, for she relished the notion
of endless work in the garden. She even suggested planting certain species for their leaf effect
alone – recommending that as they came into
flower the buds should be clipped off with
scissors daily.

Jekyll's approach to the wild and woodland
garden was to introduce carefully selected herbaceous plants into natural woodland or man-
made shrubberies and then to ensure their
survival by constant attention – weeding, watering and feeding them whenever it was necessary.
This is the technique still used by the best wild
gardeners today.

Patches of natural woodland, of the kind that
become included in new gardens, are usually
dominated by a very limited range of plants. To
become truly Arcadian and interesting, other
trees, shrubs and herbaceous plants have to be
introduced, and these often need considerable
help to survive.

Shade-loving plants such as plantain lilies,
brunnera, Solomon's seal, primulas and violets
are ideal for these conditions, although even they
may benefit from the extra light produced by
lopping branches of established trees and shrubs.
In the broken light at the edge of the woodland
or glades aconites, acanthus, aquilegia, campanulas and pulsatillas will all thrive, given some
attention. In more open situations, foxgloves,
crocosmia and hardy geraniums can be used to
enrich the lower story. Meanwhile, all areas can
be enlivened by bulbs, the less showy forms of
daffodil being particularly effective. The overall
aim is to add color and variety with plants that
look particularly good in a woodland setting –
the sort of plants you might find individually in
the wilderness if you covered a large area looking
for them.

Since the time of Robinson and Jekyll, "wild"
woodland gardening has never completely lost its
popularity among gardeners lucky enough to
have the necessary trees.

· THE VICTORIAN SHRUBBERY ·

While writers like Robinson and the designer J.
C. Loudon were making a case for less ordered,
more natural-looking gardens, the variety of
woody plants available to British gardeners was
vastly increasing. New species appeared that had
their origins in Africa, India, New Zealand, the

NATURAL BULBS
*In a Victorian wild garden,
spring-flowering bulbs were
grown in natural drifts,
rather than in formal
clumps. Bulbs were
positioned by scattering
them on the ground. They
were then planted exactly
where they fell. The
instrument used for this –
the bulb planter – made the
work easier by producing
neat holes of the correct
depth. A bulb would be
positioned in each hole, and
then the plug of earth that
had been extracted would be
crumbled over it.*

FERNERIES AND ROOTERIES

THE NINETEENTH-CENTURY PASSION FOR FERNS prompted many Victorian gardeners to create *ferneries*, or miniature wildernesses specially designed for fern cultivation. If a garden had its own source of running water, a rock fernery would be constructed on a shady bank or beside a waterfall, creating the ideal climate for these attractive moisture-loving plants.

A rock fernery is built by cementing together pieces of stone to form the basic structure. As it is pieced together, deep water-retaining pockets are included which, when filled with loam, will hold the plants. Although ferns thrive on stream banks, running water is not essential for their success. Their chief requirements are moisture and a rich soil. If planted in humus and regularly watered, they will thrive in a shady courtyard or at the foot of wall facing away from the sun.

The *rootery* is a creation from the same period. It depends on a dank and shady atmosphere to convey a feeling of wildness.

LADY FERN

ROYAL FERN

COMMON POLYPODY

HART'S-TONGUE FERN

WATERFALL FERNERY
Lifelike though it appears, this ambitious fernery (above) is entirely the result of the gardener's artifice. The ferns are bathed by the moist air surrounding a waterfall.

A SIMPLE ROOTERY
The white blooms of snowdrops (right) stand out among the shadows in this shallow rootery.

GROWING FERNS
Ferns thrive in a damp soil with a high organic content. Unlike flowering plants, ferns reproduce by spores. A spore gives rise to an intermediate plant and this in turn produces the adult fern. Fern cultivation from spores is a slow process. For the gardener, container-grown plants produce more rapid and reliable results.

SENSITIVE FERN

East and the least explored areas of the United States. The prosperous bourgeoisie vied with each other to be the first to grow them, and as a result, shrubberies became a Victorian garden phenomenon.

The typical Victorian shrubbery tended to be asymmetrical in plan, backed by a high wall, thick hedge, or perhaps standing alone as an island in a lawn. Instead of being straight, its margins would curve gently.

Of all the woody plants brought back from all four corners of the world, undoubtedly the most cherished were the rhododendrons. Mesmerized by their enormous flowers, gardeners planted them wherever their gardens contained pockets of acid, moisture-retaining soil. In, too, went other acid-lovers, such as camellias, acers and azaleas. Since these shrubs were so spectacular, they were given more and more space. Often they excluded a host of other less showy but, to

our eyes at least, more discreet and satisfying species which were also being imported at the time. However, they did provide evergreen foliage in winter.

In shrubberies on soil that would not support rhododendrons, other evergreens, such as spotted laurel, common laurel, Portugal laurel and *Viburnum tinus*, were included to give the shrubberies winter bulk.

Shrubberies today can still lend a wild, informal look to a garden, but they tend to be on a much smaller scale than their predecessors. However, after a further century of plant introductions and hybridization by talented nurserymen, the choice of shrubs available to gardeners is infinitely greater.

· **THE NEW AMERICAN GARDEN** ·

The concept of a man-made wilderness received something of a boost when, in the 1930s, a

THE WILD SHRUBBERY
A shrubbery lends a wild, informal look to a garden. Here hydrangeas form the border to a leafy walk. They thrive in the cool shade of trees and taller shrubs, and produce flowers that persist for a number of months.

MASSED WILD FLOWERS

Wild flowers often have a grace and delicacy that has been lost in plants with a long history of cultivation. Here corncockles, once a weed of cornfields but now a rare plant in the wild, have been sown in a mass alongside a path. They produce a brilliant display in return for relatively little effort.

to produce maximum visual impact. They are chosen because they die beautifully, producing intriguing seed heads and colors, to provide interest late into the autumn. The grasses are underplanted with spring bulbs whose less beautiful dying leaves are masked in late spring by the new grass.

· TODAY'S WILD GARDEN ·

Apart from Oehme and Van Sweden, there are several other successful partisans of the wilderness approach working in the United States today. Designers like Connecticut landscaper A. E. Bye make wild gardens carefully attuned to the mood of their region. In one garden on Cape Cod, Bye created a new peninsula 400 feet (120 m) wide by 800 feet (245 m) deep projecting into the bay. This was covered with thousands of tons of sand, which were bulldozed into mounds and valleys. Bayberry, black pine, juniper and yew now grow in sinuous masses around the domes of artificial dunes.

In particular environments like the Arizona desert, cacti and other drought-tolerant plants can be propagated and then assembled to form denser, more attractive arrangements around buildings. This creates a garden totally in harmony with the surrounding wilderness.

The notion of embellishing the wild by appropriate introductions, and lightly modifying it by clipping trees and mowing tracks through the meadows, has always had a great appeal for Gilles Clement, one of France's most outstanding contemporary landscape practitioners. His approach to designs of this type is a good compromise between that of William Robinson and Gertrude Jekyll. He is pre-eminent in the selection, placing and management of bold clumps of highly architectural plants such as rheums in natural, well-wooded sites. He also enriches natural areas with shrubs selected for foliage and flowers that will harmonize with and augment the natural flora.

· GARDENING FOR WILDLIFE ·

The concept of creating a wilderness within a garden is of continuing importance, because from it the humble wildlife garden of the late twentieth century has developed. Over the past decade, many gardeners have set aside a portion of their plots as miniature wildernesses. The aim of this kind of gardening is to create havens for the smaller forms of wildlife – insects, birds, small mammals and reptiles – which are losing habitats in overdeveloped landscapes.

In smaller urban gardens, the most popular type of wildlife garden is the wild flower meadow. This can be created in two ways. In the

German nurseryman, Karl Foerster, proposed the use of ornamental grasses in what he called "wild garden design."

In the 1950s, Wolfgang Oehme saw such a wild garden which had survived in a Hamburg park. When he emigrated to America, he took the idea with him. He and his partner James Van Sweden have subsequently built the reputation of their Washington-based architectural practice on what has become known as the New American Garden.

The speciality of this team is to provide gardens needing very low maintenance, composed of a series of highly ornamental grasses mixed with carefully chosen perennials which require little attention. Rudbeckias, sedums, astilbes and coreopsis are used in very large drifts first, land is dug and cultivated and specific seed mixtures, including the seeds of grasses and a broad spectrum of wild flowers, are sown on to the bare earth in the same way as a normal lawn is sown.

The second method, which is generally more successful, is the "checkerboard" technique. An outlying portion of lawn is allowed to go unmown. At intervals, 2-foot (60-cm) square patches of the turf are removed and, after the soil has been lightly cultivated, wild flower seed mixtures are sown on to it.

The checkerboard technique has been used quite successfully in the Cambridge Botanic Garden – flowers that were established in the small plots soon spread their seeds over the surrounding area to produce a homogeneous-looking flower meadow.

· MANAGING A WILD FLOWER MEADOW ·

As many gardeners have found to their cost, managing an artificial wild flower meadow is not easy. Nature has selected the plants which thrive in truly wild meadows and that can cope with regular grazing. The gardener can only find that plants cope with garden meadow conditions by trial and error. One of the major problems when working with an existing lawn is that lawn grass has been bred for vigor. If the soil is too fertile, the grass may swamp introduced wild flowers and prevent their growth.

In theory, a wild flower meadow should be topped in late spring, after the early flowers have set seed and before the later flowers have put up their flower stalks. In autumn, the whole area should then be well mown and the hay removed. This tidies it up and gives the spring flowers a good chance to receive as much light as possible early in the season. It also keeps the soil poor in nutrients, which helps to subdue species that tend to dominate.

Timing these operations is crucial, and can sometimes be difficult. Of the 30 species present in a seed mixture which I sowed on a 1-acre (0.4-ha) site, fewer than half were in evidence five years later. This is despite the fact that each species was included in the sowing mixture because it was believed that it would enjoy the particular combination of soil and climate encountered in that garden. Those species which have survived seem to host a fine range of butterflies whose caterpillars readily devastate other plants in the garden!

Such are the ecological dilemmas facing the modern wilderness maker. Earlier gardeners, in their longing for a free, more natural way of life, were happily spared such difficulties.

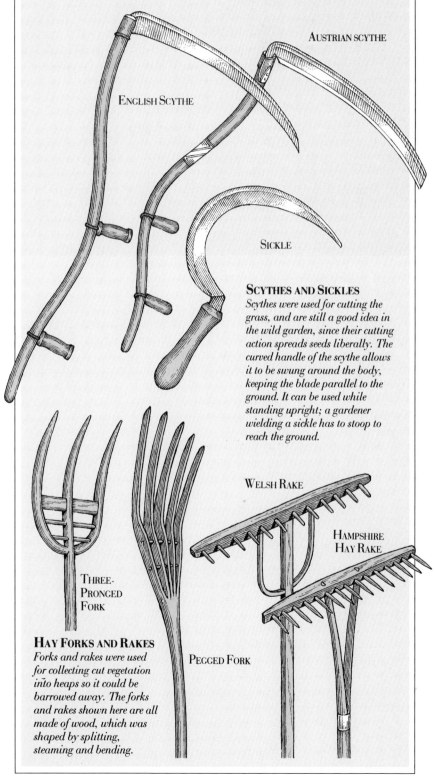

MOWING A MEADOW

Rough grass of the kind found in wilderness and wild gardens cannot be left to itself year after year. Without grazing animals, grass often reverts to scrub and then to woodland. Cutting it not only removes the season's hay crop, but also kills any saplings that may have sprung up. Today, mowers make quick work of rough grass. In earlier times, it was kept in trim with the same tools that were used for maintaining lawns.

AUSTRIAN SCYTHE

ENGLISH SCYTHE

SICKLE

SCYTHES AND SICKLES
Scythes were used for cutting the grass, and are still a good idea in the wild garden, since their cutting action spreads seeds liberally. The curved handle of the scythe allows it to be swung around the body, keeping the blade parallel to the ground. It can be used while standing upright; a gardener wielding a sickle has to stoop to reach the ground.

WELSH RAKE

HAMPSHIRE HAY RAKE

THREE-PRONGED FORK

PEGGED FORK

HAY FORKS AND RAKES
Forks and rakes were used for collecting cut vegetation into heaps so it could be barrowed away. The forks and rakes shown here are all made of wood, which was shaped by splitting, steaming and bending.

THE
WATER GARDEN

From irrigation to decoration — The stew pond —
Raised ponds and basins — Aquatic follies and fantasies
— Romantic water gardens — The Victorian water garden
— Informal water in the modern garden

THE AIR IS ALWAYS HOTTEST A COUPLE OF HOURS AFTER NOON ON STILL days in high summer. That is when, in places like Granada in southern Spain, the sun remains menacingly high in the sky and the rock, after hours of irradiation, generates air-shimmering thermals that distort the horizon with mirages. The white glare seems to drain the whole landscape of its color and reduce it to a numbed silence. It is too hot for busy lizards to scurry about. They retreat into cracks in the wall to doze, and even the crickets stop their fidgeting in the parched grass.

At times like this the genius of the Arabs who built what is arguably the finest water garden on Earth becomes apparent. For despite the torrid conditions elsewhere, the lofty arcades and shady courtyards of the Alhambra Palace in Granada remain a haven of cool. They epitomize what is, to a desert people, a notion of paradise.

It is perhaps because Western civilization owes its origins to the achievements of people from sunbaked lands that water has been in gardens since gardening itself began. Water certainly appeals to something fundamental in us. It can soothe or excite, bore or amuse, charm or repel,

THE MIRRORED GARDEN
The reflective quality of still water increases the impact of plants in and around it, and creates a new visual dimension within a garden.

terrify or enchant. Unlike the static earth beneath us, it is a dynamic medium, but one which can be controlled. By damming rushing streams, it can be made to form placid lakes. By using rocks to impede its flow in streams, it can be made to chuckle and gurgle. By allowing it to rush in volume over falls, it can be made to thunder.

The different ways in which water can be impounded, channeled or guided can be used by the gardener to develop the mood of a particular area.

Moving water brings animation. Confined in a pool, it introduces color and reflects features and plants to double their impact. Tumbling over cascades or pushed through fountains, it serves as a decorative eye-catcher, while in the cool depths of a grotto, it positively chills the atmosphere. In long narrow canals, water beckons for attention and lures the eye along its margins to give the illusion that vistas are more extensive than is actually the case.

· FROM IRRIGATION TO DECORATION ·

Tomb paintings from Thebes in Egypt dating back to 1400 BC show gardens with rectangular ponds, with what appear to be marshy areas around their margins. Egyptian water garden planners used both plants and animals to add a satisfying variety to the scene. Lilies and lotuses are shown in the water, with plants resembling papyrus growing in the boggy margins.

These early gardens had very practical origins. Civilization in the Middle East would hardly have been possible without irrigation. The notion of plants without water would have been inconceivable, and it would not have taken much imagination for a workaday irrigation channel or ditch to become converted into a more decorative feature such as a basin or formal canal. Once the idea of decorative water had become widespread, no new garden would have been complete without it.

There is little doubt that Roman gardens contained formal water features based on Middle Eastern models, seen first in Greece and then, as the empire spread, at first hand. Relics of these can still be seen in the atria of houses at Pompeii, where water was often made to splash into rectangular basins, producing a soothing sound and refreshing the air with its vapor.

The more modest Roman water features — their fountainheads and basins — are fairly easy to replicate in a modern garden. However, some Roman water gardens were highly sophisticated, and would be costly and difficult to imitate today. Among the most exciting must have been that made by Pliny the Younger in the Apennines. In 62 BC, his nephew described it in a letter as having at its upper end "a semicircular bench of white marble, shaded with a vine, which is trained on four small pillars of white Carystian marble. Water, gushing through several little pipes from under this bench, as if it were pressed out by the weight of the persons who repose themselves upon it, falls into a stone cistern underneath, from whence it is received into a fine polished marble basin, so artfully contrived that it is always full without overflowing." The water was not designed simply to be looked at. At mealtimes, plates of food were even floated on it like "little ships and waterfowl."

As always, the Romans were masters of indulgence. So too were the Persian shahs many centuries later, who built enclosed water gardens for relief from the summer heat. Their formal tiled pools and fountains were arranged on geometrical lines, as were the cypress trees and roses that scented the air.

Most Persian water features were fed by *qanats*, which are underground tunnels dug to conduct water from deep in the water table at the foot of mountains. They would be considered extraordinary feats of engineering even today. Many of the tunnels were several miles long, and they would run at up to 300 feet (90 m) below ground. They were dug by sinking vertical breather and spoil excavation shafts at 150-foot (45-metre) intervals and then linking the bottoms of the shafts by tunneling between them.

· KEEPING WATER IN ITS PLACE ·

Whenever possible, the makers of early water gardens dug their lakes, ponds and basins down below the water table to avoid water loss from leaks. But in warmer parts of the world, the water table can drop spectacularly during the drier months. In these conditions, the designers of water gardens had somehow to keep the water up to the required level.

One obvious way of overcoming the problem of leakage or a falling water table was to ensure a constant supply of water to keep a basin or pool topped up. But such wasteful means were not often resorted to. It can only be assumed that the cement that they used to render their masonry was so waterproof that losses were minimal.

Certainly, the evidence to be seen on the Greek island of Delos points to this conclusion. Here, rendered cisterns designed to catch rainwater have been revealed among the ruins of houses. They still retain water two thousand years after they were built, providing homes for innumerable frogs, which produce a deafening croaking at sundown.

Today, waterproofing basins and ponds does not present many problems. Heavy-duty

BASINS AND FOUNTAINS

IF YOU HAVE NATURAL RUNNING WATER, CONDUCTING IT INTO a tank or cistern provides a decorative dipping tank that can be used for a variety of practical purposes from plunging potted plants to filling watering cans. It is from such workaday spouts and tanks that the tremendous diversity of traditional decorative fountains developed. At one time, the pressure required by fountains would have been that of a natural head of water. Today, electric power provides an alternative that is suitable for all gardens. In a high-pressure fountain, the escaping water fragments, creating droplets that sparkle as they fall through the air. If less pressure is applied, the water column remains intact. This creates a gurgling flow endlessly changing in form that can be viewed from close quarters. Although fountains powered by electric pumps simply recirculate water, they do need topping up to compensate for the losses caused by evaporation. This can be allowed for by incorporating a hidden sump.

LEAD CISTERN

GROTESQUE HEAD

TORTOISE

LION ON PEDESTAL

LION WITH BASIN

DOLPHIN CONSOLE

BOY WITH DOLPHIN

FIGURED FOUNTAIN

REGENCY FOUNTAIN

MOORISH FOUNTAIN

SHELL ON PEDESTAL

A SPECTRUM OF SCALE
*Water makes an effective
garden feature on any scale.
Where space permits, an
extensive pool (above) can
be used as a place to grow a
tangle of luxuriant water
plants. By contrast, this
small pool (right) is just
large enough to support a
single waterlily, seen here
emerging in spring. With its
formal stone surround, this
pool is the work of the
Scottish garden designer
and sculptor Ian Hamilton-
Finlay.*

A CANAL GARDEN
*The imposing ornamental
canals at Buscot Park in
Oxfordshire (opposite) form
a stepped corridor leading
away from the eighteenth-
century house. This is water
gardening at its most
formal, with perspective
being the paramount feature
of the design.*

great decline. In abbeys and monasteries, modest decorative water features like fountains were probably found in cloisters and the "paradises" provided for contemplation, but there was nothing approaching the elaborate water features of earlier times.

One practical use of water that was widespread was the *stew pond*, a body of water used to keep bream, roach, carp, trout and other fine-tasting fish, which were fed on kitchen waste. This early form of fish-farming probably went on in most monasteries. Since the monks were good masons, many of their ponds would have had well-cut coping stone surrounds, if not more ambitious decoration.

Ponds of this type have been restored at the twelfth-century monastery at St. Guilhem le Desert near Montpellier in southern France. They show how attractive a pond surrounded by simple masonry can be. Fed constantly from a spring tapped high up in the valley above the cloister, the water is always well enough aerated to allow giant trout to prosper. Their appetites are so voracious that their feed vanishes within the space of a few minutes to leave the water in the ponds crystal clear.

· RAISED PONDS AND BASINS ·

Some of the most pleasing and successful water features that have been built through the ages are those in which the water's surface is brought closer to the observer's eye by confining it to basins standing proud of the ground. It is a form that has been recurrently adopted since the twelfth century, and many fine examples still survive in traditional gardens. Their size, shape and style vary from simple circular basins, through hexagons to long raised canals. But they all embody a certain element of surprise because the discovery of water above ground level is unusual, and commands attention.

At its most successful, this surprise is sprung at the last moment, as at Hidcote in Gloucestershire. Here a large circular basin is set within an outdoor room surrounded by thick, tall hedges. Visitors only become aware of it as they walk through the entrance archway.

In raising the water level, garden designers discovered that it became exposed to more intense light, and had more than its usual glitter. Plants floating upon it, such as waterlilies, or fish moving just beneath the surface, could be more easily seen and enjoyed. Perhaps the most striking of their experiments with raised water were canals. These have the advantage that both their retaining walls and the water beckon for attention, drawing the eye along their surface to distant vistas.

polyethylene or butyl rubber sheeting can be satisfactorily welded to make strong linings of almost any size. Alternative materials such as resin-impregnated fiberglass sheet, or sealing powders, which are mixed with an earth lining, also make simple and effective waterproof barriers. Concrete can be used, but it has a tendency to crack, and forming it in the required shape can be difficult for the amateur.

Early gardeners, of course, had none of these materials, and this makes their spectacular achievements in the art of water gardening all the more impressive.

· THE STEW POND ·

Throughout the Dark Ages, which followed the eclipse of the Roman Empire in the West, water gardening, in common with other forms of ornamental gardening, seems to have suffered a

DESIGNING A FORMAL POOL

F ORMAL POOLS HAVE A DISTINCT SYMMETRY, AND ARE designed to exploit water for its architectural impact and for its ability to reflect light. Although often built to great sizes in the past, they are equally effective on a small scale. By using modern materials such as concrete, a traditional formal pool can become a distinctive feature in today's garden.

In general, formal pools are of two types – those in which the water level is below the ground, and those in which it is impounded by raised walls. Making a pool of the first type is fairly simple. After the hole has been excavated, it is fitted either with a rigid liner or lined with plastic sheeting laid over sand. Raised pools are harder to construct because the walls must not only be watertight, they must also be pressure-proof. Rendered concrete blocks make satisfactory walls if a plastic liner is also used. For safety, it is advisable to keep the water level no higher than 2 feet (60 cm) above ground. If the pool is extended below ground, this will help to prevent the water freezing solid in areas that experience cold winters.

FRAMED BY COLUMNS
This formal pool (above) in an English garden was designed by the landscape architect Harold Peto. It successfully features classical ornament both in and around the water.

RENAISSANCE-STYLE LILY POND
This raised pond shows how the use of decorative detail, such as stone finials and a fountain within a curved bay, can transform a simple rectangle of water into something much more alluring.

TRAILING PLANTS

ORNAMENTAL STONE
Care needs to be taken to ensure that the decoration is used sparingly. Ornaments such as finials should match the pond's walls, so that they do not look like an afterthought.

BALL FINIALS

SOLID STONE OR SLABS ON CONCRETE BASE

CIRCULAR RAISED POOL WITH FOUNTAIN

ROUND-ENDED RAISED POOL

OCTAGONAL RAISED POOL IN BRICK

RECTANGULAR POOL WITH SUNDIAL

PERIOD STYLES
Simple round and rectangular pools have been used since Roman times. The octagonal pool was often favored in Moorish water gardens, while pools that combine a rectangular overall outline with one or more curved bays have been popular since the Renaissance. Pools like this need a drainage channel to prevent the water overflowing down their sides after heavy rain. The closer this maximum level is to the top of the surround, the more reflective the water's surface will be.

· MAKING RAISED BASINS ·

In the past, raised water features were usually built in stone or brick, with a stone coping of varying degrees of sophistication. They were thickly lined with render, which in cold regions frequently needed renewing after being damaged by heavy frost.

Nowadays, heavy-duty ultraviolet-resistant plastic or butyl rubber liners can be used to overcome that problem. Steel panels that bolt together, and which are used to make small reservoirs or lagoons on livestock farms, can be used to make circular retaining walls for water features. These form the structure that holds the water in. Their unattractive looks can be hidden by cladding them with a masonry wall in old brick or stone that is non-structural, and therefore easily laid. Earth can be used to fill the gaps between the two layers of the wall.

If stone coping is put in place so that it overhangs the water's surface, it then masks the materials used in waterproofing, and the result is a particularly attractive water garden, especially if it is planted with vigorous waterlilies that create rafts of leaves. If gaps are left in the cladding wall and coping, plants can be inserted to festoon the wall and tumble over the coping.

A basin of this type obviously occupies a lot of garden space. But gardeners short of room need not be deprived of the pleasure that raised water can bring. All that is needed is a watertight container of the right shape. A heavy-duty dustbin or even an extra-large plastic bowl, half sunk into the ground, can be disguised by cladding them with masonry walls. Although these basins will be too small for really vigorous water plants, they will comfortably accommodate those varieties of waterlily that thrive in shallow water.

Less demanding aquatic plants will survive in porcelain or earthenware domestic sinks. There is no reason why you should not have a miniature water feature even on a balcony. However, the smaller a container is, the more widely the water's temperature will fluctuate. In zones subjected to heavy frost, small basins should be taken indoors for the winter, while in hot weather, they need to be kept topped up.

· SPLENDORS OF THE ALHAMBRA ·

The efforts of the monks in the Dark Ages may have done little to progress water gardening, but towards the end of that period came the heyday of Moorish garden planners in southern Spain. Their achievements are some of the highest expressions of the art. Despite their often grand scale, their inward-looking and formal designs

THE LILY GARDEN
Waterlilies are the roses of the water garden. Traditionally, they are often grown to the exclusion of all other plants. Some wild species, such as the water fringe and yellow waterlily, grow well in garden ponds, but pride of place goes to the many cultivated varieties of Nymphaea species. The largest of these can be planted in 4 feet (1.2 m) of water, and will reach a spread of up to 5 feet (1.5 m). Dwarf waterlilies can be planted in as little as 6 inches (15 cm) of water, making them suitable for the shallowest of ponds.

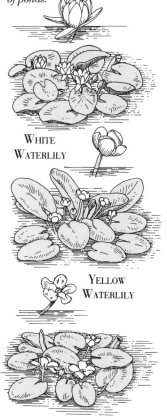

WHITE WATERLILY

YELLOW WATERLILY

WATER FRINGE

suit them well to small gardens today. The Spanish Moors were ruled by the Muslim Umayyad dynasty, which was founded by North African Berbers. By the early tenth century, the Umayyads had severed their links with the Middle East and begun to develop Spanish towns such as Granada into regional administrative and cultural centers. There the caliphs built the palace-fortress of the Alhambra, which remains one of the world's marvels.

The designers of the Alhambra used techniques learned in their homelands to tap the ice-cold water from springs high up in Spain's Sierra Nevada mountains and conduct it through endless channels, basins, fountains and courtyards in the palace far below. Perhaps the greatest achievement of their hydraulic engineers was the economy with which they used their hard-won water. They were clever enough to be able to confine it in channels in marble paving which are only a fingernail's depth and often less than 1 foot (30 cm) across, and which provide a continuous sparkling ribbon of water when fed with only a trickle.

These channels frequently run from the margins of shady courtyards to their centers, meeting in wider central basins that are only fractionally deeper, before running away to feed other features at lower levels. Filled with the sight and sound of water, these courtyards have offered a refuge from the furnace-like Andalusian sun for a thousand years.

Modern materials make it easy for gardeners to make "rills" — narrow and fairly shallow water channels similar to those used to such great effect by the Muslim masters of the Alhambra. Pre-cast concrete culvert sections, of the kind used in making roads, and rigid plastic canal-liners are both suitable for forming the basis of these features. Although of the right scale for the smaller garden, they seem to transform it into something larger. Since many aquatic plants such as yellow flag and flowering rush need only constant moisture rather than total immersion, they will thrive in this situation as long as severe frost is not a problem.

· AQUATIC FOLLIES AND FANTASIES ·

Northern Europe had to wait until the great seventeenth-century houses were being built before water gardening approached the heights it had reached hundreds of years before at the Alhambra. By that time, different sources of inspiration had been tapped as travelers brought back descriptions of the wonderful water gardens they had seen in Moghul India. The water features at places like the Shalamar near Srinagar and the Taj Mahal were on a gigantic

scale, with lines of sparkling fountains, broad canals with weirs and cascades, and octagonal basins. These were all set with finely patterned tiles or stonework that, although reminiscent of their Persian antecedents, had a more ponderous style that was quite their own.

With the accession of Louis XIV, Europe had a monarch who was able to work on a comparable scale. At Versailles, his gardener André Le Nôtre used water in myriad ways, thanks to the help of an enormous team of talented sculptors and hydraulic engineers. On the higher terraces, the water is confined in shallow basins as a reflective ingredient in intricate parterres. Elsewhere, it flows through a plethora of fountains and tumbles over statuary figuring everything from gorgons to gods, mythological beasts to buxom matrons. There are dams, falls, pools and stepped cascades, with the most spectacular achievement of all being a broad and lengthy canal on which mock naval battles could be fought to amuse the courtiers on festive days.

ADDING ORNAMENT
A solitary figure (above) gives a classical touch to a pool surrounded by autumnal foliage. Statues are particularly effective where opaque water or deep shade conceals the means of support.

PLANTING A POOL
The banks of an informal pool (opposite) make a perfect stage for displaying plants, especially where, as in this case, the water lies a little below ground level. Here purple loosestrife, day lilies and astilbes thrive in the damp ground, while bogbean and waterlilies clothe the water's surface.

GARDEN GROTTOS

ALTHOUGH IN CLASSICAL TIMES GROTTOS WERE OFTEN USED AS A respite from heat and the glare of the sun, their role in gardens has since become a symbolic one. Their function is to convey an atmosphere of mystery, and this can be created by anything from a majestic, gloomy cavern to an overgrown recess set into a wall. Traditionally, grottos were built of rock, including tufa, a compressed volcanic ash, and also stone that had been *rusticated*, or chiselled to give it an eroded or pock-marked appearance. Today, concrete can be used if it is disguised with a surfacing of stone that is then covered by climbing plants. Shells cemented to the inside walls create a glittering spectacle when the dank interior is illuminated by candlelight.

ENTRANCE TO THE UNDERWORLD
The sepulchral air of a grotto set in a bank (right) is emphasized by the ornate masonry surrounding the entrance to its dark interior.

WALL GROTTO
A wall grotto (below) makes an ideal source for flowing water in a garden. Here, a fountain issues into a scalloped basin, and from there into a pool before flowing out into the garden.

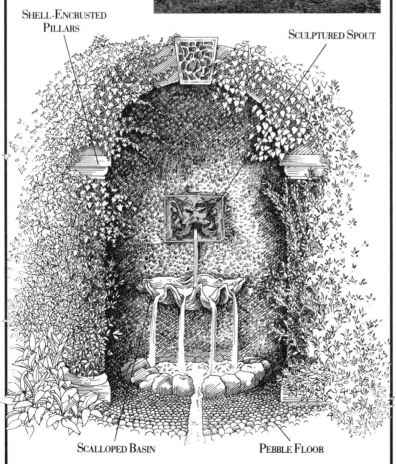

SHELL-ENCRUSTED PILLARS

SCULPTURED SPOUT

SCALLOPED BASIN

PEBBLE FLOOR

· ROMANTIC WATER GARDENS ·

Today's natural-looking "wild" water gardens have their roots in the eighteenth-century romantic movement, which had little time for any garden feature that smacked of geometry or artifice. In the romantic approach to gardening, water was introduced with less apparent intervention by man.

Whenever possible, gardeners of the romantic period would use existing streams and rivers in the design without modification, and the informal layout of their garden paths enabled the water to be glimpsed from many different angles. Sometimes natural springs would be used to make narrow winding rills through woodland, punctuated occasionally by wider deep plunges, in whose icy waters the bold could immerse themselves on hot days. It seems unlikely that visitors did so very often – the plunges appealed more to the imagination than the spirit.

Garden designers of the romantic period made much use of grottos. Under their guidance, they became major works with considerable lakes set beneath cavernous mounds of rock. Their interiors were often divided into several chambers, each heavily encrusted with glittering shells set in stucco, which were often arranged in ambitious patterns. Although they could be entered by paths, the usual mode of entry was by boat. Once inside, refreshments could be taken on special platform areas in candle- or lamplight, eerily reflected from the surface of the water, the mother-of-pearl in the shells, or the features of water gods and their attendant sprites. These grottos were deliberately damp and cool places designed for use in hot weather. They derived their inspiration from the much more formal Italian *nymphaea*, which on the outside were built like large, windowless single-story classical buildings. Inside, they contained basins and fountains, and were romantically lit during the day by shafts of light from small oculi in the roof above. Sometimes, as at Hadrian's Villa near Tivoli, one wall of the nymphaeum would be missing, offering people dining in its cool recess a view of the garden.

· WATER IN THE LANDSCAPE ·

In England, all these watery conceits were swept away whenever "Capability" Brown was called upon to renew a garden design. He, too, considered water an essential element in any parkland vista, and he was prepared to convince his clients that it was worth shifting millions of tons of rock and earth to introduce it. But he did not want artificial basins or canals. What he prescribed, and frequently got, were vast reaches of water in the form of lakes, which he made by damming streams or by excavating enormous holes in the ground. He would often use the spoil from these excavations to make the gradients of steep slopes more gentle, or even to create slopes where none existed before.

In cases where the water table could not be easily reached, and it was doubtful whether the subsoil would retain water, the excavations to make lakes would be lined with hundreds of tons of puddled impervious clay. Marl – a chalky clay that had been oven-dried and crushed into powder – was preferred for this work. Scattered as a thin layer over the soil to be lined, it was wetted and then hammered with large wooden mallets until it formed a congealed, impervious and uniform lining.

Like the designers of smaller romantic gardens, Capability Brown arranged that his lakes could be glimpsed not only from the house but also from several other angles, particularly along the long, winding approach drives that he favored. However, he ensured that it was never possible to judge the full extent of the water by making the far reaches of a lake swing out of sight behind a slope, or by hiding its end beyond some masonry feature such as a bridge.

· THE VICTORIAN WATER GARDEN ·

Over the last hundred years, fashion in water gardening has wavered between two quite different traditions – the formal and geometrical use of water, as epitomized by the works of the Moors and at Versailles, and the "natural" use of water, long favored in the Far East but initiated by the romantic movement in the West.

Formal water garden features look good in compact modern gardens, especially where they can be seen against the backdrop of walls or fences. The Victorians were the first to experiment with formal water gardening on a reduced scale, and fountains and basins began to appear in town gardens with the revival of interest in formal designs.

Many of the best Victorian fountains were made in cast iron. As suburban villa gardening grew in importance, manufacturers modified their techniques to produce smaller versions of the fountains and basins which they had first made for large gardens and public parks. Many of these designs were over-fussy, but the best are still copied today.

· INFORMAL WATER IN THE MODERN GARDEN ·

Modern materials make informal water gardening a possibility in all sizes of garden, even courtyard gardens in towns. Pre-formed liners

and miniature falls and cascades enable the gardener to create small ponds in an afternoon. Small basins with built-in jets, made out of resin-bonded fiberglass, terracotta or even porcelain, can easily be set into walls. Only a modest understanding of electricity and plumbing is needed to assemble quite ambitious features, in which water, powered by a submersible pump, tumbles in cascades.

It is surprising how little water is needed to create an effective garden feature. This is demonstrated by the traditional Japanese *ping* fountain, in which single drops of water provide the focus of attention. As water emerges from a spout, it is allowed to fall into a pool in the slightly hollow top surface of a stone projecting from a wall. It eventually overflows from this hollow and moves down a tiny groove to spill over the edge of the stone, to drip into a similar stone emerging from the wall below.

The *ping* fountain is a charming and easily constructed feature which will fit into the smallest garden. The sequence of drips as water moves down several of these stones set as steps makes a noise which will either soothe or infuriate, depending on the temperament of the listener.

In Japanese tradition, dripping water prompts tranquillity and reflection. To a participant in a caravan from Isfahan to Damascus, where so much Western water gardening originated, they would sound like intimations of paradise.

THE PLANTED POOL
Water plants can be used to introduce a great variety of flower forms and foliage into a relatively small area of garden. Here, the informal planting contrasts with the structured appearance of the pond margin, which is bounded by timber.

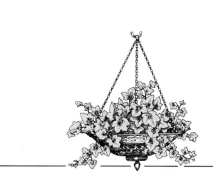

CONSERVATORIES & GREENHOUSES

*The orangery — The conservatory from within —
Traditional conservatory plants — The modern period
conservatory — Window gardens and Wardian cases —
Gardening under glass — The traditional greenhouse*

I N 1816 THE DESIGNER J C LOUDON MADE AN ENGINEERING BREAK-through that was to change the face of Victorian gardening. His invention was the thin iron glazing bar, a lightweight structure for supporting glass. Simple though it was, it heralded a golden era in conservatory building. Loudon's glazing bar allowed a maximum of light penetration and could easily be bent and assembled into huge and often beautiful structures, varying in size from modest annexes for suburban houses to huge buildings resembling crystal cathedrals.

Today's conservatories and greenhouses owe much of their design to the Victorian ironmasters who took up Loudon's invention. But the art of growing plants indoors is by no means Victorian in origin. In fact, in tending greenhouse-grown tomatoes, today's gardeners echo a tradition whose roots go back much further than the nineteenth century, to a time when Renaissance gardeners were determined to stamp their authority on nature. They also commemorate the discovery by northern Europeans of a

GARDEN UNDER GLASS
*The equable climate of a cool greenhouse provides ideal conditions for Victorian favorites
such as fuchsias, ferns, hydrangeas and azaleas.*

THE PRESTIGIOUS PINEAPPLE
Until the end of the last century pineapples, or pines as they were also known, were a favorite hothouse fruit of wealthy English landowners. Their gardeners would plant "winter pines" and "summer pines", guaranteeing a succession of fruit throughout the year. Such was the prestige attached to growing pineapples that they were often depicted in stone ornaments (see p.89).

CHARLOTTE ROTHSCHILD

LAMBTON CASTLE SEEDLING

host of hitherto unknown plants that were to change the range of foods in their diet.

· FOOD FROM AFAR ·

Until the end of the sixteenth century, most European gardens yielded few crops that could be eaten during the winter. Even in the households of the rich, the diet during the winter months was appallingly low in fresh produce. Onions, some root crops and a few overwintering cabbages were the only fresh vegetables available in quantity. Potatoes were as yet unknown. A few apples and pears, many of which were rotting by Christmas, were the only fresh fruit, and these had to be eaten alongside flesh that was nearly always dried, salted or smoked.

Although they did not know it, the people's short stature, life expectancy and poor health were due as much to the poor quality of their diet as to their open drains and lack of sanitation.

INSIDE A PINERY
Pineries, or glasshouses wholly devoted to pineapples, had to be kept at high temperatures if the plants were to fruit successfully. They were heated from below either by the hot-bed principle (see p.60) or by hot-water pipes buried in the soil. The plants were propagated from cuttings, and were usually grown in pots plunged into deep beds. These were sometimes arranged so that they sloped steeply to catch the maximum amount of sunlight.

SMOOTH-LEAVED CAYENNE

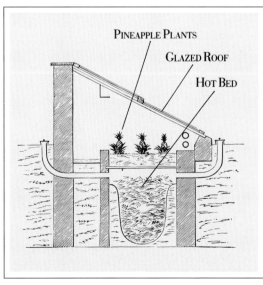

PINEAPPLE PLANTS

GLAZED ROOF

HOT BED

When reliable ocean-going vessels were built in the sixteenth century, great navigators made landfalls in remote places that often had a warmer climate, which nurtured strange and frequently delectable crops. Having feasted on this bounty, it was natural that the ships' crews would want to repeat the experience after their return home to more familiar fare.

Some of these crops, when harvested a little early, could be shipped long distances without their quality being lost, because nature had packaged them well. Pineapples from the Caribbean, pumpkins, squashes and marrows from the Americas, melons, peaches, apricots and citrus fruits, originally from India and the Far East, could be brought from the Mediterranean to where they had spread overland.

There must have been many attempts to grow these new crops outdoors, but most of them would have failed because winters were, on average, much colder than they are today. By persisting and protecting crops from the cold, gardeners did succeed in coaxing some through the winter months.

In England, Henry VIII's gardener, Lovell, successfully grew fruit such as figs, peaches and apricots against the warm, south-facing brick walls at royal palaces. Not much later, Sir Francis Carew was growing orange trees outdoors in Surrey. But the cold climate of southern Britain meant that extraordinary measures were needed to keep these delicate trees alive. In winter, wooden huts were erected around the trees, and these were heated with stoves whenever frost threatened.

· THE ORANGERY ·

By the late seventeenth century, temporary structures to protect tender fruit trees growing in gardens began to disappear in favor of permanent glazed buildings constructed to house plants. One of the first of these was built at Kensington Palace. Structures of this kind became known as orangeries, because this was the crop that they most frequently protected.

The trees in an orangery were grown in tubs, which were laboriously moved out into the garden in spring and brought back inside again each autumn. This spell outdoors in summer must have been quite useful because, compared with today's conservatories and greenhouses, the light level indoors was very low. The glass available at the time, although very expensive, was frequently imperfect and varied greatly in its ability to allow light to pass unhindered. But, more important than this, early orangeries were designed with as much attention to form as to function. They were built as adjuncts to great houses, and this meant that they had to be beautiful as well as useful. Although they had large windows facing the sun, they were heavily pedimented and pilastered. Their roofs were solid and this, together with their attractive but bulky masonry, meant that the facade through which light could penetrate was greatly reduced.

· HEAT *VERSUS* LIGHT ·

Eighteenth-century gardeners can hardly be blamed for thinking that, as a stimulant to growth, heat was far more important to indoor plants than light. Cold could be fatal to tender plants; heat was the obvious antidote.

Initially, heat was provided with coal-burning stoves and flues. Fuel was used in huge quantities, and over a period, vast amounts of ash from the orangery furnaces were used to make paths or sunken ash beds, in which hardy potted plants were stationed during the winter.

It was not until the nineteenth century that the value of light was fully understood. Glass roofs, designed to improve illumination, seem to have been pioneered by the great Regency architect John Nash when he designed a conservatory at Barnsley Park where he worked between 1805 and 1810. Early glass roofs could be weighty structures. But when Loudon's glazing bars were widely manufactured, they became much lighter and more graceful, and the art of building with glass could gain its full expression.

· BUILDING WITH GLASS ·

In the 1840s, advancing technology, together with the development of cheaper and more uniform glass, led to the development of a whole range of buildings, from domestic conservatories to structures whose cast-iron beams bridged immense spans. From relatively humble beginnings, they became large enough to make permanent homes for mature trees such as palms, and they housed exotic plants from all over the world. They formed important centers for botanical education (a great Victorian enthusiasm) or, as at the Royal Botanic Gardens at Kew, staging posts for the transfer of tropical crops from one region to another.

Great glass palaces were often funded by philanthropic industrialists anxious to educate their workforce. As well as containing plants whose labels stressed their peculiarity, origins and economic importance, they also housed paved areas, seats and stages that could be used as the venue for edifying concerts and lectures. A fine example of such a "People's Palace" has been lovingly restored in Glasgow, and the Du Pont family built a beauty in Delaware that still attracts thousands of visitors each year.

Domestic conservatories also underwent a metamorphosis. By the end of the 1850s, the conservatory had become an almost mandatory feature in new houses of any size. Apart from its original function as a place to grow and display some of the more spectacular tropical and subtropical plants, it also acquired an important social role.

· THE CONSERVATORY FROM WITHIN ·

In the bright atmosphere of a conservatory, the formal protocols that governed activities and behavior in the normally cluttered and stuffy Victorian interiors could be relaxed a little. It was not long before most conservatories in towns were also equipped with gas lighting, which allowed them to be used in the evenings as well. It was a room for escape. While smoking was not usually acceptable in the *salon*, gentlemen could enjoy their pipes and cigars among the plants.

The design of furniture used in Victorian conservatories was also in harmony with the more relaxed atmosphere. Woven willow was, as it is today, much in demand for the production of

BOXES AND BARROWS
The traditional method of growing oranges in a cool climate calls for them to be kept indoors in winter, and to be moved outside for the summer months. The elegant boxes used for growing oranges sometimes featured handles or wheels to ease the task of moving the trees. McIntosh's Patent Box had a hinged side to allow the tree to be removed for root-pruning.

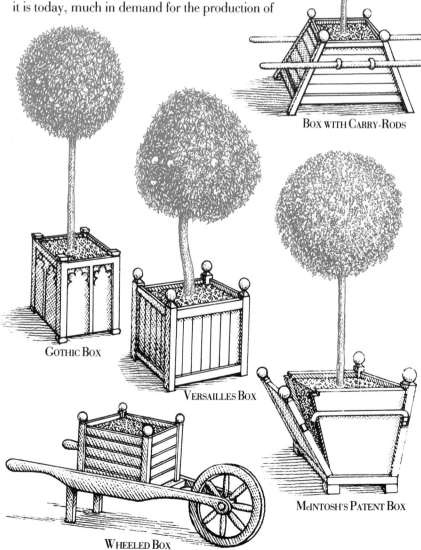

BOX WITH CARRY-RODS

GOTHIC BOX

VERSAILLES BOX

WHEELED BOX

McINTOSH'S PATENT BOX

loungers and armchairs that were both durable and comfortably yielding. They were often arranged in tandem with footstools; indeed, their catalogue specifications referred to their "total stretch", showing that they were truly intended for leisure. Higher willow chairs were available for dining, and two-seater sofas offered opportunities for more intimate exchanges. The woven willow furniture was usually upholstered with billowing cushions, which were removed for airing to a drier atmosphere every night.

For activities such as eating and playing cards, conservatories were equipped with highly decorative openwork cast-iron tables and chairs, which were commonplace during the second half of the nineteenth century. No doubt they were frequently preferred to willow because they provided more opportunity for elaborate decoration, which the Victorians so enjoyed.

· FIXTURES AND FITTINGS ·

The Victorian taste for ornament was not confined to furniture. As the century wore on and casting techniques improved, features such as doors and windows became more and more complicated. From the simple and rectangular, they evolved through early and high Gothic to Tudor, Moorish and even Moghul.

Matching motifs were used in exterior features such as finials, which resembled everything from pine cones (frequently confused with pineapples) to onion domes and spires, which were used to terminate lines of fretted cresting in cast metal or wood set along the roof ridge.

The same spirit permeated the work of the designers who produced the supports for hanging baskets of plants, or the pots and planters used to grow plants on the floor. Often made of cast metal, these could mimic materials as various as cut logs, plaited rope or terracotta. Many of the hanging baskets' supports resembled the kind of lamp favored in mosques or harems. Their festooning of foliage and flowers echoed the flickering glow from burning oil.

While part of the floor area was usually devoted to deep beds capable of supporting large plants, much of the rest was covered with colourful ceramic tiles, which the Victorians used

FACING THE SUN

When this eighteenth-century orangery (above) was built, glass could only be produced in panes of relatively small dimensions. As a result, its large windows are divided by many glazing bars, shaped in sympathy with the arches above.

THE PERFUMED GARDEN

Poet's jasmine (opposite) frames a mirror in the conservatory at Dunster Castle in Somerset. One of the great pleasures of conservatory gardening is that the perfumes of fragrant plants such as this are contained and accentuated by the still, moist atmosphere.

so frequently in their entrance porches and hallways. Figuring formalized plants, they were often arranged to form highly complicated patterns into which the openwork cast-iron gratings and heating pipes were integrated. A well-furnished conservatory even had its own piano, for musical entertainments. Since piano stringing could be badly affected by prolonged exposure to the high humidity prevalent in many conservatories, special compact instruments were developed that could be wheeled away when not in use.

· TRADITIONAL CONSERVATORY PLANTS ·

While it is easy to scoff at the Victorian mania for applied decoration, it must be admitted that in

FURNISHED WITH CANE
Cane furniture (above) looks very much at home in the semi-tropical environment of the conservatory. It is suitable for all conservatories except those maintained at high humidity levels.

DRAWN TO THE LIGHT
At a time when fashionable interiors were heavily curtained and furnished, conservatories were a valued escape from such somber conditions. Their bright light would have been useful for reading (above).

DOMESTIC FANTASY
Victorian architects were not noted for their stylistic restraint, especially when designing spacious conservatories. This flamboyant structure (left) shows the unabashed eagerness to experiment that was typical of the period.

the conservatory it matched the flamboyance of the plants they grew, which would have seemed quite alien if they could have been outdoors against the cool, temperate backdrop of an English garden. Favorite plants were monsters like the prickly *Echinocactus grusonii* – great barrel-shaped globes from Mexico which will grow to nearly 3 feet (1m) in diameter, the polyp-like prickly pears such as *Opuntia microdasys*, or the staghorn fern *Platycerium bifurcatum*, which has fronds that resemble the antlers of a drunken reindeer. Great clumps of shoulder-high bird-of-paradise flowers jostled in the beds, and it almost appeared that the more bizarre a plant's form, the more readily it was seized on by Victorian gardeners..

Happily, there were plenty of beauties to restore the balance. The elegant leaves of cocos or phoenix palms and *Davallia* ferns, the fragrant jasmines and glowing oleanders, the hanging chains of ivy-leaved geraniums and asparagus ferns, and the skyward scramble of the purple-flowered cup-and-saucer vine, *Cobaea scandens*, made a fine background for evening singing of the sentimental ballads the Victorians so adored.

· THE MODERN REPRODUCTION ·
· CONSERVATORY ·

Following their apogee in Victorian times, conservatories gently decayed in their tens of thousands as the First World War swept away the society that created them. However, after decades of neglect, they are now enjoying a period of rediscovery. Countless designs, many Victorian in inspiration, are now made in pre-formed metal or fiberglass-reinforced plastic sections that are ready for assembly and glazing on-site.

The fact that some of these are mass-produced should not be a deterrent to anyone buying them. During the heyday of the Victorian conservatory, suppliers of garden buildings produced "off-the-rack" conservatories in huge numbers, as evidenced by their weighty catalogues.

However, reproduction conservatories have to be chosen with care. A heavily ornate conservatory of the style prevailing in the 1880s will look very well on a building that dates from that time, but if the same structure is attached to a house built when more severe lines were in vogue, the effect will be an uncomfortable one. From their earliest days, conservatories were designed to be regarded as an integral part of the houses they adorned. If a conservatory departs very much in style, it will have the unfortunate look of an inappropriate afterthought.

Modern conservatories do have many advantages that their predecessors lacked. One of these is ease of maintenance. Victorian conservatories

THE MODERN CONSERVATORY

THE GROWING INTEREST IN THE CONSERVATORY HAS BROUGHT ABOUT a revival of many traditional designs from the last century. The simplest of these is the lean-to conservatory, which has the advantage that it loses less heat than styles that feature proportionately more glazing. Hexagonal-ended conservatories are more suitable where the length of available wall is limited. A clerestory, containing a series of vertical windows, may be fitted to the roof for additional ventilation. The gable-ended conservatory gives a broad view of the garden beyond it.

LEAN-TO CONSERVATORY

HEXAGONAL CONSERVATORY WITH CLERESTORY

GABLE-END CONSERVATORY

THE FURNISHED CONSERVATORY
The degree to which a conservatory is planted and furnished determines its relation to the house and the garden. The conservatory at Barnsley House in Gloucestershire (above) *is furnished in the manner of a living-room.*

A GARDEN ROOM
Standen in West Sussex (opposite) *is a late Victorian house, built in 1892. Its tall conservatory is very much a room for plants, with a high back wall providing space for vigorous climbers.*

uncomfortable places. Really keen plants-people ran them at temperature and humidity levels that were designed to produce the best support for their plants, regardless of the comfort they offered to people. Lovers of tropical orchids in particular kept conditions so warm and sultry that their conservatories were tolerable only for short visits, during which the visitor gasped for breath in the steamy atmosphere.

People for whom the conservatory was principally a social asset aimed for much less humidity, and accordingly restricted the plants that they grew. It is probably true to say that most modern conservatories are run on these lines. Most foliage plants will have no difficulty with a moderately dry atmosphere, as long as their roots are well watered, and the same is true for such traditional favourites as strelitzias, jasmines and of course geraniums. However, plants that obtain most of their water through aerial roots, such as tropical orchids, will often find these conditions too dry.

The traditional answer to this problem is either to spray the moisture-loving plants with water every day, or to move them into the conservatory only at certain times. In the past, orchids would often be raised by the gardener in pots in greenhouses and simply brought into the conservatory for the period during which they were in full bloom.

· WINDOW GARDENS AND WARDIAN CASES ·

The Victorian passion for natural history was such that plants found their way not only into conservatories but also into their houses as well. Only a few plants, the aspidistra being pre-eminent among them, could survive in the dark recesses of a heavily curtained sitting-room. However, nearer the light of a prominent window, many a Victorian house contained what at first glance looked like a miniature conservatory, filled with a jungle of lush growth.

These objects, originally designed to ensure the safe passage of delicate plants on long sea voyages, were known as Wardian cases, after their inventor, Nathaniel Bagshaw Ward. Ward's original cases were workaday affairs, but once they had made the jump from ship to shore and become indoor curiosities, they grew more and more elaborate. In many ways, their design echoed that of conservatories, with arched "windows" and elaborate decoration. The inhabitants of these cases were almost invariably ferns, which Victorians collected in such great quantities that they seriously endangered many wild species.

By the 1870s, the Wardian case fell from grace, although the practice of growing plants in closed containers is still with us. However, the

were often made of cast-iron, which was subject to gradual rust and needed frequent re-painting. Today's equivalent is made of aluminum alloy or plastic, neither of which will rust. Glazing has also greatly improved. Modern glass admits much more light for plant growth, and when installed as double or triple glazing, it makes it possible to grow truly tender plants in cold climates with the minimum of heat. Early conservatories consumed, and therefore wasted, great amounts of heat in maintaining sufficiently high temperatures, especially on winter nights. Today's conservatory suffers far less heat loss.

· CONSERVATORY PLANT CARE ·

Because they come from so many different climatic regimes, traditional conservatory plants vary in the conditions needed to make them thrive. Some, such as the long-suffering Kentia palm, the ubiquitous aspidistra and Norfolk pine, are tolerant of a wide range of temperature and humidity. Others, especially orchids and ferns, are much more demanding. In the nineteenth century, some conservatories were very

MAKING A WINDOW CONSERVATORY

A VICTORIAN WINDOW CONSERVATORY CREATES AN opportunity for gardening under glass in almost any situation. There are two types, one of which – the half-sash conservatory – is designed to fit over the lower half of a sash window. More ambitious, but more appropriate to modern windows, is the oriel-style conservatory. This is fitted on a wall so that it entirely covers an existing window.

When installing an oriel-style conservatory, some modification to the existing window is often necessary, because an outward-opening window does not allow access to plants beyond it. To solve this problem, the window can be removed in its entirety, or replaced with sliding panes.

HALF-SASH WINDOW CONSERVATORY WITH SLOPING ROOF

HALF-SASH WINDOW CONSERVATORY WITH DOMED ROOF

PROVIDING VENTILATION

Without ventilation, the air temperature inside the conservatory may fluctuate widely if it receives direct sunlight. A hinged external window will allow ventilation to correct this. If the conservatory is built on a wall that faces away from the sun, no extra ventilation will normally be needed.

FRAME AND GLAZING BARS

The conservatory's frame and glazing bars should be made either of a durable hardwood, or of a softwood that has been treated to prevent decay.

PLANTING BENCH

The plants inside the conservatory can be grown in pots on dishes. Placing these on a tray of moist gravel will help to maintain high humidity.

SUPPORTING THE CONSERVATORY

The base of the conservatory can be made to sit on a windowsill. If your windows do not have projecting sills, a pair of decorative brackets can be bolted to the wall.

FLASHING

Waterproof flashing is essential to prevent rain penetrating the point where the conservatory meets the wall. Flashing is usually made of metal or bitumenized sheeting.

WINDOWS

Double glazing is essential in areas that experience severe winters. Arched frames lend a period flavor to vertical windows. Wooden arches can be attached to the glass, avoiding the need to cut curves.

PLANT SPRAYS

Spraying conservatory plants prevents their leaves suffering excessive water loss. Plants should not be sprayed when direct sunlight is falling on them.

ever-ingenious Victorians did continue to indulge in another method of indoor horticulture which was especially popular in town houses that lacked gardens. This centered on the "window conservatory," a glazed structure that was attached to a window frame, allowing plants a good deal of light in which to grow.

Window conservatories, or window greenhouses, were within the reach of those of fairly modest means. The basic structure could be embellished to form "all manner of ornamental projections," according to *Beeton's Garden Management*, the plants being "watered and arranged from the room within."

The window conservatory is a thoroughly practical idea for growing plants in confined spaces, and it also makes a very decorative feature. The conservatory can be either an adjunct to the lower part of a window, projecting like a box, or it can form a glazed alcove the full depth of the original window frame. The treatment of the glazing bars – whether real or sham – gives much scope for period detail. By applying a design cut out of thin board, what is simply a glazed box can become a Gothic fantasy half obscured by a tangle of luxuriant growth.

· GARDENING UNDER GLASS ·

Unlike conservatories, greenhouses have always been very much working buildings, structures that belonged very much to the garden rather than the house. In large gardens a century ago, greenhouses were put under the charge of a gardener who was skilled at raising plants under glass. Those with sufficient resources might have a range of greenhouses, each maintained at a different temperature. Most plants intended for the garden or indoors required only modest heat during the winter months; some, such as alpines, needed little or no heat, but depended on special attention to moisture levels. Tropical orchids, which had pride of place in any garden, often had a greenhouse entirely devoted to them, with many of the plants being hung in slatted boxes from the roof-beams.

Greenhouses were built either free-standing or leaning against sunny walls. They were often substantial structures, and usually had brick bases supporting walls that reached to waist height. Inside, a single or double row of staging supported a medley of plants in containers of all shapes and sizes. As always, an extraordinary amount of attention was paid to the details of the design. In some greenhouses, the staging was supported on metal pillars that had water-cups built into them. These acted like little moats, preventing slugs and insects from climbing up the supports and attacking the plants above.

FREE-STANDING WARDIAN CASE
WITH TURNED LEGS

WARDIAN CASES

The Wardian case was the elegant forerunner of the modern terrarium – a sealed container in which plants could flourish with little or no attention. Palms and cacti (left) thrive in a dry case. Non-flowering plants such as ferns (below) and mosses make the most successful subjects for growing in a humid case. They enjoy moisture, and do not suffer from fungal diseases that often attack flowering plants in very damp atmospheres.

TABLE-TOP WARDIAN CASE

· CLEANING UP ·

Work in the greenhouse continued on a strict timetable throughout the year, one which started not in spring but in autumn. In a well-stocked greenhouse, this was the time when all but the most cold-sensitive plants were put outside for a few hours, while the inside of the house was tidied and scrubbed to kill lurking insects and fungal spores. This scrubbing extended to all the equipment, including the seed-boxes and pots, and was carried out on a bright day when everything could be left to dry in the sanitizing sunlight. For several days afterwards, the air would be permeated with the powerful aroma of phenolic disinfectant.

In places that experienced cool summers, the role of the greenhouse was to extend the growing season and to provide some indoor color in the winter months. Clearing out the greenhouse was a task that had to be completed before the chrysanthemums, which had been growing in beds outdoors, could be brought into the house and planted in the ground to provide flowers in

CUCUMBER CULTIVATION

I**N NINETEENTH-CENTURY BRITAIN THE CUCUMBER** was *de rigueur* as a constituent of sandwiches. In the cool climate, cucumbers were usually raised under glass, either in a greenhouse or in a frame. As with many greenhouse crops, cucumbers were the subject of competitive cultivation and much experimentation with new varieties. Great importance was attached to the straightness of the fruit, with cucumber glasses being used to prevent prize specimens from curling.

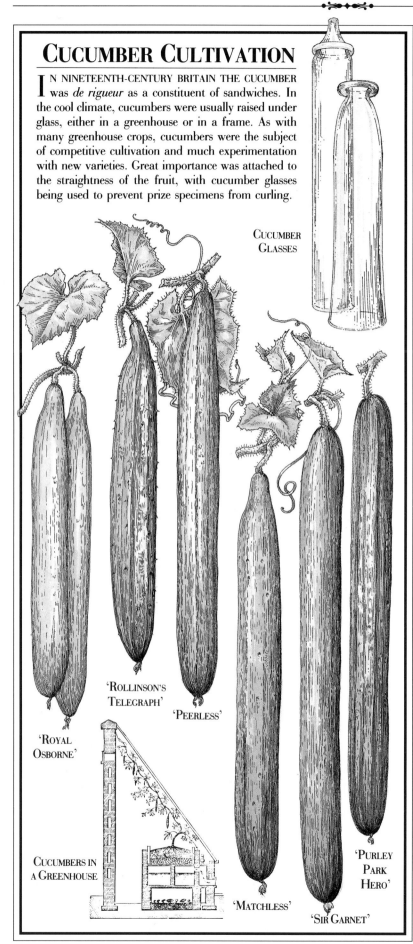

CUCUMBER GLASSES

'ROLLINSON'S TELEGRAPH'

'PEERLESS'

'ROYAL OSBORNE'

CUCUMBERS IN A GREENHOUSE

'MATCHLESS'

'SIR GARNET'

'PURLEY PARK HERO'

early winter. Traditionally, they always went into the ground previously occupied by the tomatoes.

There was little danger of scorch from the lower autumn sun, and the limewash previously applied to offer shade was washed off.

· MANAGING AN INDOOR CLIMATE ·

Heating a greenhouse today is a simple matter of flicking a switch or lighting a match. In greenhouses with thermostatically controlled heating, even this is unnecessary. But in earlier times, as winter approached, an extraordinary range of furnaces, stoves, pipes, boilers and burners sputtered or burst into life.

Water- and steam-boilers with piped radiator systems were introduced during the first quarter of the nineteenth century. The pipes usually ran underneath the staging, and if high humidity was needed, flat tanks above the pipes allowed water to evaporate into the rising air. In places where piped town gas later became available, many greenhouse owners turned to this as a source of fuel. Then, when fuel oil prices became very competitive, many of those furnaces were converted to burn oil.

In greenhouses that had coal-fired heating, the onset of winter brought with it the daily chore of tending the fire. Raking out and stoking was the last job to be carried out every evening and the first to be accomplished every morning.

Since the sun could still be warm on some days, the gardener had to be careful to see that the vents were open and closed as necessary. This required great vigilance, because the aim was to try to keep the temperature as even as possible, using only experience and the regular reading of thermometers as guides. Anyone familiar with an old-time greenhouse gardener will remember those moments when, during a conversation, the gardener would pause momentarily, sense a change in atmosphere and then automatically decide what corrective action to take.

· PREPARATIONS FOR WINTER ·

Autumn was not solely a time for bringing the year's growth to a close. The seeds of plants such as pansies, violas, clarkia, godetia and schizanthus needed to be sown, and suckers from calceolarias and cinerarias were also potted, and seedlings transplanted. Rooted cuttings of pelargoniums, scheduled to flower the following summer, would be moved to their final flowering pots, and stocks previously sown in the nursery areas outdoors would be ready to be brought indoors and planted into pots.

Vegetables, too, needed attention. Tomato seed sown for an early crop in the following spring would be sown into small individual pots

A FLORAL TOWER
Geraniums (left) are one of
the traditional favorites of
the greenhouse gardener. In
this cool greenhouse, some
geraniums have been
allowed to grow to a
statuesque size.

A PLETHORA OF POTS
*Before the turn of the last
century, terracotta plant
pots were nearly all thrown
on a potter's wheel. The fact
that they were made by
hand often gave them a
slight asymmetry that
added to their earthy charm.*

and both cauliflower and lettuce seed would be
sown in trays. Endive and lettuce would be ready
to prick out to become plants for an early indoor
crop. The age of air transport of fruit and
vegetables may not have arrived, but greenhouse
gardeners managed to stretch the supply for as
long as possible.

· THE TRADITIONAL GREENHOUSE IN SPRING ·

As spring approached, the traditional timetable
for greenhouse gardening called for greater
urgency as operations for the coming season
became more pressing. Achimenes and gloxinias
for early flowering would be started by watering
and moving them to a bright, warm spot, while
potted roses would be pruned. The seed of
cannas, freesias, fuchsias and gloxinias would be
sown, while bedding stock destined to produce
cuttings would be brought into the heat. Hip-
peastrums would be repotted, as would pelargoniums and houseplants that had outgrown
their pots. In order to get vegetables off to a
quick start, many of them would be brought on
or "forced" under glass.

The first days of spring were by far the busiest
time in the greenhouse year. In a large garden,
up to sixty types of annual, biennial and perennial flower seed, and usually a dozen types of
vegetable seed, needed sowing. It was also the

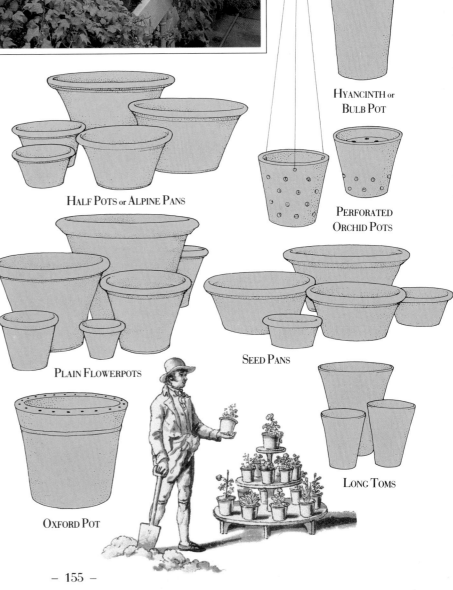

HALF POTS or ALPINE PANS

HYANCINTH or BULB POT

PERFORATED ORCHID POTS

PLAIN FLOWERPOTS

SEED PANS

OXFORD POT

LONG TOMS

WATERING POTS AND CANS

The development of gardening under glass produced a need for watering cans capable of producing a fine spray that would not damage young plants. Some early watering pots were made of earthenware, while later watering cans were made of zinc or tinplate.

time when a great many cuttings were taken every year of such plants as abutilons, carnations and petunias.

Most plants would be given a spring feed of manure to support their increased growth. Potted shrubs like azaleas would be moved to shady areas of the greenhouse to hold back their flowering. This would ensure that they would maintain a succession of flowers once in the house. Summer bedding plants sown earlier would have their tops pinched out to make them strong and bushy, cuttings would be taken of the

soft stems of woody plants and the half-hardy annuals, plants such as ageratum, asters, auriculas, nemesias and phlox would be sown in boxes, in readiness for the approach of warmer weather, when the young plants could be cautiously moved outside.

Once the first days of spring were past, the burden of work for the greenhouse gardener began to slacken. His main jobs were watering, ventilating and damping down. The crush of pots and trays within the greenhouse would be eased as more and more of them were moved outside. As the sun grew stronger, the heating could be reduced until, for the first time since the previous autumn, the furnace was finally allowed to die out.

· MODERN GREENHOUSES IN PERIOD GARDENS ·

After the First World War, mass production techniques led to a revolution in greenhouse gardening. From being a pursuit of the gardeners of the privileged, it was thrown open to almost anyone with a small patch of land.

Today, a serviceable greenhouse, made of alloy supports with transparent plastic sheets, can be built in an afternoon with relatively little cost. Unlike earlier greenhouses, these can be fitted out so that they almost look after themselves. Automatic blind systems, controlled by photo-sensitive switches, prevent plants from being scorched by the sun in summer. Double glazing, or sheets of insulating plastic, cut down heat loss at night. Heating can be controlled by thermostats, and plants can be watered automatically through drip nozzles whose supply valves can be operated either by an electronic clock, or by a switch operated by a humidity sensor.

Unfortunately, with this increasing sophistication has come a gradual decline in the greenhouse's aesthetic appeal. Shiny aluminum cannot compete with the more traditional brick base and painted or stained wood frame.

Although little can be done to alter the appearance of a modern greenhouse, it can be screened so that it does not clash with more traditional features in a garden. A surround of old roses, growing on an open framework, will conceal the house in summer, and if left open on the sunward side, will not unduly reduce the amount of light reaching the plants inside. A trellis screen or hedge will serve the same function, but as these cut out more light, they need to be positioned further away.

In areas with cool climates, modern greenhouses can be extremely valuable. Dealt with imaginatively, there is no reason why they should spoil the appearance of a traditional garden.

WATERING POT

WATERING POT

LONG-SPOUTED CAN

REVERSED ROSE CAN

STEP-SPOUTED CAN

"PAXTON" CAN WITH FEET

BARREL SPRINKLER

PEST CONTROL AND PLANT CARE

BEFORE THE ADVENT OF MODERN PESTICIDES, THE TWO most frequently used substances for controlling greenhouse pests were sulfur and tobacco. Sulfur dust was scattered over foliage with bellows-like sulfurators. Tobacco was burned in fumigators, producing smoke containing nicotine, a highly effective insecticide. Syringing and spraying also helped to keep plants in prime condition. Syringes suffered from the disadvantage that they needed frequent filling. If a suitable source of water was available, hand-pumps and "aquajets" could be used to create a continuous spray.

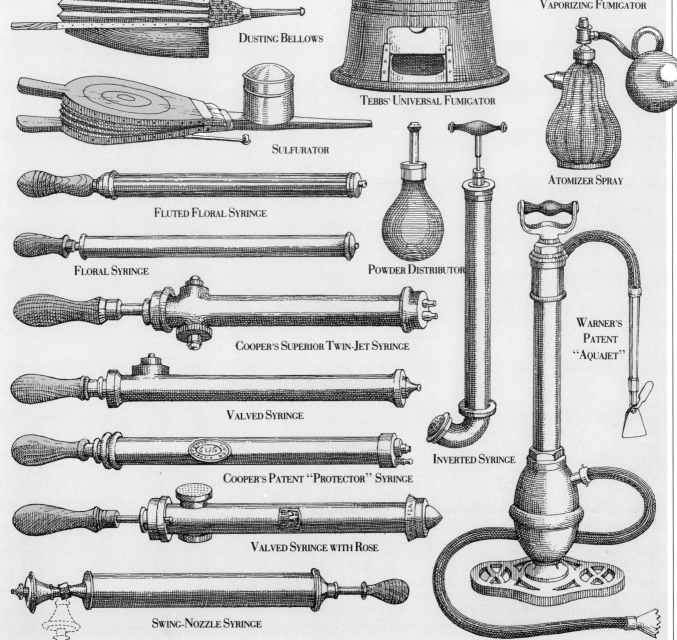

VAPORIZING FUMIGATOR

DUSTING BELLOWS

TEBBS' UNIVERSAL FUMIGATOR

ATOMIZER SPRAY

SULFURATOR

FLUTED FLORAL SYRINGE

POWDER DISTRIBUTOR

FLORAL SYRINGE

WARNER'S PATENT "AQUAJET"

COOPER'S SUPERIOR TWIN-JET SYRINGE

VALVED SYRINGE

COOPER'S PATENT "PROTECTOR" SYRINGE

INVERTED SYRINGE

VALVED SYRINGE WITH ROSE

SWING-NOZZLE SYRINGE

TERRACES & STEPS

Catching the sun — The terrace as a focal point —
Techniques of terrace-making — Decorative devices —
Ramps and inclines — Steps and their decoration
— Planting a flight of steps

GARDEN TERRACE-MAKING IS A BRANCH OF AN EXTRAORDINARILY ANCIENT art. It has its origins in subsistence farming, and indeed it could be said that the first subsistence farmers, who each tended just enough land to provide for their families, were the earliest gardeners.

It cannot have taken long for these farmers to discover that if they cultivated the soil on steeply sloping land, a heavy rainstorm would erode it into gulleys and sweep the best of the topsoil down the hill. Somehow, this topsoil had to be retained. Gradually, a technique developed. Flat areas of land were created by moving the topsoil aside and shifting the subsoil to form wide level steps. Walls, either of subsoil or stone, were then built on the outer margins to hold back the earth. The topsoil, once returned and leveled, was then safe from the threat of erosion.

Terrace-making of this kind has been going on for so long that in parts of the world its has molded entire landscapes. In the Far East, whole mountainsides are stepped right up to altitudes where conditions are too

A CHANGE OF LEVEL
Whether in the form of short flights of steps or bold terraces, changes in level give the gardener unrivaled opportunities for planting and creative decoration.

bleak for crops to grow. Similar if less spectacular evidence of early terracing can be seen in places like the hilly areas of Crete, as relics of the Minoan civilization, or even on the soft undulations of what has latterly become Dorset meadowland, where the terraces are known locally as *lynchets*.

At first sight, the practical considerations that brought about these farming terraces might seem to have little relevance to domestic gardens. But the terrace's advantages are many, and through the centuries gardeners have come to appreciate that they can be far more than a way of cultivating sloping ground.

· VARIED VIEWPOINTS ·

The vistas in a garden can be changed dramatically if the sight line is raised, even by a small amount. This is something that garden designers have long realized, and indeed some of the finest terraced gardens have been created on what was originally perfectly flat ground. In such gardens, the contours are varied by excavating some parts to create sunken areas and using the spill from the excavation to make raised terraces elsewhere. This procedure, which is frequently used in modern landscape architecture, gives three viewing levels: the floor of the sunken garden, the normal level of the land and the higher terraced area.

Terraces where the ground is sloping offer more advantages still. In hot climates they are more exposed to cooling breezes, and they also make it possible to enjoy the strange but enchanting experience of walking at the level of the crowns of quite tall trees growing on the terrace below. This was a feature of the Hanging Gardens of Babylon, which were in fact a flight of high terraces. Visitors to the Generalife Gardens at the Alhambra in Granada can still enjoy walking the high terrace in a hanging garden where, in hot weather, the Moorish caliphs used to sip mint tea or take their evening stroll, perhaps leaning out to pick oranges still warm from the sun.

A less obvious advantage of terracing a sloping garden is the lofty seclusion that the higher terraces can provide. Anyone standing or sitting on the inner margins of a high and relatively wide terrace cannot be seen and can barely be heard by anyone on the terrace below. This fact has long been used by garden designers and architects to ensure the privacy of their patrons. Houses were built on high plateaux that formed the upper surface, giving an uninterrupted overview of the garden and the landscape beyond. The owners could survey without being seen — something that may have daunted approaching

enemies and must certainly have intimidated their gardeners and farm workers. A fine example of this type of terracing can be seen at Powis Castle in the Welsh Marches.

· CATCHING THE SUN ·

High terraces, like walled gardens, create a perfect environment for growth. Their retaining walls act like radiators, storing the sun's heat, and they also give shelter from strong winds. In cool climates, plants in terraced gardens often fare much better than they would if grown unprotected on level ground.

Large-scale kitchen gardens in undulating country often took advantage of the heat-storage effect of terraces. The terraces made the ground easier to work, and they also produced early-maturing vegetables.

Terraced fruit gardens had the same advantages, and they were common in cooler climates where under normal conditions trees such as peaches and nectarines only rarely produced ripe fruit. Grown against a terrace wall, the fan- and cordon-trained fruit would be bathed by the heat retained by and gradually liberated from the masonry of the walls.

Sometimes, in more northerly locations, the faces of terraces were used as a backing to support a framework of temporary glass panels during the winter. The glass protected the delicate buds of climbers and fruit trees from damage by frost. A fine example of this can be seen at the Sanssouci Palace in East Berlin, where winters can be bitterly cold. Here, frames are used to front the faces of a series of shallow terraces on the southern side of the palace.

· CASCADES AND FOUNTAINS ·

It may well be that the early use of terraces to aid irrigation inspired later garden designers to plan multi-level water features in ornamental gardens. In terraced irrigation systems, water that was initially confined to the higher terraces was slowly channeled down over dams to terraces below.

Some of the great Renaissance gardens certainly contained very ambitious waterworks which employ these principles. A fine working example can still be seen at the Villa d'Este, Tivoli, near Rome. Here water spills down a series of terraces through cascades or spouts set in the mouths of animals, gorgons and other grotesque figures.

A smaller-scaled and much earlier example can be seen at the Generalife Gardens. On flights of steps, the open-topped hollow stone handrails are used as water conduits. The water makes a splendidly soothing sound on a hot day and it has a distinct cooling effect on the air. Its rush is

halted as the channel widens out into basins on each landing. Here, the caliph could cool his brow in water still carrying the chill of the Sierra Nevada mountains.

· THE TERRACE AS A FOCAL POINT ·

In a garden that is split into different levels, the one on which the house itself stands is naturally a focus of attention. As terrace-making developed, the terrace adjoining the house evolved into part of its structure, becoming a surfaced and often ornate platform from which the garden could be viewed without encountering either mud or gardeners.

In many great houses of the eighteenth and nineteenth centuries, the entire garden is designed to be seen at its best from the terrace. In the formal garden, the terrace often overlooks a parterre, with avenues leading away to distant gates or obelisks. In later less formal designs, the terrace offers a panoramic view of a rolling landscape: clumps of trees stand out boldly in the middle distance, dense woodland hangs on more distant hillsides and lakes spanned by bridges curve tantalizingly out of sight, their true extent being artfully concealed.

It might be thought that, since these terraces are in essence outward-looking, depending for their effect on great expanses of park or garden, they would be quite out of place in today's gardens. But, as many of this century's gardeners have discovered, this is not entirely true. Even deprived of the views they command, many period terraces are works of art in their own right. By reproducing some of the details of their construction and planting, it is possible to create an inward-looking terrace that captures something of the character of its traditional counterparts.

· TECHNIQUES OF TERRACE-MAKING ·

While the procedures involved in making a terrace have not changed much over the ages, the materials available to make their retaining walls have become more diverse. Loose stone walls are an easy and attractive way of holding back the earth when making terraces not more than about two feet (60 cm) high. This kind of wall is ideal for a smaller garden where the aim is to make a terrace adjoining the house, or to break up an originally level surface. As long as the walls are more than one foot (30 cm) wide and carefully built, they will be solid enough to withstand the

AN ELEVATED VIEWPOINT
Terraces and steps allow a garden to be appreciated from a variety of angles. These Edwardian ladies are seen on an unusually expansive landing – almost a terrace in its own right – that connects two flights of steps.

THE ART OF TERRACE CONSTRUCTION

T ERRACING IS AN ASPECT OF GARDENING WHERE MISTAKES IN construction or the selection of materials can be difficult to correct. For this reason, careful planning is needed before embarking on the work. The key to good terracing is to ensure that the retaining walls sit on well-prepared foundations, and that they are correctly drained. Traditionally, the choice of materials for terrace walls was governed by local geology. If a good supply of local stone was available, then this would be used, giving a wall whose character would be in sympathy with its surroundings. If no local stone could be obtained, brick or brought-in stone took its place.

BUILT-IN STABILITY

While low walls are usually made to be exactly vertical, high walls benefit by being made to lean slightly towards the soil they are holding back. This slope, or batter as it is known, gives the terrace greater strength. It also makes the retaining wall look less overwhelming than it would otherwise be.

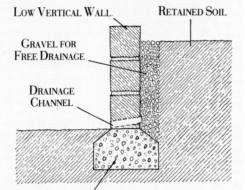

LOW VERTICAL WALL RETAINED SOIL
GRAVEL FOR FREE DRAINAGE
DRAINAGE CHANNEL
CONCRETE FOUNDATIONS

MATERIALS FOR FACING A TERRACE

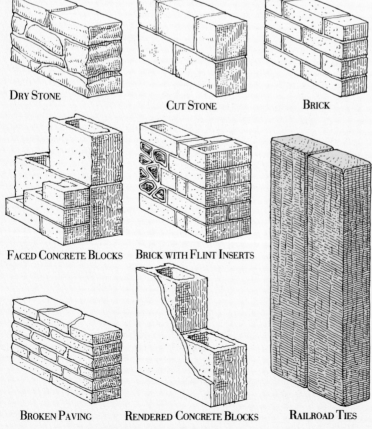

DRY STONE

CUT STONE

BRICK

FACED CONCRETE BLOCKS

BRICK WITH FLINT INSERTS

BROKEN PAVING

RENDERED CONCRETE BLOCKS

RAILROAD TIES

outward pressure of the soil behind them. A similar effect can be produced by using irregularly broken parallel-faced paving slabs which sit tightly on top of each other.

In a garden where the ground slopes steeply, the terrace walls need to be higher and therefore stouter. If you can afford it, regular-cut stone, closely spaced, still makes the most attractive and satisfactory material for a high retaining wall. In earlier times, high walls depended for their stability on deep foundations. Today the work is made easier by setting the first course of stones on a concrete base. The concrete should be poured into a trench in the soil at least 18 inches (45 cm) wide and 9 inches (20 cm) deep.

Cheaper and quite attractive walls can be made from old weathered brick, or from some of the newer bricks that are deliberately molded to give them a weathered appearance. Strong and economical walls can be made from large concrete building blocks. These would look very ugly if left in view, but they can very easily be masked by a simple non-structural facing layer of brick or irregular walling stone fixed in cement to simulate dry-stone walling.

· TERRACING WITH TIMBER ·

Stone is not the only material worth considering. Stout baulks of preserved timber, such as heavy railroad ties, can be used without reinforcement to edge low terraces when laid flat on top of one another. If sunk upright into the ground like palisading, timber can be used to retain higher terraces, although they need to be supported internally by buried "dogs." These are lengths of stout iron set deep in the subsoil below the inner edge of the terrace. They are connected by chain or wire hawser to U-shaped bolts fixed to the inside of the timbers.

Although ultimately such timber retaining walls will rot, if the wood is originally very well preserved they will last for many years. They have a softer appearance than masonry walls and this can be an advantage if you have a garden where a more rustic appearance is appropriate.

· DECORATIVE DEVICES ·

For safety, high terraces were always edged with some form of railing, and this decorative device was developed by garden designers and used in terraces attached to houses. Traditionally, those in nobler gardens had turned stone balustrades with variants such as fine wrought-ironwork between brick or stone pillars.

Stone balustrading has always been very expensive, but these days there is the alternative of cement-based simulated stone. The quality of these copies varies enormously. Some have seams and burrs that make it quite clear that they are molded rather than turned in the traditional manner. The best, however, will bear the closest inspection and can be artificially aged (*see p.86*) to resemble natural stone even more closely. Even a small length of this balustrading can be most effective.

In less grand terraces, simpler brick walls or plain iron railings were used. These were often reinforced with a line of hedging. Yew was the species most frequently chosen for this work because it grows relatively quickly, is evergreen and makes a thick and meaningful barrier.

Terrace surfacing has varied with the styles of gardening favored through the ages. Nearly all of the styles can be adapted for use in a modern terrace of limited dimensions. Lawn, the simplest surfacing, wears too rapidly to be used on its own in a small-scale terrace, but is quite satisfactory if protected by paths. These can be of solid stone, brick, plain paving, or paving punctuated by beds of shrubs and flowers. If you wish to follow more recent informal styles, a surface such as coarse grit, gravel or stone paving with small gaps will allow mound-forming plants to grow, giving a delightful feeling of controlled neglect.

· SUPPORT AND DRAINAGE ·

The pressures that the soil can apply when expanding as it becomes damp can be very great. For this reason, high masonry walls usually need some reinforcement at approximately 10-foot (3-m) intervals. This normally takes the form of buttressing, in which the thickness of the wall is increased by an extra layer of firmly keyed-in brick or stone.

In traditional retaining walls, buttresses, when they were not left plain, were developed into some form of decorative feature, like a pilaster, which reduced the bareness of the wall surface by breaking it down into obvious panels of a pleasing shape. If you have a buttressed wall, you can further decorate its panels by attaching trellises to support climbing plants.

Whichever technique you use to make a terrace's retaining walls, proper drainage is essential. Usually this involves leaving passage-ways for water through the wall at intervals. If your soil is heavy, it is wise to build up a vertical seam of gravel or broken stone immediately behind the wall as the terrace is being filled. This ensures that water moving towards the terrace edge will immediately sink to the lowest drainage holes rather than build up to exert high pressures at the top of the wall.

To ensure good drainage and evenness of surface, traditional hard terracing was nearly always laid on a thick layer of sharp sand packed

SURFACING A TERRACE

TERRACE SURFACING HAS TO BE HARD-WEARING, AND IT ALSO HAS TO be able to resist the effects of the weather. The way a surface is laid depends on the result that is required. In very formal terraces the surfacing should be laid in a precise pattern. For more informal terraces, the surfacing can be irregular and may include gaps through which plants can grow.

Surfacing materials are of two kinds – man-made and natural. Brick is probably the most attractive of all man-made materials. Purpose-made pavers, or frost-resistant walling bricks, can be laid as paving in a number of different patterns or *bonds*, and if of good quality and bedded down well on to sand, will provide an almost indestructible surface. Simulated stone slabs made out of concrete are generally less expensive and are increasingly used for surfacing in today's gardens.

Stone, the most popular natural material, varies in its durability. Some of the softer sedimentary stones, such as sandstone and limestone, will flake to produce a surface that has great character. Igneous rock, such as granite and flint, is much harder. Water-worn pebbles of flint can be arranged in patterns held together by cement. Granite can be obtained in the form of cobblestones, which were once widely used for surfacing city roads. They make a durable if rather urban surface.

BASKETWEAVE BRICK

HERRINGBONE BRICK

FORMAL STONE SLABS

FLINT PEBBLES IN FAN FORMATION

SIMULATED STONE CONCRETE SLABS

GRANITE COBBLESTONES

MAKING AN ITALIANATE TERRACE

T HE ARCHITECTURE OF RENAISSANCE ITALY HAS HAD a profound influence on garden design both in Europe and in North America. The gardens of Italian houses in the sixteenth century were highly formal, with ornate symmetry symbolizing the triumph of civilized man over unruly nature. Few gardens would have been without a terrace, and these were often built on an expansive scale. Today, more a restrained version of the Italianate terrace can provide a delightful classical touch to a formal garden.

The terrace shown here includes the basic architectural elements that would have been considered essential four centuries ago. It can be raised above a sloping garden, or, as a purely decorative feature, can be modified to suit a garden that is level. The surface is made up of square-cut slabs. These are laid on a layer of sand that is spread over the base of the terrace. Originally, these slabs would have been of natural stone, but today you might well find that simulated stone is a more easily obtained alternative. The most important architectural detail is the balustrading, which runs between low pillars, giving a sense of enclosure. Again, this can be of natural stone or a modern alternative. Ornament is provided by statues, vases, troughs and stone sphere finials.

The plants used in this scheme are formal to harmonize with the style of the terrace. Suitable plants to stand on the terrace itself include mop-headed bay trees, grown in terracotta pots, and clipped box in containers. The vases can be used for trailing flowering plants whose more informal appearance contrasts with the rest of the terrace.

PLANTS IN POTS
Potted plants on a Renaissance-style terrace should be trimmed into formal shapes with the emphasis on symmetry. Box is the ideal subject for this, as are woody herbs such as sages and lavenders. Herbs have the advantage of giving off a pleasing scent when anyone brushes past them.

VASES
Vases and bowls provide an opportunity to introduce plants into the terrace at eye-level. Originally these would have been made of stone, with marble being particularly popular. Modern artificial stone vases make good substitutes, but if you live in an area subject to frost, make sure that they are able to withstand freezing.

ALTERNATIVE STEP ARRANGEMENTS
If the depth of the terrace is limited, the best way to include steps is to extend them from the terrace, as shown in the main illustration. If the terrace is sufficiently deep, the steps can be partly or wholly inset. A double flight of steps provides an interesting change of direction.

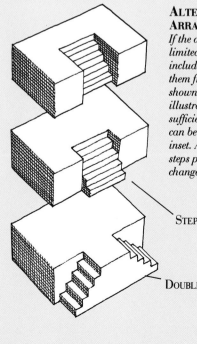

STEPS PARTLY INSET

DOUBLE FLIGHT OF STEPS

PAVING
The original material used for surfacing this kind of terrace – stone slabs – can be replaced by concrete if it is realistically textured and colored. Here the slabs are inset with a mosaic and laid linearly. A more elaborate alternative is to lay the slabs diagonally. Although elegant, this does entail more work as each edging slab has to be cut to fit.

TOPIARY TREES

The classic plant for decorating a terrace of this type is bay, clipped into standard trees with ball-shaped or "mop-headed" crowns. These can be grown in terracotta pots (see pp.174–5) or traditional wooden containers (see p.145). Orange trees make an attractive alternative where the climate is warm enough.

STATUARY

In Italian gardens, statues provided references to classical myths and legends and were a common sight. Because statues are rarer today, they need to be selected with care. Modern reproduction statues that are too tall or bulky should be avoided, as should any that have visible seams that result from poor molding.

BALUSTRADES

Traditional balusters are made of stone turned on a lathe to produce a variety of distinctive patterns – the bulbous-based type being the most common where the stone was sufficiently soft to be worked. In period balustrades, the individual balusters were fixed at the top and bottom by dowels – iron or stone pegs that were slotted into holes in the wall and rail.

BULBOUS-BASED BALUSTER

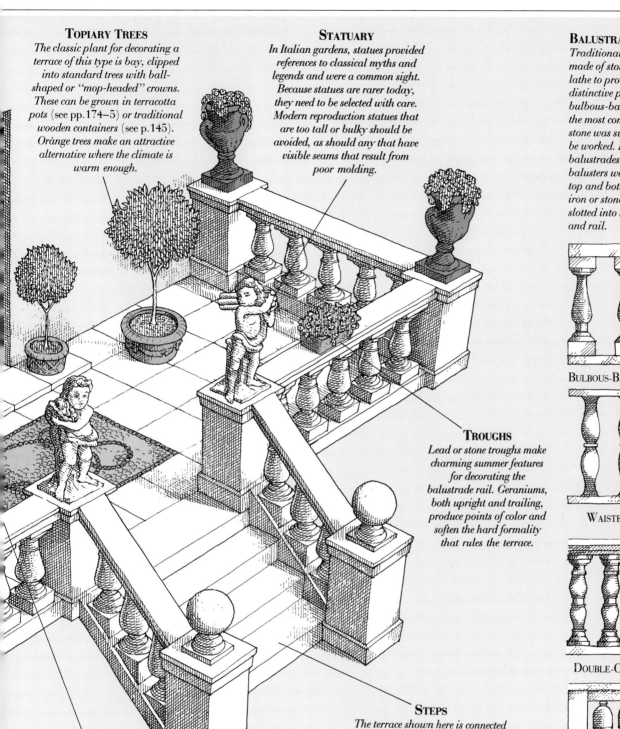

TROUGHS

Lead or stone troughs make charming summer features for decorating the balustrade rail. Geraniums, both upright and trailing, produce points of color and soften the hard formality that rules the terrace.

WAISTED BALUSTER

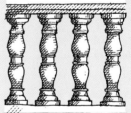

DOUBLE-CUP BALUSTER

STEPS

The terrace shown here is connected to the garden below by a short single flight of steps. In a terrace that is level with the rest of the garden, there is obviously no requirement for steps, and so the pillars topped with statues mark the entrance to the garden. The greater the difference in level between the terrace and the garden, the wider are the opportunities for making the terrace more elaborate.

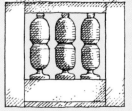

CYLINDRICAL BALUSTER

PEBBLE MOSAIC

Mosaic work provides a focus just beyond the doors opening on to the terrace and prevents the paving from seeming too bland. A simple patterned mosaic can be made out of water-worn pebbles of different colors. Traditional colored mosaic tiles allow more complex decoration.

GRASS STEPS

Steps surfaced entirely with turf are usually seen only in short flights, because they need almost constant maintenance. The sweep shown here is exceptionally grand. In summer it would have needed many hours of painstaking shearing, all of which had to be carried out by hand.

ramp could be made wide enough not to require any form of lateral walling, the edges of the walkway being simply sloped down to the surface of the terrace from which it rose.

More elaborate narrower ramps were provided with lateral walls, which were either solid or balustraded above the level of the ramp's surface. To prevent the bare ramp topping from becoming too eroded, transverse lines of stone would be set just clear of its slightly convex surface at intervals. Shallow stone water runnels in its margins were made which would allow the water to spill away quickly.

It could be that corpulent and well-fed Roman senators found ramps easier to negotiate when they strolled their villa gardens half drunk and satiated by their gargantuan meals. Or perhaps the horses found them easier going if the senators felt too lazy to walk.

In formal situations, ramps certainly require a good deal less expensive cut stone for their construction than do steps. If you have shallow terraces to link, this, combined with the fact that they are easy to make, might make them an alternative worthy of consideration.

· GARDEN STEPS ·

Ramps are only practicable for gentle inclines. Abrupt changes in level call for steps, one of the great eye-catching features of any garden.

The great garden designers have always fully exploited the visual appeal that steps undoubtedly have. In some of the magnificent formal gardens of the sixteenth and seventeenth centuries, the steps were often so wide and so grand in appearance that processing up or down them had something of the character of a notable event. Even today mounting them in casual clothes seems to be an affront to their grandeur. The forms of these feature flights of steps have not changed much over the past three hundred years but, with a few exceptions, their scale has greatly diminished during the last century.

At their simplest, steps in gardens can be just a few stout square-sectioned timbers, stones or bricks laid straight on the ground and arranged as a few steps to join shallow terraces. In woodland gardens, the steepest sections of narrow paths on rising land have traditionally included log steps. These are held in place by metal or wooden stakes driven into the ground.

In building flights of steps to link high terraces with the ground below, garden designers have always had a number of approaches to choose from. Most simply, they could leave the area of the top terrace completely intact by building their flight of steps entirely on the lower ground. Conversely, they could leave the lower ground

down level on to a base of broken rock above well-compacted soil. In recent years the time-honored paver's tools — the sand shovel, roller and heavy tamping hammer — have been replaced by mechanized devices such as vibrating rollers. These are highly efficient in leveling and compacting each layer after it has been spread.

· RAMPS AND INCLINES ·

For as long as gardeners have been making raised terraces they have been obliged to make ramps or steps to link them.

Provided the difference in height is not too great, the ramp is the simplest way of progressing from one level to another. It certainly seems to have been the one favoured by the practical and economical Romans. Made by raking broken stone into an incline and then binding it with gravel and coarse grit, their ramps were either left bare or grassed over. Where space allowed, a

PLANTS FOR PAVING

A SUNNY PAVED SURFACE PROVIDES A COMBINATION OF relatively dry soil with unimpeded exposure to light. These are ideal conditions for the growth of alpines and other rock plants. Paving restricts competition between plants, so once a plant has become established, it will usually thrive without further attention.

In existing paving, the technique used for planting depends on whether or not mortar has been used in the construction. With unmortared brick paving, whole bricks can be extracted and then broken in half. The resulting square gaps left by replacing the half-bricks are then used for planting. In unmortared stone paving, it is usually a simple matter to lever up a slab. Plants can then be inserted alongside the adjoining slabs before the lifted slab is replaced. If the joints are too close to permit this, chipping off the corner of a slab will provide sufficient room for planting.

FLORAL PATH
Established plants in paving (right) produce an abundant display but need little maintenance apart from occasional shearing to keep them in check.

PROPAGATING PAVING PLANTS
Some paving plants, such as Welsh poppy, will self-seed so profusely that propagation is never a problem. Many of the saxifrages can be increased by taking cuttings, each consisting of a single rosette of leaves. Mat-forming plants with numerous stems, such as the thymes, are propagated by division. To divide an established plant growing between pving slabs, the paving must be lifted so that sufficient root can be removed.

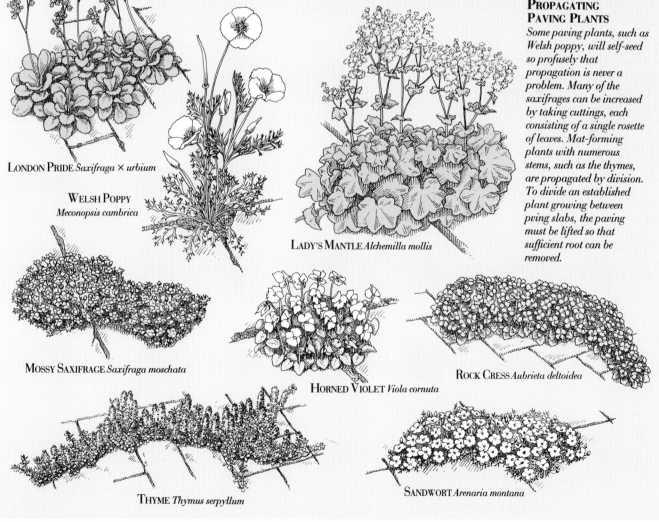

LONDON PRIDE *Saxifraga × urbium*

WELSH POPPY *Meconopsis cambrica*

LADY'S MANTLE *Alchemilla mollis*

MOSSY SAXIFRAGE *Saxifraga moschata*

HORNED VIOLET *Viola cornuta*

ROCK CRESS *Aubrieta deltoidea*

THYME *Thymus serpyllum*

SANDWORT *Arenaria montana*

FLIGHTS OF FANCY

THE DECORATIVE USE OF STEPS IS SEEN AT ITS HEIGHT IN gardens of the early eighteenth century, where they became an art form in their own right. Although most gardens today do not have a large enough range of levels for long flights, even three or four shallow steps can make a real contribution to the appearance of a garden. In all but rustic steps, the rise between successive steps in a flight (the *riser*), together with the width of each step (the *tread*), is constant. By making the risers small, the number of steps in a flight can be increased. The shallow steps that result from this can be difficult to negotiate if they form part of a busy path, but in quieter parts of a garden, having steps that slow down progress is often an advantage.

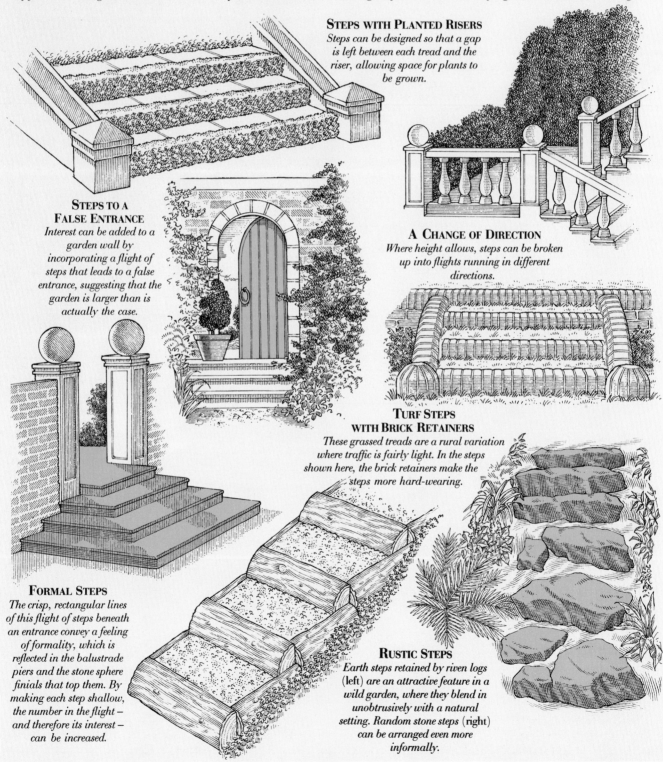

STEPS WITH PLANTED RISERS
Steps can be designed so that a gap is left between each tread and the riser, allowing space for plants to be grown.

STEPS TO A FALSE ENTRANCE
Interest can be added to a garden wall by incorporating a flight of steps that leads to a false entrance, suggesting that the garden is larger than is actually the case.

A CHANGE OF DIRECTION
Where height allows, steps can be broken up into flights running in different directions.

TURF STEPS WITH BRICK RETAINERS
These grassed treads are a rural variation where traffic is fairly light. In the steps shown here, the brick retainers make the steps more hard-wearing.

FORMAL STEPS
The crisp, rectangular lines of this flight of steps beneath an entrance convey a feeling of formality, which is reflected in the balustrade piers and the stone sphere finials that top them. By making each step shallow, the number in the flight — and therefore its interest — can be increased.

RUSTIC STEPS
Earth steps retained by riven logs (left) are an attractive feature in a wild garden, where they blend in unobtrusively with a natural setting. Random stone steps (right) can be arranged even more informally.

free by excavating the steps entirely into the margin of the upper terrace. Finally, they could compromise, offering perhaps the most satisfactory feeling of a linkage by building the lower section of the flight on the lower ground, and insetting the remainder in the upper terrace.

The opportunities for elaboration did not finish there. The main axis of the flight could run parallel to the margin of the upper terrace or at right angles to it, and the flight itself could be interrupted by one or more broader landings on which people could pass, pause or view the garden from a high point.

· STEPS AND THEIR DECORATION ·

Over the years, garden designers have often varied the shapes of individual steps and landings. They made them simple and rectangular in plan, convex or concave in form, or a mixture of both. A favorite arrangement was to have concave steps inset into the upper terrace leading down to a circular landing from which the convex protruding steps led down to the lower terrace in a series of elegant arcs.

This is a form frequently seen surfaced with either brick or an edging of brick with a grit infill. In the past fifty years, solid paving has become a widely used alternative.

Many older flights of garden steps were constructed with double or even triple (one in the middle and one at each side) sets of steps leading to a landing with either multiple or single flights leading from it up to the terrace. In some highly decorated seventeenth-century baroque gardens, even sinuous wavy edged steps were built. And such fantasies were not restricted to early gardens. In the United States, one of the most interesting garden designs of this century was made by Thomas Church at his home in California. Several curved double flights of stairs kept parting and uniting from a series of landings rising up a steep hillside clad with white-barked birch. What is most notable about these steps is that their curved metal banister rails are painted pale blue — an unexpected choice which sounds dreadful and looks wonderful.

Steps, like any other change of level or direction, need beacons of some sort to indicate their presence and prevent accidents. Whether or not they are furnished with any sort of banister, they are usually signaled by pillars at both the top and the bottom of the flight, often topped by urns or vases *(see p.172)*.

On the whole, designers liked to include banisters — frequently of stepped and decorative balustrading — in their designs. They provided a good opportunity for stamping a print on the overall design by repeating masonry themes used

elsewhere in the garden or on the house. These could often be repeated in the treatment of the surface of the steps which in some cases were given highly sophisticated patterns including such items as crest motifs.

· PLANTING A FLIGHT OF STEPS ·

Plantsmen have always found it difficult to overlook the opportunity and the challenge presented by a flight of steps. Their flanking walls can be used to support climbers, which can ultimately be trained to ramble over and through the balusters. The risers, too, can be clad with small clinging plants set in cracks between the paving of the treads which will mark them with bright flowers.

Perhaps the most delightful form of planted steps are those which are made of rough stonework of the kind favored by Edwin Lutyens and Gertrude Jekyll. The plants that flourish in these situations are those commonly found on or at the feet of walls. Red valerian and yellow corydalis are two favorites which, once established, will sow themselves freely. Mounds of moss in damp corners will act as a foil for their bright summer color.

CIRCULAR STEPS
This unusual flight of steps departs from the idea that steps have to be rectangular. Instead, the flight is designed on a circular plan, making an attractive and novel feature out of a change of level that is actually quite modest.

DECORATIVE FEATURES

*Pots, urns and vases — Troughs and sarcophagi —
The art of treillage — Seats and benches — Follies and
temples — Statuary — Geometrical ornaments —
Instruments and eye-catchers*

GARDENERS DIVIDE NATURALLY INTO TWO GROUPS THE FIRST CONTAINS dedicated plant enthusiasts, who can hardly see anything in a garden except plants, and whose overriding passion is collecting and growing them. When visiting gardens, they disregard all exhortations and warnings, and clandestinely snip off cuttings or snatch at seed heads, slipping them into bags or pockets.

People like this often have gardens packed with botanical wonders, and because they grow their plants so well, they have a vital role in conserving the most exquisite species for future generations. But, in truth, their gardens are frequently a mess. Any structure that they may originally have had vanishes because the passion to collect causes more and more of the area to be lost to the spade, as longer and larger beds are needed as homes for plants The second group attaches almost as much importance to a plant's color and form as the first does to its rarity. These gardeners treat plants as only one component in a well-structured scheme that also includes features

PERIOD PIECE
Paired obelisks, decorated with chiselled trelliswork, lend a note of distinction and formality to this otherwise simple brick terrace.

URNS AND VASES

URNS AND VASES ARE TRADITIONALLY USED AS FEATURES TO adorn balustrades and steps. In the past, they were valued primarily for their architectural qualities. Even when their design allowed them to be planted, they were more likely to be filled with gravel instead, as it was believed that plants detracted from their form. While few gardeners today are this severe, it is advisable to exercise restraint when planting a masonry container. Plants should be selected with care, the aim being to complement the container rather than to produce a riot of color and foliage. In areas that experience severe frost, a waterproof cover will prevent damage to the container in winter.

BALUSTRADE VASE

FINIAL URN

FLANKING A DOORWAY
Urns and vases add a note of grandeur to an informal garden.

FLUTED BOWL

GARLANDED URN

SCALLOPED VASE

HEXAGONAL PLANTER

STONE BASKET WITH FLINTS

BALUSTRADE VASE

LEAD VASE

such as pots, benches, pergolas, and perhaps statues and sundials to add embellishment. In the best examples of their gardens, flowers and foliage contrast with ornamental structures. Instead of being crammed together, the plants are sometimes isolated and used to balance a composition in counterpoint to masonry or water.

Gardeners who place a high value on outdoor ornament have much in common with earlier gardeners who had far fewer plants to use in their designs. Before plants began to arrive from North America in the seventeenth century, and later from India and South Africa, European gardens depended for their beauty as much on manmade decoration as they did on flowers.

· POTS, URNS AND VASES ·

Many of the earliest pictures we have of gardens show pots, urns and vases being used to grow plants, and it is known that today's common Mediterranean custom of growing plants in pots on balconies was well established by the inhabitants of the crowded tenements of ancient Rome. While Renaissance and eighteenth-century designers have added a few embellishments to their design, most of the shapes and decorations of the pots, urns and vases available today derive from earlier models, which early citizens of Rome would have recognized. With the exception of what could be called the "gas-station plastic" versions, they would also have been familiar with the materials used.

Although carved stone vessels would have been ordered by the rich, the Romans were renowned for their talent as makers of mortars and also for their ability to simulate stone. They often made important features such as structural columns out of brick or rubble, which was then given a cladding of stucco.

Throughout the ages, terracotta has been the favored material for making cheap, attractive pots. Its unsophisticated charm and earthiness still makes it popular for use in small gardens – particularly surrounding houses of modern design where clay seems less alien than the more pretentious stone.

· SUBSTITUTES FOR STONE ·

While pots, urns and vases in imitation stone can look very convincing, their major snag is that they tend to crack, especially in cold climates, where water penetrates their crevices and then freezes, expanding and thereby shattering them. In an attempt to overcome this problem, Mrs Eleanor Coade in England patented and manufactured a substance called *Coade stone*, which was in fact a mixture of clays, ground stone and ground glass. When dried out and fired like an

LEAD CISTERN

STONE TROUGH

STONE BOX

STONE TROUGH ON SUPPORTS

CISTERNS, TROUGHS AND BOXES
Because they are deeper than most garden containers, decorative cisterns, troughs and boxes can be densely planted. However, as with all containers, the soil within them has a tendency to compact through frequent watering, and this can retard the growth of the plants. Compaction can be prevented by using a planting mixture of loam and horticultural grit.

unglazed ceramic in a kiln, this mixture became very hard and durable, and had the great virtue of being frost resistant. From the 1770s onwards, it was widely adopted for making both urns and vases, and also for architectural details such as the capitals for pilasters to be applied to buildings. Such was the texture and colour of Coade stone that, once in place, it was indistinguishable from stone itself.

Sadly, after Mrs Coade's patent lapsed, Coade stone became simply a fashionable generic name for objects made from stone substitutes. Most of these substitutes today are not fired, and, as many gardeners have discovered to their cost, many are not frost resistant.

Undoubtedly, the best hope for gardeners looking for reasonably priced ornaments lies in the development of resin technology. It is spawning a new class of materials that are very convincing substitutes for real stone and terracotta, and which can be cheaply molded to produce final forms without the need for kiln firing and the expense that this brings.

BAKED EARTH: THE CHARM OF TERRACOTTA

IN A GARDEN, FEW THINGS SO RELATIVELY INEXPENSIVE LOOK better than terracotta. Its appeal is ageless. In Sicily, terracotta is still made on the site of kilns that date back for two and a half thousand years, testifying to the continuing popularity of this simple material. Unglazed terracotta is highly porous, and this has important consequences for the gardener. It absorbs water, allowing rapid evaporation from the soil within it, and also creating a danger of cracking in frosty weather. Frost-proof terracotta is available, but some of it is glazed, rendering it less attractive.

PASTRYWARE FLOWERPOT

TERRACE POT

GARLANDED HALF-POT

THREE-LEGGED POT

ROUND TERRACE POT

ROSE FLOWER POT

ROSE BOWL

TERRACE POT

LILY POT

JAR

BARREL POT

BASKETWARE FLOWERPOT

ITALIANATE POT

PASTRYWARE POT

POT WITH SWAGS AND ROPEWORK

ITALIANATE POT

RUNNING LEAF POT

JAR

BARREL FLOWERPOT

SCALLOPED BOWL

FLAT-BACKED WALL POT

DOUBLE-RIMMED POT

PERSIAN JAR

PEDESTAL VASE

BASKETWARE FLOWERPOT

OVAL-ENDED TROUGH

INSCRIBED VASE

TALL PEDESTAL VASE

TROUGH

GARLANDED URN

PEDESTAL VASE

ORANGE POT

TREILLAGE FOR TODAY'S GARDEN

LITTLE ORIGINAL TRELLISWORK SURVIVES FROM ITS HEYDAY in the eighteenth century, most having succumbed to the natural processes of decay or to changes in fashion. However, the most popular eighteenth-century designs were recorded in contemporary pattern-books, and today these provide the inspiration for much modern *treillage*. Trelliswork provides a pleasing way to transform a small garden.

FRENCH FANTASY
The Temple de l'Amour *at Chantilly in France* (left) *exemplifies the skill of French trellismakers.*

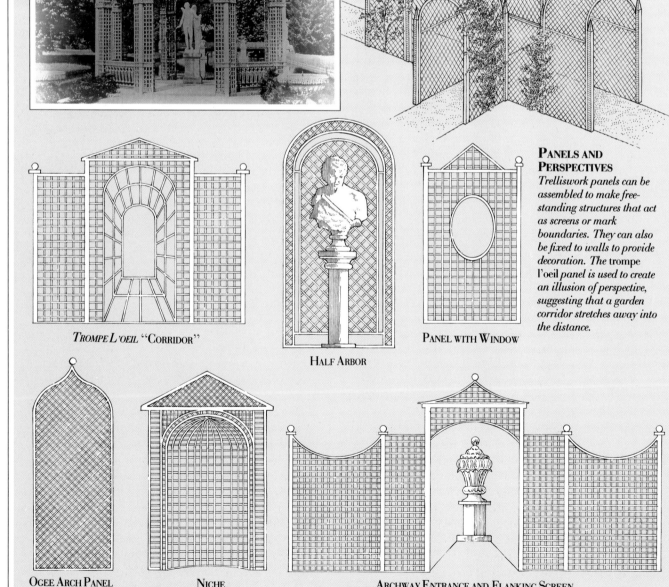

COVERED *TREILLAGE* PATHWAY

TROMPE L'OEIL "CORRIDOR"

HALF ARBOR

PANEL WITH WINDOW

PANELS AND PERSPECTIVES
Trelliswork panels can be assembled to make free-standing structures that act as screens or mark boundaries. They can also be fixed to walls to provide decoration. The trompe l'oeil *panel is used to create an illusion of perspective, suggesting that a garden corridor stretches away into the distance.*

OGEE ARCH PANEL   NICHE   ARCHWAY ENTRANCE AND FLANKING SCREEN

· TROUGHS AND SARCOPHAGI ·

Early Persian and medieval paintings show rectangular troughs in gardens fed from water jets. They were presumably placed there as decorative features, although they were also no doubt used as dips for buckets and jugs when watering pot-grown plants. When Renaissance excavations revealed a multitude of early Roman stone sarcophagi embellished with beautiful and detailed relief sculptures, it is understandable that some designers adopted them as forms of garden decoration.

Having found their way into gardens, it is easy to see why some gardeners could not resist using some of them as planters. But their usefulness as reservoirs was never quite forgotten, and in the seventeenth and eighteenth centuries, when the art of casting lead became highly refined, they were often filled with water. Since lead is so durable, many fine eighteenth-century lead troughs are still in use today, often richly planted. Apart from the particular patina that two centuries of use has given them, they are frequently beautifully decorated, with their panels showing either mythological scenes or intricate compositions of fruit, foliage and flowers.

By packing the outermost layers of resins with lead powder, the manufacturers of fiberglass reinforced troughs have now managed to make very convincing reproductions that, when planted, can ennoble any garden.

· THE ART OF *TREILLAGE* ·

As a substitute for walls and hedges, simple trelliswork must have been used quite early in the history of gardening. A picture dating back to the fourteenth century shows two lovers in a garden surrounded by a low, diagonally trellised fence which was made by binding thick poles together. This is shown acting as a support for a climbing rose. An attractive variant on the conventional trellis is shown a century later in an illustration to the fifteenth-century book *Le Roman de la Rose*. It depicts a very stout, rectangular-section framework filled by dense panels of much lighter, diagonally crossed timber laths. In the same picture, there is a glimpse of a two-railed fence, supported by closely stationed light timber posts being used to support roses.

In the sixteenth century, English knot gardens were frequently surrounded by trellis of what was called "carpenter's work," which greatly resembles today's rectangular cross-spar trellises.

There is no doubt that the high point of trellis-making occurred in the last years of the seventeenth century in France. In the gardens of the great châteaux, particularly at Versailles, it was developed into the art of *treillage*. The features that were produced were every bit as majestic as the buildings in whose gardens they were located. Alcoves, doorways, archways and decorative backing walls were all made by the intricate arrangement of fine wooden spars, supported by well-disguised strong wooden posts. The *treillage* makers were so clever that they could mimic perfectly the details of the capitals, pediments and other motifs used by architects when building in stone. When the *treillage* was viewed from a distance, visitors were snared into believing that they were approaching a work that was made of the finest masonry.

The miracles at Versailles were soon copied elsewhere in Europe. At the same time in China, simpler trellis was being used very much as we often use it today, as free-standing fencing to support climbing roses.

· TRADITIONAL TRELLISWORK TODAY ·

Since the eighteenth century, the popularity of trelliswork has waxed and waned as garden designs have fluctuated between informal schemes, in which it can be seen somewhat out of place, and formal and semi-formal layouts, where it can be very useful in delineating a garden's structure. At present, it seems to be undergoing one of its many revivals, with ready-made wall panels in which the woodwork is used to play perspective tricks becoming increasingly popular in smaller gardens.

Sadly, a good deal of ready-made trellis panelling is of poor quality, made of thin timber or of unattractive plastic. But assembling cheaper and more robust trelliswork is well within the

TRELLISED SEATS
Trelliswork is sometimes used to screen seats, providing privacy without completely obstructing the view. The role of trelliswork in this context parallels that of pierced screens in Arabia and the Far East.

CLASSIC TRELLISED SEAT

GOTHIC TRELLISED SEAT

SEATS AND BENCHES

RUSTIC BENCH

O**F THE THREE TRADITIONAL MATERIALS AVAILABLE FOR GARDEN** furniture – stone, wood and iron – the last is the one that has provided designers with the greatest scope for introducing fresh styles into the garden. The elaborate patterning of iron seats and benches is accentuated by painting them, a necessity since, without some sort of protective covering, iron furniture soon becomes disfigured by rust. Wooden seats and benches may be painted, stained or oiled. Painting wooden garden furniture is by no means a new practice, and serves to make a seat or bench catch the eye in a distant vista.

PERPENDICULAR-STYLE BENCH

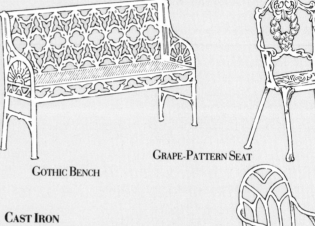

GOTHIC BENCH

GRAPE-PATTERN SEAT

FERN-FROND BENCH

CAST IRON

Cast iron garden furniture was in great demand throughout the nineteenth century. The elaborate patterns were first carved in hardwood formers, and these were then used to make molds in fine casting sand. When cool, the separate metal parts would be slotted or bolted together. Today, the same designs are reproduced in lighter alloys.

GOTHIC CHIPPENDALE SEAT

WROUGHT IRON

Wrought iron, which is fashioned by hammering, is less brittle than cast iron, but allows for less intricate and fussy decoration. Precisely because it is wrought, the iron takes on an almost organic form. At its most elaborate, its twists and curves mimic in metal the twining stems of growing plants.

SPRUNG SEAT

GOTHIC SEAT

SCROLLED BENCH

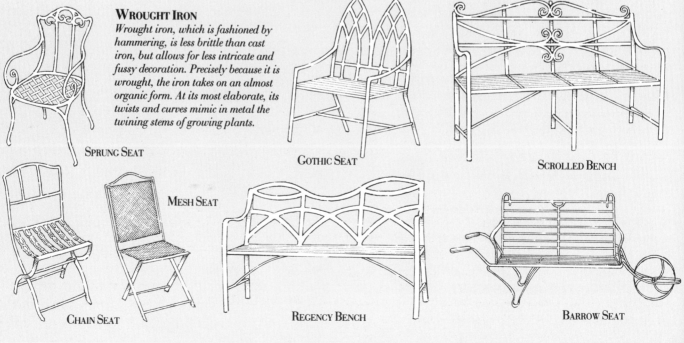

MESH SEAT

CHAIN SEAT

REGENCY BENCH

BARROW SEAT

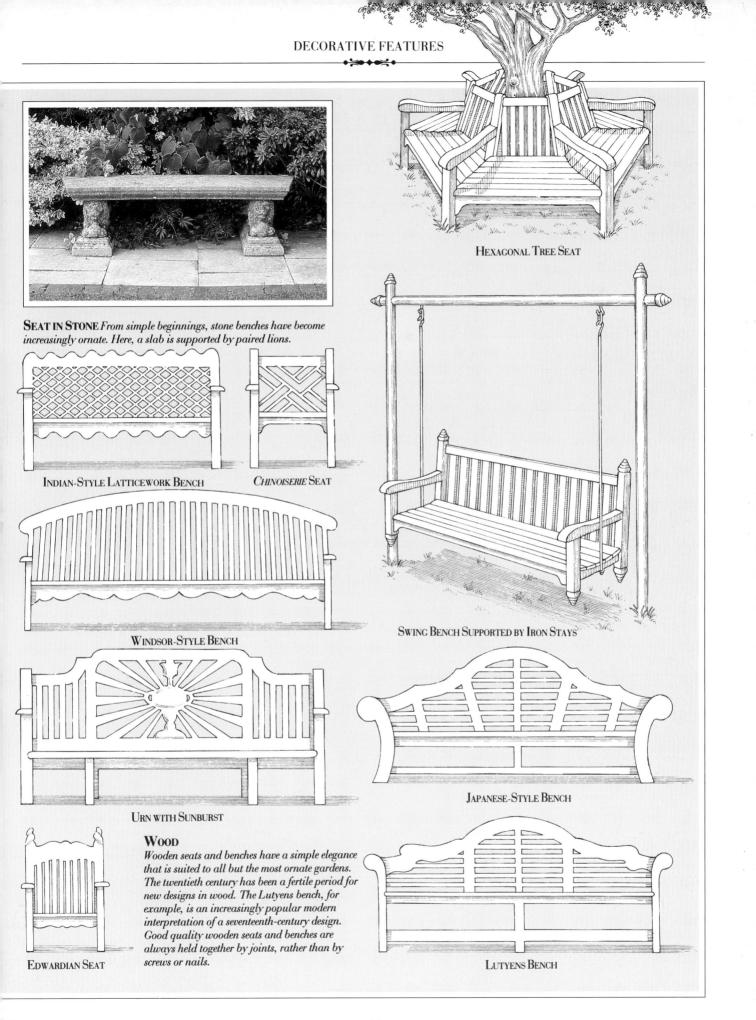

HEXAGONAL TREE SEAT

SEAT IN STONE *From simple beginnings, stone benches have become increasingly ornate. Here, a slab is supported by paired lions.*

INDIAN-STYLE LATTICEWORK BENCH

CHINOISERIE SEAT

WINDSOR-STYLE BENCH

SWING BENCH SUPPORTED BY IRON STAYS

URN WITH SUNBURST

JAPANESE-STYLE BENCH

EDWARDIAN SEAT

WOOD

Wooden seats and benches have a simple elegance that is suited to all but the most ornate gardens. The twentieth century has been a fertile period for new designs in wood. The Lutyens bench, for example, is an increasingly popular modern interpretation of a seventeenth-century design. Good quality wooden seats and benches are always held together by joints, rather than by screws or nails.

LUTYENS BENCH

FOLLIES AND MONUMENTS

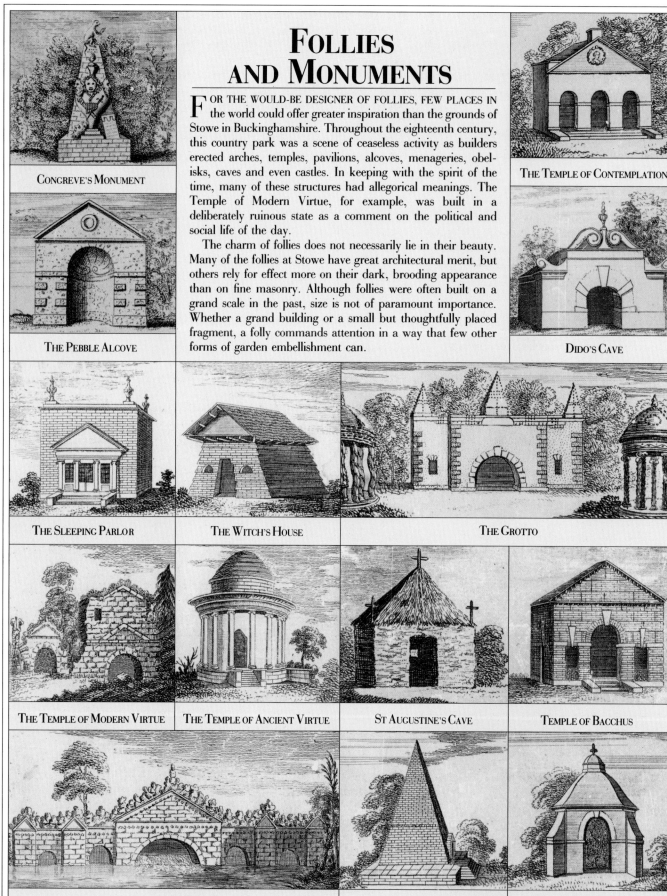

FOR THE WOULD-BE DESIGNER OF FOLLIES, FEW PLACES IN the world could offer greater inspiration than the grounds of Stowe in Buckinghamshire. Throughout the eighteenth century, this country park was a scene of ceaseless activity as builders erected arches, temples, pavilions, alcoves, menageries, obelisks, caves and even castles. In keeping with the spirit of the time, many of these structures had allegorical meanings. The Temple of Modern Virtue, for example, was built in a deliberately ruinous state as a comment on the political and social life of the day.

The charm of follies does not necessarily lie in their beauty. Many of the follies at Stowe have great architectural merit, but others rely for effect more on their dark, brooding appearance than on fine masonry. Although follies were often built on a grand scale in the past, size is not of paramount importance. Whether a grand building or a small but thoughtfully placed fragment, a folly commands attention in a way that few other forms of garden embellishment can.

CONGREVE'S MONUMENT

THE PEBBLE ALCOVE

THE TEMPLE OF CONTEMPLATION

DIDO'S CAVE

THE SLEEPING PARLOR

THE WITCH'S HOUSE

THE GROTTO

THE TEMPLE OF MODERN VIRTUE

THE TEMPLE OF ANCIENT VIRTUE

ST AUGUSTINE'S CAVE

TEMPLE OF BACCHUS

THE SHELL BRIDGE

EGYPTIAN PYRAMID

THE BELVEDERE

capabilities of most gardeners. Once you have tried making a simple trellis panel, it does not require much more talent as a handyman to make trellis with quite intricate curved features such as rounded archways. These are produced by gluing together several layers of flexible wooden lath, stretched around simple jigs.

· SEATS AND BENCHES ·

A seat can be both the most useful and the most decorative feature in a garden. Because of the invitation to rest that they mutely offer, seats act as eye-catchers that beg for attention. In this role their appeal is always strongest if their color is light and their design elaborate, and it is important that they are carefully positioned. Good designers have always ensured that they offered a view of something interesting, perhaps beautiful plants close at hand, or long, attractive vistas.

The noblest of traditional garden seats were made of light stone or marble, with heavily ornamented carved backs to exclude all draughts. Generous arms, mounted on pedestals, were carved to incorporate architectural motifs or animals, both real and mythological. Seats of this character were made by the Romans and similar designs occurred in many Renaissance gardens. They gradually developed into much more elaborate structures, either backed by walls or completely integrated with them.

After carpentry became fashionable in gardens in the eighteenth century, highly decorative timber seats began to appear. Many designs from this period are still copied now, and other seats are made today which are clearly influenced by these earlier models. These include mobile bench seats equipped with wheels and shafts which can be moved about like wheelbarrows.

Later, as the romantic movement grew in popularity, and then when woodland gardening gained a wide appeal, seats became much less formal. They were often made from rough-cut timber, and they could be as simple as a beam mounted on bricks, cut stone or heavy logs. More complicated "rustic" seats were made from twisted branches, carefully selected so that when they were combined they became frames with supporting backs, arms and legs to which smoother seat timbers could be fixed.

Loving their comfort, the Victorians produced countless types of garden seat. They exploited their technology to great effect in using cast iron to make many of the designs previously pioneered in wood and stone. Having mastered the art of casting, they developed many designs of their own. These were often highly decorated, featuring twisted stems, foliage, flowers and fruit. During the present century, gardeners have relied

relied heavily on traditional designs for their permanent garden seating. Portable seats of various degrees of ugliness have been made in wood and canvas, tubular aluminum alloy and plastic. Their usefulness cannot be said to have improved the beauty of gardens. The best modern portable seats are often the simplest, painted in an unobtrusive dark green.

Perhaps the most attractive simple seats can be made by sitting heavy timber railroad ties on two pillars of brick or stone against a wall for backing. These have the advantage that they take up little space. For the same reason, seats built into brick or stone boundary walls are well worth considering in a town garden.

· FOLLIES AND TEMPLES ·

In the seventeenth century, landscape designers of the romantic period used temples to stimulate contemplative thought and create an atmosphere of fruitful melancholy. The fact that many of their temples were used as mausoleums helps to confirm this serious purpose, as does their high architectural merit. These characteristics are evident not only in temples, but also in the follies that simulated ruins. These "ruins" became popular because it was realized that a fragment could often be more eloquent and thought-provoking than a completed artifact, and that grandeur in decay could have a special beauty.

The ruins of ancient Rome, which were revealed during the Renaissance, or those of monasteries sacked by Henry VIII in Britain, must certainly have provided the models that inspired the building of ruins in gardens by the romantics. However, many of their works were in turn wiped out by the landscape movement during the eighteenth century, and when the building of temples and follies became popular again in the nineteenth century, most of its formerly serious motivation had been forgotten.

Temples became unashamed eye-catchers, interpreted in a host of lighthearted and inventive ways. They varied from facsimiles of classical models in stone or stuccoed brick, to simple kiosks over which climbing plants like wisteria could clamber. In these, hexagons, octagons or circles of wooden, masonry or iron columns supported dome-shaped iron roof frameworks. Their forms became giddier as their designers strove for originality, using as their models everything from the palanquins of Persian potentates to the temples of Chinese emperors.

Follies, too, lost most of their symbolic purpose and generally became visual jokes of greater or less wit. One of the best survivors was made at Biddulph Grange in Staffordshire. Here, great blocks of yew are clipped to resemble masonry.

FOLLY IN MINIATURE
In an age when so much store is set by practicality, any departure from this rule always engages the interest. A folly in miniature, made by a capital and part of a fluted column clothed in ivy, has precisely this effect.

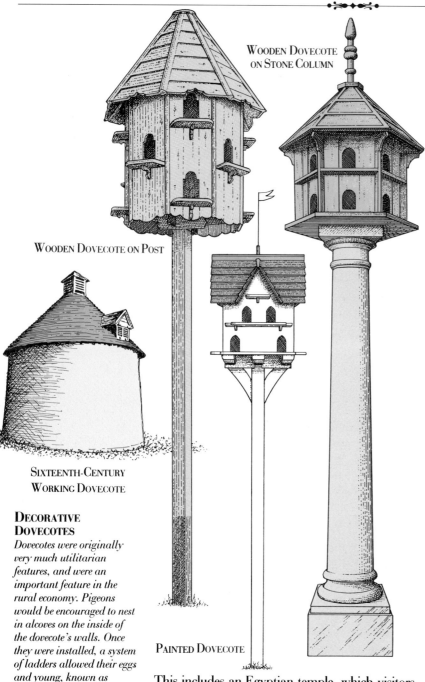

WOODEN DOVECOTE
ON STONE COLUMN

WOODEN DOVECOTE ON POST

SIXTEENTH-CENTURY
WORKING DOVECOTE

PAINTED DOVECOTE

DECORATIVE DOVECOTES

Dovecotes were originally very much utilitarian features, and were an important feature in the rural economy. Pigeons would be encouraged to nest in alcoves on the inside of the dovecote's walls. Once they were installed, a system of ladders allowed their eggs and young, known as squabs, to be removed to the kitchen. Purely decorative dovecotes became fashionable in later times. They were used to accommodate not only white doves, but also fancy pigeons, including highly bred varieties such as pouters, fan-tails and tumblers.

This includes an Egyptian temple, which visitors approach down an alley between two pairs of genuine Egyptian *couchant* stone sphinxes. But if they look back after having passed through its tomb-like interior, they realize that they have emerged from the facade of a Victorian version of a typical half-timbered cottage. The effect is anything but serious.

· THE MODERN FOLLY ·

Today, simple temple-like structures continue to be popular as plant frames, much as they have been for the last hundred years. More ambitious stone or simulated stone structures have had recurrent periods of popularity in larger gardens whenever the taste for formality has re-emerged. This is reflected in the supply of simulated stone

products, including columns and entablatures, which can be used to make the twentieth-century equivalent of a romantic temple. These days, instead of being dedicated to a particular deity, temples can be useful eye-catchers, which also make attractive alternatives to summerhouses and arbors for shady seating.

In the corner of a small modern garden, something as simple as the broken capital from a Corinthian column, poking out of a ground planting of ivy, with perhaps a fragment or two of column barrel elsewhere, can act as a provocative folly. If you have a larger, rural garden and a source of scrap masonry – perhaps a demolition site – you have all the makings of a modern folly. The surrounds of nineteenth-century neo-Gothic windows from old office blocks, and other fragments of chiselled stone, can be built into walls, towers and gateways and surrounded by convincing rubble. When clad with creepers like ivy, Virginia creeper or Russian vine, they can soon look as though they have been present for hundreds of years.

· STATUARY ·

Statuary for gardens must have consumed more of sculptors' modelling, polishing, mold-making and casting time than any other outlet for their art. That is possibly why so many of the best garden designers today were trained initially as sculptors, and why throughout history gardens have provided homes for some of their most impressive works.

Statues were initially confined to the gardens surrounding the homes of the powerful or the patrician. The gardens of Roman emperors, generals and senators featured figures of the popular deities, great characters from mythology, or great men from their own or former times. Megalomaniacs like Nero were keen to display heroic portrayals of themselves. However, mingled with this pomposity there were more satisfying and poetic interpretations of goddesses like Diana and Aphrodite, Flora and Ceres or rascals like Pan and Bacchus to dominate fountains and occupy other prominent positions and decorate the garden. The works used in Roman gardens were frequently faithful copies of Greek models or even originals pillaged from Greece or her colonies and carried away.

The themes for sculpture widened with the dawning of the Christian era. Gentler, more appropriate figures such as St. Dorothy, or St. Francis with his doves, began to appear in the gardens of the laity. But it was not until the romantic movement in the seventeenth century that more workaday people and their activities were commemorated. Gamekeepers, gardeners, shepherds, shepherdesses and woodsmen fashioned out of terracotta, lead, wood, stone and bronze began to populate gardens. These, together with a few older heroes and animals such as fawns and frogs, have continued to peer out of our shrubberies and terraces until today.

The scale of statues has dwindled with the size of gardens. These days, twentieth-century materials such as resin-bonded fiberglass often takes the place of masonry or metal. When appropriate fillers are used, the mixture can produce a very effective imitation of weathered traditional materials.

Nowadays, more emphasis is placed on the use of sculpture purely as eye-catchers in garden designs, but the best works still have the capacity to charm or provoke thought. This can be enhanced by subtly planning their location so that they are not immediately obvious. A mask of Triton, for example, can generate a great feeling of surprise when he is spotted hidden in dripping ivy backing a basin, into which a jet of water is allowed to trickle. A lifelike figure encountered suddenly when entering a glade can provoke the embarrassing notion that your private remarks may have been overheard when approaching his or her hiding place.

· GEOMETRICAL ORNAMENTS ·

Obelisks, pyramids, cubes and spheres have been used as garden ornaments since Roman times. It is possible that the Romans became excited by these new geometric shapes after the conquest of Egypt. The obelisk is the least usual among them, and it has long fascinated the more imaginative garden designers.

Until the seventeenth century, obelisks appeared in many sizes and were usually constructed in stone. But with the development of skilled *treillage*, it was then quickly adopted by masters of the art. It is the trellis obelisk which has persistently appealed to gardeners since the seventeenth century because it makes an attractive support for climbing plants. Trellis obelisks are still available as ready-made decorative features. Metal trellis obelisks, which were made when iron became much cheaper to produce in the nineteenth century, are harder to find. In Victorian gardens, these were used as frames for climbers, and were particularly favored as supports for roses.

Spheres, with their obvious symbolic reference to the sun and moon, must have been used to decorate gardens long before the Romans conquered Egypt, and they have certainly been used by garden designers since the sixteenth century. They have a traditional role as finials to top off such features as impressive gate posts or, on a

A SUITABLE SCALE
A small lead statue on a pedestal (above) *provides an object for contemplation near this stone bench. Statuary does not necessarily depend upon scale for effect, and a statue that is too large for its setting may easily overstep the line that separates the imposing from the overpowering.*

PARTLY OBSCURED
By allowing plants to partially hide a statue (left), *a feeling of antiquity and mystery can be created. Here, this is accentuated by positioning the statue on the ground, without a pedestal.*

GARDEN OBELISKS

Obelisks are traditionally used in symmetrical arrangements where their formal lines are exploited. They are valuable for defining areas, such as alleys and courtyards, which are otherwise lacking in vertical features. Solid stone obelisks are most suitable for highly formal gardens, and are particularly effective when placed on stone paving. Treillage obelisks, which have a more delicate appearance, make attractive eye-catchers in almost any situation, from terraces to decorative vegetable gardens.

WOODEN *TREILLAGE* OBELISK ON PLANTER

PAINTED STEEL *TREILLAGE* OBELISK ON PLANTER

SOLID STONE OBELISK

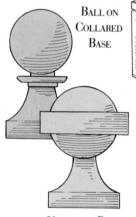

BALL ON COLLARED BASE

VANBRUGH BALL

BALL WITH FRILLED BASE

BALL FINIALS

In ball finials, the ball was often attached to the base by a metal rod that was pushed home into a plug of molten lead in the base. When the lead solidified, base and ball became locked together. Ball finials are traditionally used to crown pillars, gables and walls.

smaller scale, as knobs to top the corner posts of wooden planter tubs or seat backs. Made in a variety of materials including stone, wood and crystal, they have been traditionally used as free-standing features mounted on columns or plinths or, when obelisk design was developed, to perch aloft on their pinnacles.

Square-based pyramids, made of masonry, fulfilled the same function as obelisks where squatter features seemed more appropriate. They were mounted on cubic plinths or simply rose directly from the ground.

· INSTRUMENTS AND EYE-CATCHERS ·

From the earliest days of ornamental gardening, designers have used small eye-catchers to draw attention to particular areas of the garden, or away from less desirable vistas. Among those most frequently used are sundials. These can be set in walls or positioned free-standing on plinths in the center of paved areas, or the lawn at the junction of paths.

Sundials seem to have been popular since man first realized that the shadows cast by the sun could be used to tell the time. In the past, the decorative style of the figuring on their faces and the blades of their gnomons tended to harmonize with the prevailing architectural styles of the time. Today, however, the tendency is to reproduce on a smaller scale models that were popular

in gardens in the late eighteenth and early nineteenth centuries.

Scientific instruments and other optical eye-catchers make arresting decoration in a garden. Armillary spheres, fascinating and unusual constructions designed to help astronomers understand the workings of the cosmos, consist of a number of rings representing the principal circles of the celestial sphere, such as the equator and the meridian. They were invented by the Greeks in approximately 250 BC and were used by Ptolemy to determine the position of the stars. Because of their inaccuracy, they were little used after the sixteenth century, but they have such beautiful and intriguing spherical forms that they have been used to embellish gardens in a similar way to sundials. Unfortunately, reproductions of these early spheres are costly to make and so, as decorative devices, they are rare.

The crystal spheres beloved of fortune tellers can be mounted on columns in a garden, where they sparkle to attract attention and produce strangely distorted images when examined closely. If a sphere is surrounded by flowers, anyone peering into it sees their colors jostle enchantingly. Mirrored spheres, similarly mounted, also glint in the sunlight, and their curved surfaces distort the images of surrounding features in a similar way. Like the mirrors common at fairgrounds, they lure people towards them and never fail to provoke interest and amusement.

· CLOCKS AND WEATHERCOCKS ·

Before the invention of the pocket watch, clocks served a very practical purpose in gardens. Some of the most attractive have four faces, and were set into lanterns crowning buildings. Humbler versions were stationed high on the gable ends of buildings such as barns. Although some of these old clocks had fantasy faces, most of them had decorative ironwork figures that were either black on a white enamelled or porcelain face, or white or gold on a black lacquered face. In the latter case, the figures were usually painted in gold.

Clocks can be useful eye-catchers in a modern garden. Traditional clocks can be costly, although sometimes bargains become available when buildings—like old schools or hospitals—are demolished. However, anyone good with their hands can use the workings of a battery-driven kitchen clock as the basis for something more traditional.

Before the days of the weather forecaster, weathercocks and vanes served the useful purpose of warning gardeners about wind changes, which could herald chilly days or imminent rain. All they need is a reasonably free bearing on which to spin, and a high place where they can catch the wind.

SUNDIALS AND ARMILLARY SPHERES

Although rendered obsolete long ago, sundials and armillary spheres have an architectural charm that has secured them a continuing place in gardens. The three basic elements of any sundial are a supporting post or pedestal, a dial and a *gnomon* that casts the shadow on the dial. Armillary spheres use concentric hoops of metal to indicate the path of the planets across the heavens.

Throughout the centuries, sundials and armillary spheres have undergone a process of evolution to become elaborately decorated structures. Unlike most other garden ornaments sundials, of necessity, have to be placed in an open, unshaded position. They can be used as a focal point in terraces and lawns, or at the heart of a formal rose garden. Because they do not take up an excessive amount of space, they are as effective in a small garden as a large one.

FRAMED IN BRICK
An armillary sphere at Polesden Lacey makes an arresting feature when glimpsed through a circular aperture in an old wall.

CUPID SUNDIAL

KNEELING SLAVE SUNDIAL

EIGHTEENTH-CENTURY FACETED SUNDIAL

BALUSTER-STYLE SUNDIAL

NEO-CLASSICAL SUNDIAL

EMPIRE-STYLE SUNDIAL WITH GARLANDS

EARLY VICTORIAN SUNDIAL

SUNDIAL ON CIRCULAR PLINTH

PERIOD PLANTING

THROUGHOUT THE HISTORY OF gardening, the popularity of different plants has waxed and waned in accordance with changing tastes. In addition to this, the introduction of exotic species and the breeding of both new hybrids and cultivars has constantly provided gardeners with new opportunities, some of which have been seized on with extraordinary enthusiasm.

The plants listed on these two pages give a flavor of some characteristic plantings from different eras of gardening stretching back over the last five hundred years. All the plants are available today as seed or as nursery stock.

· MEDIEVAL PHYSICK PLANTS ·

Many of the plants in medieval gardens – most of them from Europe and the Near East – were grown for their medicinal properties. One suspects that in many cases these were more imagined than real, particularly for plants that bore some superficial resemblance to the part of the body they were supposed to cure, such as lungwort. However, the usefulness of a number of medieval physick plants is still recognized today and the efficacy of feverfew, for example, against headaches and migraines, is presently being studied by pharmaceutical companies. Traditional physic plants that make an attractive contribution to a herb garden today include:

Angelica *Angelica archangelica*
Birthwort *Aristolochia clematitis*
Chamomile *Chamaemelum nobile*
Catmint *Nepeta cataria*
Comfrey *Symphytum officinale*
Creeping Jenny *Lysimachia nummularia*
Feverfew *Chrysanthemum parthenium*
Foxglove *Digitalis purpurea*
Germander *Teucrium chamaedrys*
Ground ivy *Glechoma hederacea*
Holy thistle *Carduus benedictus*
Houseleek *Sempervivum tectorum*
Lungwort *Pulmonaria officinalis*
Mandrake *Mandragora officinarum*
Milk thistle *Silybum marianum*
Valerian *Valeriana officinalis*
Woodruff *Galium odoratum*

· ELIZABETHAN PLANTS ·

Most plants in European gardens during Elizabethan times were native to Europe or the Near East, although a few Old World plants from farther afield were grown. The first American introductions such as tobacco, agave and yucca started to arrive during this period. Plants such as the ones listed here would have been spaced at even intervals in beds and borders with soil showing between, and would have been studied closely for the beauty of their flowers rather than for overall effect:

Acanthus *Acanthus mollis*
Bachelor's buttons *Ranunculus acris* 'Flore Pleno'
Bearded iris *Iris germanica*
Canterbury bells *Campanula medium*
Christmas rose *Helleborus niger*
Columbine *Aquilegia vulgaris*
Common peony *Paeonia officinalis* 'Rubra Plena'
Crown imperial *Fritillaria imperialis*
Garden pink *Dianthus plumarius*
Hyssop *Hyssopus officinalis*
Lavender cotton *Santolina chamaecyparissus*
Madonna lily *Lilium candidum*
Martagon lily *Lilium martagon*
Pheasant's eye narcissus *Narcissus poeticus*
Rosa Mundi *Rosa gallica* 'Versicolor'
Rose, White Rose of York *Rosa* 'Alba Semiplena'
Rose, apothecary's *Rosa gallica officinalis*
Snapdragon *Antirrhinum majus*
Stock *Matthiola incana*
Sweet rocket (including double forms) *Hesperis matronalis*
Wallflower *Cheiranthus cheiri*

· FLORISTS' FLOWERS ·

Although the majority of garden plants in the seventeenth century would have been the favourites of the Elizabethan age, a handful of sorts were transformed by plantsmen and nurserymen into increasingly gorgeous and more commercial varieties by persistent cross breeding and selection. To the original "florists' flowers" – carnation, tulip, anemone, ranunculus and auricula – were added hyacinth and polyanthus in the late seventeenth century, the pink in the late eighteenth century and dahlia, chrysanthemum and pansy in the nineteenth century.

Each sort of florists' flower had its own devotees and shows and feasts were held at which prizes were given for the finest plants showing the most intricate doubling, the best markings or the richest colours. Many varieties were raised. For instance, by 1770 there were said to be over 2,000 varieties of double hyacinth.

The best sorts were immensely expensive and had to be kept out of the reach of light-fingered gardeners and unscrupulous house guests, often in a walled garden immediately adjoining the house. It would not be unusual for the contents of such a garden to be worth the equivalent of several million pounds at today's prices. In the late seventeenth-century flower garden, plants would be grown in a "fret", a geometric pattern of beds small enough to allow close inspection.

Few plants today can match the finest show anemones of old, their blooms muddled and velvety or precise and formal; the gloriously symmetrical striped or picotee ranunculus have also completely disappeared and only a few varieties of double hyacinth remain:

Anemone *Anemone coronaria* and *A. pavonina* hybrids
Auricula *Primula auricula*
Carnation *Dianthus caryophyllus*
Chrysanthemum *Chrysanthemum* hybrids
Dahlia *Dahlia* hybrids
Hyacinth *Hyacinthus orientalis*

Pansy *Viola* hybrids
Pink *Dianthus* hybrids
Polyanthus *Primula* × *polyantha*
Ranunculus *Ranunculus asiaticus*
Tulip *Tulipa* spp. and hybrids

· TULIPS AND TULIPOMANIA ·

Of all the florists' flowers the story of the tulip is the most extraordinary. Originating from Turkey in the mid-sixteenth century, bulbs were brought to Vienna and Venice and thence to Holland and Britain. Bulbs infected by virus produced striped flowers, and those that were deemed to be particularly well marked could command outrageously high prices. By the 1630s in Holland speculation in such bulbs was rife and fortunes were gambled on the value of bulbs in much the same way as they may be on stocks and shares. One bulb of the tulip 'Semper Augustus' is said to have sold for the huge sum of nearly 5,000 florins plus a new coach and pair.

The crash came in 1637 when the market was flooded with bulbs of the most desirable varieties. Nevertheless, the best remained very expensive and a good new English variety could cost as much as $350 in the nineteenth century. The following species and hybrids were available in the seventeenth century and are still grown today:

Tulip 'Amiral de Constantinople'
Tulipa clusiana
Tulip 'Columbus' (syn. 'Gala Beauty')
Tulip 'Duc van Tol'
Tulipa gesneriana
Tulip 'Insulinde'
Tulip 'Lac van Rijn'
Tulip 'Lutea Major'
Tulip 'Paragon Everwijn'
Tulip 'Perfecta'
Tulipa schrenkii (syn. *T. suaveolens*)
Tulip 'Zomerschoon'

· LANDSCAPE TREES ·

The eighteenth-century landscape garden as typified by the designs of Lancelot "Capability" Brown depended on very few tree species. Native English species such as beech and oak often provided the backbone of the planting, although fast-growing species such as larch could be used as *nurses* to protect saplings and evergreens such as yew and holly used to provide the understory.

Tastes changed towards the end of the century when more picturesque, rugged and varied planting was preferred to the classic simplicity of Brown landscapes, allowing a much wider variety of tree species. These included the following:

Ash *Fraxinus excelsior*
Beech *Fagus sylvatica*
Cedar of Lebanon *Cedrus libani*
Common linden *Tilia* × *europaea*
Corsican pine *Pinus nigra* var. *maritima*
Elm *Ulmus procera*
English oak *Quercus robur*
English walnut *Juglans regia*
Hawthorn *Crataegus monogyna*
Holly *Ilex aquifolium*
Red-twigged linden *Tilia platyphyllos* 'Rubra'
Scots pine *Pinus sylvestris*
Small-leaved linden *Tilia cordata*
Spanish chestnut *Castanea sativa*
Yew *Taxus baccata*

· VICTORIAN WILD GARDEN PLANTS ·

The Victorian age saw a flood of plant introductions from plant hunters abroad and nurserymen at home. The vast range of plants available included many that were suited to the geometric bedding schemes so characteristic of high Victorian architectural gardens, a type of gardening not so suited to the limited range of more transient and less showy flowers available to the Georgians. This brash and highly artificial style of gardening was fiercely criticized by William Robinson, who longed for a return to a more natural style and pioneered the wild garden. However, his wild gardens were by no means natural and demanded a great deal of labor, perhaps not a major consideration when this was so cheap and plentiful. The flowers he recommended included:

Acanthus *Acanthus mollis*
Bellflower *Campanula trachelium*
Bindweed *Calystegia* spp.
Columbine *Aquilegia vulgaris* forms
Cranesbill *Geranium* spp. and cultivars
Ferns, hardy
Foxglove *Digitalis purpurea*

Globe thistle *Echinops* spp.
Hogweed *Heracleum sphondylium*
Honesty *Lunaria annua*
Knotwort *Reynoutria* spp.
Lupine *Lupinus polyphyllus* cultivars
Monkshood *Aconitum* spp. and cultivars
Oxeye daisy *Leucanthemum* spp.

· VICTORIAN CONSERVATORY PLANTS ·

Cheaper glass and cast-iron glazing bars made the conservatory an affordable luxury for many middle-class Victorians as well as for the very rich. A vast number of conservatory plants was available and the amateur could specialize according to the aspect of his or her glasshouse, whether in sun or shade, temperate or tropical. Here could be found orchids for a lady's corsage, gardenias for a gentleman's buttonhole, and stephanotis to festoon the dining table:

Bougainvillea *Bougainvillea glabra*
Cranesbill *Geranium* spp. and cultivars
Gardenia *Gardenia jasminoides*
Lady fern *Athyrium felix-femina*
Orchids *Cattleya* spp., *Cymbidium* spp., *Odontoglossum* spp., *Paphiopedilum* spp., *Vanda* spp.
Solomon's seal *Polygonatum* spp.
Stephanotis *Stephanotis floribunda*
Strelitzia or **Bird-of-paradise flower** *Strelitzia reginae*
Tree peony *Paeonia* 'Elizabeth'

· MODERN SHRUB ROSES ·

Most old roses flowered only in early summer and many were prone to disease. These drawbacks were only partly overcome in the China, Hybrid Perpetual and Tea roses of the Victorians. Twentieth-century developments include the many-flowered, sweetly scented Hybrid Musks, the ground-cover roses and David Austin's English roses, which combine the flower form of the old roses with the color range, vigor and more compact habit of modern varieties. Modern Shrub roses also include colors such as bright scarlet not found in truly old roses. Among the best of these roses are:

Austin's English roses 'Chaucer', 'Constance Spry', 'Gertrude Jekyll', 'Graham Thomas'
Ground-cover roses 'Pheasant', 'Scarlet Meidiland', 'Swany'
Hybrid Musk roses 'Buff Beauty', 'Cornelia', 'Prosperity'
Modern Shrub roses 'Fred Loads', 'Kassel', 'Magenta'

INDEX

ACKNOWLEDGMENTS

Dorling Kindersley would like to thank the following for their help in the preparation of this book: Andrew Crace Designs; Forsham Cottage Arks; Haddonstone Limited; Jim Keeling, Wychford Pottery; Machin Designs Limited; Ollerton Limited; Stuart Garden Architecture; The Landscape Ornament Company. Special thanks are also extended to Vanessa Luff for artwork research and to Kathie Gill for proofreading.

Production: Fenella Smart
Indexer: Hilary Bird
Picture research: Jenny Faithfull

Illustrators

Brian Delf: 66, 74–75.
Vanessa Luff: 18–19, 26, 32–33, 35, 38–39, 45, 48, 50–51, 52, 58–59, 67, 72, 81, 88–89, 100–101, 104, 110–111 (*after Brian Delf*), 114, 117, 133, 137, 140, 154, 167, 172–173, and chapter opening drawings.
Andrew Macdonald: 64, 144–145.
Gillie Newman: 27, 36, 61, 91, 116, 181, 182, 184–185.
Richard Phipps: 24, 28, 92, 109, 112–113, 121, 136, 152, 156–157, 162–163, 164–165.
Richard Phipps/Peter Wyndette and Associates: 155, 174–175.
John Woodcock: 20–21, 37, 40–41, 56, 68, 76–77, 78, 80, 105, 125, 129, 149, 168, 176–177, 178–179.

Typeset in UK by Tradespools Limited, Frome, Somerset

Reproduction by Reprocolor Llovet, Barcelona, Spain

Picture credits

All photographs by **Geoff Dann** except where otherwise stated

8 (**top**) Royal Horticultural Society; **10** (**bottom**) Museum of English Rural Life, University of Reading; **12** (**center**) Mansell Collection; **13** (**bottom**) Museum of English Rural Life, University of Reading; **14–15** National Trust/Eric Crichton; **17** Greenaway Collection – from an original in the collection of the late Mr. A. Hancock; **20** Mansell Collection; **22** National Trust/John Bethell; **25** Mansell Collection; **32** Royal Horticultural Society; **34** National Trust/Neil Campbell-Sharp; **39** National Trust/Eric Crichton; **42–43** Jacqui Hurst/Boys Syndication; **44** Museum of English Rural Life, University of Reading; **46** (**top**) Jacqui Hurst/Boys Syndication; **73** (**top**) Jacqui Hurst; **73** (**bottom**) Country Life; **74** North of England Open Air Museum, Beamish, Co. Durham; **75** North of England Open Air Museum, Beamish, Co. Durham; **76** Royal Horticultural Society; **77** Museum of English Rural Life, University of Reading; **79** Royal Horticultural Society; **81** North of England Open Air Museum, Beamish, Co. Durham; **88** Royal Horticultural Society; **97** (**top**) National Trust/Mike Williams; **98** National Trust/Neil Campbell-Sharp; **98–99** Steven Wooster; **103** National Trust **105** (**top and bottom**) Museum of English Rural Life, University of Reading; **120** Museum of English Rural Life, University of Reading; **122** (**top**) Jacqui Hurst; **123** Royal Botanic Gardens, Kew; **124** Museum of English Rural Life, University of Reading; **127** Jacqui Hurst; **128** Jacqui Hurst; **134** (**bottom**) Steven Wooster; **136** Royal Horticultural Society; **141** Steven Wooster; **142–143** Michael Boys/Michael Boys Syndication; **146** National Trust/Charlie Waite; **147** National Trust/Geoff Morgan; **148** (**left**) Hulton Picture Library; **148** (**right**) North of England Open Air Museum, Beamish, Co. Durham; **153** Royal Horticultural Society; **155** Steven Wooster; **155** Museum of English Rural Life, University of Reading; **156** Museum of English Rural Life, University of Reading; **161** Royal Horticultural Society; **166** Royal Horticultural Society; **167** Jacqui Hurst; **176** Royal Horticultural Society; **180** Museum of English Rural Life, University of Reading; **186** Steven Wooster.